Writing Back

RETHINKING THEORY
Stephen G. Nichols and Victor E. Taylor, *Series Editors*

Writing Back

American Expatriates' Narratives of Return

SUSAN WINNETT

The Johns Hopkins University Press

Baltimore

© 2012 The Johns Hopkins University Press
All rights reserved. Published 2012
Printed in the United States of America on acid-free paper
9 8 7 6 5 4 3 2 1

The Johns Hopkins University Press
2715 North Charles Street
Baltimore, Maryland 21218-4363
www.press.jhu.edu

Library of Congress Cataloging-in-Publication Data

Winnett, Susan.
    Writing back : American expatriates' narratives of return / Susan Winnett.
        p. cm.
    Includes bibliographical references and index.
    ISBN 978-1-4214-0740-1 (hdbk. : alk. paper) — ISBN 978-1-4214-0782-1 (electronic) —
ISBN 1-4214-0740-X (hdbk. : alk. paper) — ISBN 1-4214-0782-5 (electronic)
        1. American prose literature—20th century—History and criticism. 2. Autobiography. 3. James,
Henry, 1843–1916—Criticism and interpretation. 4. Stearns, Harold, 1891–1943—Criticism and
interpretation. 5. Cowley, Malcolm, 1898–1989—Criticism and interpretation. 6. Stein, Gertrude,
1874–1946—Criticism and interpretation. 7. Expatriate authors—Psychology. 8. Identity (Psychology)
in literature. 9. United States—In literature. 10. Europe—In literature. I. Title. II. Title: American
expatriates' narratives of return.
    PS366.A88W56 2013
        810.9'492—dc23   2012008909

A catalog record for this book is available from the British Library.

Note on Translations: Unless otherwise noted, all translations are by the author.

*Special discounts are available for bulk purchases of this book. For more information, please contact
Special Sales at 410-516-6936 or specialsales@press.jhu.edu.*

The Johns Hopkins University Press uses environmentally friendly book materials, including recycled
text paper that is composed of at least 30 percent post-consumer waste, whenever possible.

For Gerd, Noah, and our "little dog" Dido
Elaine and George Winnett in memoriam

CONTENTS

Acknowledgments   ix

Introduction   1

1 Framing the Un-Scene/Writing the Wrongs: Henry James's Text of
   America   43

2 An Intellectual Is Being Beaten: The Escape and Return of Harold E.
   Stearns   96

3 Wo Mama war, soll Dada werden: Malcolm Cowley's Odyssey of
   Legitimation   155

4 *Everybody's Autobiography*: The Remaking of an American   203

   Postscript   234

   Notes   239
   Works Cited   265
   Index   277

ACKNOWLEDGMENTS

There is a photograph of the Queensborough Bridge, taken when its middle section had been anchored in the East River but not yet connected to either shore. This image reminds me what my own situation would look like were it not for the people and institutions on both sides of the Atlantic who have granted me the gift of connection and to whom it is a pleasure finally to express my indebtedness.

Bettina Friedl took a wild and generous risk when she agreed to supervise this project as a *Habilitationsschrift* at the Universität Hamburg; without her support, friendship, and wisdom in all things *amerikanistisch*, *Writing Back* would never have gotten written. My gratitude extends to the members of the *Habilitationskommission*, whose comments have been very helpful in the process of revision: Kurt Dittmar, Norbert Finzsch, Ortrud Gutjahr, Peter Hühn, and Joseph Schoepp. Peter Brooks, Nancy K. Miller, and the late Carolyn G. Heilbrun made decisive suggestions at this project's inception for which I continue to be thankful. I have benefited enormously from the careful attention that Sabine Broeck, Robert J. Corber, Herwig Friedl, Renate Hof, Roger Lüdeke, A. Deborah Malmud, and Donald E. Pease invested in the manuscript.

Although written as a *rite de passage* addressed to a German academic *Heimat*, *Writing Back* is about America and Americans and would never have come into being without the American community that has sustained me during my years of expatriation. William V. Spanos is, more than anyone, responsible for my choice of profession. His engagement with and advocacy of this project is only the most recent of his decisive interventions in the life of my mind. The most loyal of friends and most encouraging of colleagues, Marianne Hirsch has contributed to this project in more ways than I can enumerate. It was at her instigation that I attended the Dartmouth College Summer Institute, "The Futures of American Studies," a forum that that served as my initiation into transatlantic American Studies and inspired productive reconsiderations of the parameters of this study. I wish to thank the Dartmouth College Department of Comparative Literature for its hospitality, Wanda Bachman for her transatlantic research assistance, and the friends who have helped to make Hanover, New Hampshire, a home away from home for me and my family: Jonathan Crewe, Helene Foley, Gerd Gemünden, Lotte Hirsch, Marianne Hirsch, Tom Luxon, Klaus Milich, Jeffry Robbins, Ivy Schweitzer, Leo Spitzer, Silvia Spitta, and Melissa Zeiger.

Thanks to my students in Hamburg and Düsseldorf, whose engagement with the issues of home and homecoming has been both affirmative and challenging. The German diminutive "Hiwi" trivializes the substantial contributions of the students who have assisted me with this project: Dietlind Falk donated her superb skills as a translator; Katrin Rond performed the mind-deadening task of proofreading with zealous perfectionism and inexplicable good humor; Yvonne Bothur and Eva Ritzenhoff graciously allowed me to take their research skills for granted. Thanks to Brigitte Coombs and Jutta Sonnberger for making things work. And thanks to my colleagues and co-workers at the Institute of English and American Studies at the Heinrich-Heine-Universität Düsseldorf for making my academic *Heimat* as congenial and stimulating as I could wish.

In the early stages of this project, I was supported by a *Habitationsstipendium* from the Kommission zur Vergabe von Mitteln für die individuelle Förderung von Wissenschaftlerinnen und Künstlerinnen an Hamburger Hochschulen, as well as by an External Fellowship from the Summer Humanities Institute ("The Futures of American Studies") at Dartmouth College.

Stephen G. Nichols, editor of Rethinking Theory, and the editors and staff of the Johns Hopkins University Press have supported this project with great care and daunting efficiency. I am grateful to JHUP's reader, Joseph A. Boone, for his insistence that I pursue overlooked and underformulated connections; his painstaking commentary on the manuscript inspired an extremely productive process of rethinking and revision. I have had the good fortune to work with a copyeditor, Barbara Lamb, whose engagement and wit have made the process of revision not only rewarding but also unexpectedly pleasurable. And thanks to Saul Leiter for his incredibly generous gift of the rights to the jacket photograph, an emblem of the home to which this book is written.

In *The Street I Know*, Harold E. Stearns reminds his readers that returning home is, more than anything else, returning to the people who make a place home. I'd like to thank those denizens of my German and American worlds who, by helping to make wherever I happened to be a home, supported this project more than they can imagine: Marielle Canova, Aileen and Tim Coffey, Brant Fries, Kyra Fries, Lorin Fries, Norma Harris, Jean Howard, Gesche Ketels, Eileen McMenamin, Amina Megalli and Jim Wertz, Deborah Osinsky and Bart Moore, Edith Neimark, Jass Peland and Rose Slirzewski, Teresa Pereira, Elise Salem, Barbara Wallraff, Steven Winnett and Laura Knoy, Andrea Zielinski, and the Franz-Schubert-Chor.

In memoriam: I hope that, in some small way, *Writing Home* does some justice to the thinking about *Heimat* that Marilyn Sibley Fries did not live long enough fully to bring to fruition. The late, great Mats quite literally never left my side during the writing of this manuscript and stayed alive just long enough to help me get it done. I recall with great joy the many ways in which Elaine and George Winnett were involved in the research and writing phases of this project. Whether giving me firsthand information about New York in the 1930s, helping me to hone sentences, baby- and dog-sitting, or just being the much-loved parents of a very lucky daughter, they *were* home. I dearly wish they had lived to see this book, which I lovingly dedicate to Gerd, Noah, and Dido.

Writing Back

Introduction

We wander in our thousands over the face of the earth . . . but it
seems to me that for each of us going home must be like going to
render an account.

—JOSEPH CONRAD, *Lord Jim*

Is the one who left ever the one who comes back?

—NADINE GORDIMER, *None to Accompany Me*

It's a complex fate, being an American.

—HENRY JAMES

AT THE END OF HENRY JAMES'S NOVEL *The Ambassadors*, Lambert
Strether has decided to return to America, despite the attractions
and appeals of his Parisian friends. In the course of his farewell conversation with Maria Gostrey, the expatriate American who has supervised his
Parisian adventure, her question, "To what do you go home?" initiates
the following exchange:

> "I don't know. There will always be something."
> "To a great difference," she said as she kept his hand.
> "A great difference—no doubt. Yet I shall see what I can make of it."
> (511)

For Strether, this difference lies in the changes wrought on his own
sensibility by the ambassadorship whose fulfillment was to secure his
American ties but has instead effected their dissolution. The skills he has
needed to acquire to perform the task set him by Mrs. Newsome have,
as he explains, rendered impossible any resumption of his engagement
to her:

"There's nothing anyone can do. It's over. Over for both of us."

Maria wondered, seemed a little to doubt. "Are you so sure for her?"

"Oh yes—sure now. Too much has happened. I'm different for her."

She took it in then, drawing a deeper breath. "I see. So that as she's different for *you*—"

"Ah but," he interrupted, "she's not." And as Miss Gostrey wondered again: "She's the same. She's more than ever the same. But I do what I didn't before—I *see* her." (510)

Strether never reveals *what* he now sees, but the effect on him of this new capacity for vision makes him unsuitably "different for" Mrs. Newsome at the same time as it enables him to recognize and dismiss the sameness against which this difference will manifest itself.

Strether defends his decision to return to such apparently bleak prospects by explaining that to come out "right" vis-à-vis his Parisian experience he must obey a "logic" that ensures that he "not, out of the whole thing" have "got anything" for himself (*Ambassadors* 393). This "logic" seems to suggest that, while there remains nothing in Woollett "to get," in Paris any number of fulfillments would await him. But it does not seem that James wishes to punish Strether, or indeed, that Strether regards "going home" as a self-punishment, although it might be regarded as a necessary penance for the knowledge he has reaped. In Strether's own words, it is a matter of "logic." What, then, determines this "logic," and what is its price? The question, "To what do you go home?" resonates beyond the foreseeable shipwreck of Strether's professional and marital prospects. To confront the "great difference" in such a way that one comes out "right" seems to have an attraction—one might even say, a compulsion—of its own that overrides the pleasures and comforts offered—however variously—by Paris, on the one hand, and Mrs. Newsome, on the other hand.

It is tantalizing to imagine the form and substance of a sequel to *The Ambassadors* that would explore the unfolding of the "logic" Strether invokes, the confrontation between the critical perception of difference that he calls "seeing," and a world that, he suggests, insists on remaining innocent of this faculty. Instead of pursuing such a project in a novel, James pursued it in life. In 1904, he returned to the United States for the first time in twenty years, prepared to document an adventure of seeing not unlike the one whose terms he sketched in the final pages of *The Ambassadors*. James considered himself particularly qualified for this task, boasting of both the "freshness of eye" of the "inquiring stranger" and the "advantage" of the "initiated native" (*American Scene* "Preface," n.p.). Yet neither the experience of repatriation nor the literary project he associated with it turned out to be as straightforward as James had anticipated, and the texts resulting from the ten months he spent in America between August 1904 and July 1905, *The American Scene* and "The Jolly Corner," manifest a "logic" as tortuous as the one that necessitates Strether's journey home.

Homecoming, it turns out, foils the neat ratio between distance and perspective, on the one hand, and familiarity and affection, on the other, that James projects will organize the America he reconfronts into a Jamesian "scene." For if James considers himself to have acquired in his absence the perfect qualifications to represent his native land, the country, during this same period, has developed into something that resists his representational capacities. Is there, as James contended, something specifically American about his experience of repatriation? Or does James's consternation with the America to which he returns have more to do with the experience of return per se than with the details either of his aesthetics or of what he repeatedly calls America's growth? Can one really take inventory of the "differences" that determine one's own experience of return, or does one's situation within this matrix of differences preclude a clear perspective on them? Is, as Nadine Gordimer asks in the passage cited as an epigraph above, "the one who left ever the one who comes back?"

I

I felt myself then, all serenely, not exposed to grave mistakes—
though there were also doubtless explanations which would find
me, and quite as contentedly, impenetrable.
— HENRY JAMES, *The American Scene*

This study takes as its subject the "great difference" that both separates and mutually constitutes America and the returning expatriate. In my readings of four autobiographical narratives by expatriate writers in which the return to America figures prominently—James's *The American Scene* (1907), Harold E. Stearns's *The Street I Know* (1935), Malcolm Cowley's *Exile's Return* (1934), and Gertrude Stein's *Everybody's Autobiography* (1937)—I examine how this difference manifests itself in the adventure of repatriation and, more specifically, in the texts that document this adventure. The study consists of detailed readings of these four autobiographical narratives; each reading attempts to assess not only how a particular writer represents the experience of repatriation but also, and more importantly, how, through its representation, this unsettling experience is crafted into the foundation of the writer's self-conception and, perhaps, more generally, a conception of the American artist or intellectual.

Although the texts I discuss are all first-person narratives of return to the United States, they differ in many other respects. *The American Scene* and *Everybody's Autobiography* were written by long-term expatriates who returned briefly to the United States at the height of their fame and productivity and then went home to the lives they had established for themselves in Europe. *The Street I Know* and *Exile's Return* were written after inauspicious returns that would prove to be permanent, following European sojourns that lasted eleven years in Stearns's case and two years in Cowley's. James and Stein were established writers for whom the return to America was a sort of celebration of the notoriety they had achieved during their years abroad. The Malcolm Cowley who returned to the United States in 1922 was a young and relatively unknown figure in the American cultural landscape, while the Harold Stearns who arrived back in New York in 1932 seemed to have traded the reputation for brilliant punditry he enjoyed between 1913 and 1921 for that of the Parisian bum and barfly. The accounts of their returns helped to establish—or in Stearns's case reestablish—their reputations as cultural critics.

Except for *The American Scene*, the texts I examine here were all written in the mid-1930s. (In fact, the chronology of their completion allows us to imagine Stein passing the buildings in which Cowley and Stearns were at work on *Exile's Return* and *The Street I Know* as she and Alice B. Toklas explored the streets of New York.) Although in the context of this study, *The American Scene* represents a historical anomaly, it is a precursor text for those accounts of repatriation that follow. Not only does it establish the repertoire of responses to repatriation on which the other texts will draw; it also anticipates the consequences—both literary and personal—of these responses. Stein's preoccupation with James is palpable throughout her oeuvre, and even though she nowhere alludes directly to him in *Everybody's Autobiography*, both her preoccupations and strategies in this text and her allusions to James elsewhere attest to the power of his example as well as to the centrality of his writing to her conception of American literature.[1] Stearns acknowledges his indebtedness to *The American Scene* by citing James's remarks on racial politics in the South in his epigraph to the chapter on race in *Rediscovering America* (171). Like James, Stearns is both tantalized and disturbed by the kinship between the returning expatriate and the immigrant. More generally, Stearns's attempt to recognize and document possible positive implications of situations to which his personal response is negative recalls James's approach in *The American Scene*, even if the two men's ultimate conclusions differ considerably. Cowley alone gives no sign that he is aware that others before him have tackled the issue of "return." Since he was too well-read not to know of James's book, I assume that his silence is strategic: in order to dramatize the originality and pathos of his "Lost Generation," he needs to remain silent about a figure toward whom he remained ambivalent, even in those writings in which he is most enthusiastic ("The Two Henry Jameses" 96–99).

Although all four texts are autobiographical in that they recount the experiences of their authors in the first person, they deploy the autobiographical occasion to different ends. For decades, *The American Scene* was read as a travelogue and evaluated according to the justice of its representations; only in recent decades has it been considered "autobiographical" and discussed as such.[2] James's text does not focus, as does conventional autobiography, on the development of the writer's consciousness, although this consciousness is clearly the ultimate locus of the drama of repatriation. Rather, the subject of the text is the "scene" registered by this consciousness and the difference between the country it remembers and the one it confronts. Hence, the life it ultimately records is less that of the individual, Henry James, as he returns to America than that of the *writer*, caught between representational strategies that have served him throughout an illustrious career and a world that he sees as resisting these strategies. As its title suggests, *Everybody's Autobiography* aggressively begs the question of the extent to which it is the record of its author's reencounter with America. The occasion of the text, Stein's return to her native country after thirty years, is not mentioned in the title and is actually ignored by many commentators. While its title announces the genre of the book to be autobiography, the word "everybody's" obscures and complicates the relation between the experience recorded in the book and its author. It turns out that the text is both thoroughly about Stein's trip to America and in service of her construction of herself as "everybody," the quintessential, because quintessentially "queer," American subject.

Like James and Stein, but for entirely different reasons, Malcolm Cowley renders the story of his return to America in terms that go beyond the personal. *Exile's Return* presents itself not simply as the account of one "exile's" ex- and repatriation but as that of an entire "generation" that Cowley calls into being. By incorporating his individual story into a "collective autobiography," Cowley constructs the genealogy of a Lost Generation that found itself in Europe and then returned home to transform the lessons of "exile" into an American cultural mainstream.[3]

It is ironic that only the least known of the four authors I study here—and hence the figure whose life story would not immediately solicit the interest of a contemporary reader—writes traditional autobiography. Although Harold Stearns is now virtually forgotten, prior to his expatriation in 1921, he was one of New York's most notorious intellectuals, considered by many to have been the instigator of the migration to Paris of the intellectuals and artists who would come to be known as the Lost Generation. But Stearns himself refuses to enlist himself in this cohort, writing an autobiography that focuses on the private man rather than the public intellectual and explores how even the persona of the pundit was determined as much by personal relations and neuroses as by the political and cultural issues with which Stearns was associated. Returning to New York from a life that derailed totally in the course of the eleven years he spent in Paris, Stearns compares repatriation and the opportunities to start again that America offers him with those it affords the immigrant. No longer an aloof commentator on the society that he had earlier excoriated for its vulgarity and homogenizing mercantilism, he now claims membership in the ranks of democracy's subjects. This perspective forces him to revise—but not to rescind—his critique of American society and to acknowledge the instances in which his education and pretensions had distorted his judgment. Stearns presents himself as a prodigal son whose return from Europe—and abjection—ratifies the mandate of American democracy.

II

What will they say to me and what will I say to them. I cannot believe that America has changed, many things have come and gone
but not really come and not really gone but they are there and that
perhaps does make the America that I left and the America I am to
find different but not really different, it would be impossible for it
to be really different or for me to find that it was really different.

— GERTRUDE STEIN, "Meditations on
being about to visit my native land"

Because of the very different generic affiliations, intentions, and aesthetic quality of the repatriation narratives I discuss, theoretically informed close reading is the only method that ensures that each text be engaged on its own terms and that the text, and not the life of its author, remain the subject of analysis.[4] Such readings give us access to the assumptions underlying both a text's self-constitution and our reception of it, and they represent a first step toward establishing for the subject of repatria-tion the kind of theoretical discourse that organizes discussion of such related themes as expatriation and exile, travel, and tourism.[5] I have drawn considerably on the historical, anecdotal, and theoretical material available on expatriation, although its general silence on the subject of repatriation not only limits its usefulness here but represents a concep-tual limitation as well: both the expatriate experience and the literature it has generated need to be reconsidered in light of the returns that punctu-ate or culminate them.[6] Along the same lines, while it is a commonplace in the modern and postmodern periods to regard the alienated intellec-tual as an exile, the extensive literature on creativity and exile studiously avoids the issues of repatriation and return, except as a mythic trope.[7] In the texts I examine here, the experience of return that Milan Kundera calls "the apotheosis of the known . . . a reconciliation with the finitude of life" (8) inevitably provokes both a reevaluation of the expatriate ex-perience and a critical reconsideration of the ways exile is deployed as a metaphor for certain forms of intellectual and spiritual alienation. Since there is so little scholarly literature that examines these processes, in section 3 of this introduction I generate my own topology of the subject by examining a selection of fictional and theoretical texts that represent and dwell upon the dynamics of the expatriate's reencounter with home.

In the readings of *The American Scene, Everybody's Autobiography, The Street I Know,* and *Exile's Return* that make up this study, my main concern has been to ascertain what personal drama, in each case, achieves articulation through the narrative of repatriation and to evaluate what is at stake in representing this drama via this narrative. This undertaking requires attention not only to a text's thematization of expatriation and return but also to silences, absences, inconsistencies, and details that might seem at first glance irrelevant or only marginally relevant to the study's thematic focus. These silences, absences, details, and incongruities grant us access to the particular concerns that get worked out through the repatriation narrative and help determine the theoretical framework most appropriate to each discussion. Hence, in the chapter on *The American Scene,* I follow James's cue and focus less on what he finds than on what he finds missing in America, tracing his struggle to organize the spectacle he encounters in terms of this missing quantity, the fundamentally European notion of manners that organizes his fiction. *The American Scene,* like "The Jolly Corner," a tale of repatriation written upon James's return to England, is concerned with the question of accommodating America to the sensibility of a Europeanized aesthetic temperament or, seen from a complementary perspective, with the viability of this figure in the American context. In *The American Scene,* James stages a confrontation between his representational techniques and the American medium that essentially resists them and assesses his capacity as an American writer to write America.

Whereas in the chapter on *The American Scene* I examine an absence in America that organizes James's account of his return, in the chapter on *Exile's Return* I turn my attention to an absence in the text itself that I find striking and significant. Although, as we know, women were both conspicuous and influential in the epoch and the milieu of which Malcolm Cowley writes, *Exile's Return* tells the story of the intellectual generation that came of age in the 1920s as though women had no part in it.[8] I begin my examination of the gender politics underlying this exclusion of women from the 'official' chronicle of the Lost Generation with readings of two texts about his mother that Cowley wrote late in life and that reflect on the same processes of growing up and leave-taking thematized in *Exile's Return*. These two attempted tributes to a figure who is never mentioned in *Exile's Return* reveal—as it were, retrospectively— the gender contours of the ambivalence that structures his early works. Although Cowley was candid about his ambivalent nostalgia for an authentic, rural America that sends its children into what he calls "exile," he was silent as to—and perhaps willfully unaware of—its gendering. Yet the pattern of escape, nostalgia, and return that shapes the narrative of his relation to his mother is uncannily similar to the structure of *nostos* that he imposes on the patently misogynistic *Exile's Return*. Reading the ambivalence toward his mother manifested in the late texts into Cowley's early writing enables us to see how he suppresses and ignores the issues of gender that troubled the self-styling of so many American male intellectuals in order at the end of his "literary odyssey" to instate himself and his cohorts at the vanguard of an untroubledly male American high culture.

My interest in Harold Stearns had its origin in what seemed to me to be the untoward acrimony that accompanies Cowley's every allusion to him and in my sense that Cowley had something at stake in writing Stearns out of the narrative I describe in the previous paragraph. Despite Cowley's repeated attempts to represent Harold Stearns as Elpenor to his own Odysseus, Stearns survived the shipwreck of his Paris experience not only to reencounter Cowley in New York City rather than Hades but also to tell a story that covers much of the same terrain as Cowley's. Yet the accents set by Stearns's *nostos* are anathema to the premises of Cowley's project and threaten the cultural, political, and gender hierarchies that structure and sustain Cowley's construction of the Lost Generation. Although Cowley continually calls attention to Stearns's debauchery, he is not really concerned that bums like Stearns discredit the new American cultural elite associated with him by proximity. Rather, not only does Stearns refuse to accede to the cultural generalizations that are Cowley's stock in trade, but his example disturbs the distinctions upon which *Exile's Return* depends.[9] Unlike Cowley's "tragic" icons of the 1920s, Hart Crane and Harry Crosby, Stearns hits rock bottom and then rehabilitates himself; unlike Cowley, Stearns represents the intellectual worlds of

New York and Paris as populated by women as well as men; and unlike Cowley, Stearns insists upon the personal, even neurotic motivations for actions that Cowley needs to deem culturally determined.[10]

The almost-suppressed detail in Stearns's text that goes furthest toward explaining the trajectory of his career is an intimate one that requires the kind of psychoanalytic explanation that Cowley refuses to pursue even in the cases of Crane and Crosby: the psychopathology of masochism suggested by an allusion to Rousseau turns out to structure both Stearns's private life—at least as he represents it—and the gender inflections of his public responses to his world. Reading Stearns's account of his life through the lens of a masochism whose sexual application he seems not to have pursued particularly vigorously explains the confused affection and respect for women palpable in his writing; it also helps to clarify the logic of his rebellion against and reconciliation with American society, goes far toward explaining the dereliction of his years in Paris, and suggests as well why repatriation brought an end to the abjection that governed his expatriate experience. Within the context of masochism—a pathological submission that simultaneously opposes and enforces the hierarchies constituting the individual—we can account for Stearns's challenge to and eventual resolution of the association between "femininity" and intellectual activity in American culture. As Stearns's relation to the dominant culture changes, so do his gender politics; unlike Cowley and so many other contemporaries who circumvent the threat of intellectual "feminization" through hypermasculine misogyny, Stearns, in his early writing, confronts the issue head on and, in his later works, shows how the vagaries of individual experience and cultural self-situation forced him to reconsider his relation to and attitude toward those social, racial, and gender hierarchies constituting the American individual that the expatriate seeks to escape.

It is impossible to discuss *The American Scene*, *Exile's Return*, and *The Street I Know* without reference to their occasions. However they may otherwise differ in tone, perspective, and literary quality, they demand to be, and have consistently been, read in the context of the returns to America that they chronicle. *Everybody's Autobiography* seems to invite a different kind of reception; few critical treatments of the text mention the return to the United States that is its ostensible subject, and even fewer take this subject into account in their conclusions. Instead, most commentators focus on the philosophical, antimimetic, and antinarrative premises that Stein champions in *Everybody's Autobiography* and the other texts she wrote in the wake of the commercial success of *The Autobiography of Alice B. Toklas*. Far from controverting or preempting such readings, however, a consideration of the philosophical challenge to her own aesthetic convictions posed by the trip to the United States that Stein represents as her ambivalent response to the success of *The Autobiography of Alice B. Toklas* enriches our understanding of Stein's life project and of the role she sees her Americanness as playing in her self-construction.

The textual detail that reconciles the identity-minded narrative trajectory of *Everybody's Autobiography* with an antinarrative aesthetic that rejects identity in favor of "existing" is the phrase "I am I because my little dog knows me" and the variations on this phrase that punctuate *Everybody's Autobiography* as well as the other texts Stein wrote during the same period. I trace the phrase to an old nursery rhyme, "Lawkamercyme," a dysphoric tale of "recognition and non-recognition" in which an old woman falls asleep on the way to market, is violated by a peddler, and, upon awakening to find her skirts cut off at the knee, fails to recognize herself ("this is none of I") but hopes that her "little dog" will rectify this crisis of identity by recognizing her when she returns home. The upshot of this homecoming narrative—the dog barks instead of wagging his tail—is the old woman's loss of identity. In the course of *Everybody's Autobiography,* Stein rings changes on the dynamics of recognition governing the "little dog's" responses in such a manner that, unlike the old woman, she dissociates herself from the tyranny of identity—in Stein's case, from the "outside" that expatriation had helped her to keep at bay but whose determining power had been revived by commercial success. Until the publication of *The Autobiography of Alice B. Toklas*, expatriate life in a hospitable but strange and indifferent country had enabled Stein to "be" American without being distracted by things American. Fame, however, altered her relation to her French surroundings: "It was less Paris than it had been and so it was natural that sooner or later I should go to America again" (*EA* 46). Stein represents the America to which she returns as having no use at all for the distinctions forged by "outside" and "inside" that govern social organization in France. In an America structured not by hierarchy but by degree ("In

America everybody is but some are more than others. I was more than others" [173]), Stein is able to claim the affiliation between her aesthetic and the ethos of the country. As the representative American, Stein represents the return to her country as the affirmation of everything that she had to leave it to achieve.

III

What Europe still gives an American—or gave us—is the sanction, if one can accept it, to become oneself. No artist can survive without this acceptance. But rare indeed is the American artist who achieved this without first becoming a wanderer, and then, upon his return to his own country, the loneliest and most blackly distrusted of men.

—JAMES BALDWIN, "The New Lost Generation"

Each of the writers whose work I examine in this study uses the occasion of return—more specifically, the occasion of writing about return—to evaluate a period of his or her life for which return represents at least a provisional culmination. Such an endeavor involves coming to terms with what this phase meant, and, more specifically, what it meant that this phase was spent abroad. "Who is the person who returned?" "How did I become the person who returned?" "What has become of this homeland to which I return?" "How did this country become the country to which I return?" and "How do I reconcile the changes in the 'me' who returns with the changes in the country to which I return?" are the questions most germane to this process of self-scrutiny, although these questions are as often acted out as articulated directly. Because the occasion of return crystallizes issues that predate and survive it, many of the texts that document it have less to do with return per se than with the retrospective construction of an "official" expatriation narrative. This narrative is often juxtaposed with a circumspective one that brings the critical faculties shaped through the retrospective act to bear on the present moment. This present, the occasion of writing, is a liminal moment that marks both the end of the trajectory begun by expatriation and the beginning of something new. The text of return is heavily invested in motivating this new beginning, in taking inventory of the successes and failures of the past, and in implementing their lessons in the future. But at the moment of new beginning, the text is forced to confront and take into consideration the particular ambivalences mobilized by the experience of return as well as the difficulties in identifying and negotiating what Lambert Strether in *The Ambassadors* called the "same" and the "different."

The chapters that follow explore the threat and challenge that homecoming represents to the expatriate. Before I narrow my focus to the specific nexus of issues confronting the returning expatriate, I would like to stress that it is not only the expatriate who experiences homecoming as a crisis. In the case of exile, homecoming represents both what Vladimir Janké-lévitch terms "le désir élémentaire du transplanté . . . [de] retourner à son point de départ" [the fundamental desire of the uprooted person . . . to return to his point of departure] and the reality test of this desire (284). In a discussion of exile and return that focuses on *The Odyssey*, Janké-lévitch imagines a "zero degree" narrative of repatriation that would entirely redress the experience of exile:[11] "Au degré zéro de la nostalgie le repatriement annulerait 'sans reste' (*restlos*) l'expatriement, comme le débarquement d'Ulysse à Ithaque annule, dix ans après, l'embarquement: pas de résidu incompensable, pas le moindre je-ne-sais-quoi; la liquidation de l'exil ne laisse ni regret ni rancoeur" [At the zero degree of nostalgia, repatriation would completely (*restlos*) cancel out expatriation, just as, ten years later, Ulysses' return to Ithaca cancels out his departure: not the slightest residue in need of compensation, not the smallest irrelevant detail; the canceling out of exile leaves behind neither regret nor bitterness] (283).

But, as *The Odyssey* never ceases to remind us, everything has changed: Odysseus is marked by the glories and miseries of war and exile; his son has grown up and embarked on his own quest; his mother is dead and his father wallowing in abjection; his palace is beleaguered by his faithful but restless wife's suitors. "Odysseus's homecoming," Svetlana Boym writes, "is about nonrecognition" (8). Odysseus fails to recognize his homeland when he is deposited there by the Phaeacians and returns to his palace disguised as an old beggar in order that he not be recognized before he has evaluated the loyalty of his family and subjects. Neither the Odysseus who returns nor the world to which he returns bears much resemblance to the memories that fuel the desire to return. If, as Jankélévitch claims, *The Odyssey* is the "narrative of a return that was supposed to be the infallible cure of nostalgia" (283), its narrative yield juxtaposes the processes of accommodation that *nostos* demands and the incommensurabilities that remain when these processes have taken place. In *The Odyssey*, these processes are painful and bloody, ultimately requiring divine intervention lest they overshoot their mark.

Jankélévitch writes that "le but de l'itinéraire odysséen, c'est le rendez-vous avec soi-même" [The goal of the Odyssean itinerary is the rendez-vous with oneself] (302). Even if the rendez-vous with oneself is not the intentional goal of a return home, it is an inevitable one. This rendez-vous is marked by the shocks of recognition and nonrecognition of which Gertrude Stein writes in *Everybody's Autobiography* and is perhaps figured most touchingly by the scene in book 13 of *The Odyssey*, in which the returned king of Ithaca surveys his island through the mist that Athena has produced in order to prevent him from being recognized:

> And so to the king himself all Ithaca looked strange . . .
>
> . . . .
>
> He sprang to his feet and, scanning his own native country,
> groaned, slapped his thighs with his flat palms
> and Odysseus cried in anguish:
> "Man of misery, whose land have I lit on now?
> What *are* they here—violent, savage, lawless?
> or friendly to strangers, god-fearing men?"   (HOMER 292–93)

Of course, the "they" in "What *are* they here?" is in reality a "we" or "I," and Odysseus turns out to be asking these anguishing questions of himself. Instead of settling into the home life he has anticipated, he has first, through his deeds, to answer this question. And in answering the question "What *are* they here?" through his deeds, Odysseus is revising the working definition of himself and his realm that had sustained him throughout exile. Thus, the question of identity is not only a question of deeds and attitudes but one of growth or development; the rendez-vous with oneself that is homecoming also involves a coming to terms with time.[12] It is significant that the only beings in Ithaca who recognize Odysseus before he reveals himself are Argos, the dog whose life term is sealed by his master's return, and Eurycleia, the nurse who identifies the beggar as Odysseus because of a wound he suffered as a child. The ties with home signified by the dog and the scar are ties to the past; the task of return is to make a comparable mark in the present that is enduring and true to the person one has become, that reconciles the landscape of nostalgia with the realities of the present.

The dynamics of recognition and their effect on the returnee's sense of self trouble the sense of home canonized in memory. Hugo von Hofmannsthal's "Die Briefe des Zurückgekehrten," a set of fictional letters written by a business traveler upon his return to Germany, traces the returnee's inability to locate the *Heimat* that had sustained him on his travels. Thinking back on his travels, the returnee recalls how particularly intense impressions—be they exotic or seemingly banal—evoked "home" to the extent that they expressed their own inner truth: "Wenn mir da ein guter Zug vor den Augen trat, was ich einen guten Zug nenne, ein etwas in der Haltung, das mir Respekt abnötigt und mehr als Respekt, ich weiss nicht, wie ich dies sagen soll. . . . Wenn etwas der Art mir unterkam, so dachte ich: Zuhause!" [When I noticed a good feature, something that I call a good feature, something in a person's bearing that exacts respect from me and more than respect—I don't quite know how to put it. . . . Whenever I came across something like that, I thought: home!] (281–82). The integrity of the "foreign" gesture recalls an integrity of feeling to which the traveler gives the name "home" ("Zuhause"):

Alles, was etwas Rechtes war, worin eine rechte Wahrhaftigkeit lag, eine reine Menschlichkeit, auch im Kleinen und Kleinsten, das schien mir hinüber zu deuten. Nein, meine ungeschickte Sprache sagt Dir wieder nicht die Wahrheit meines Gefühls: es war nicht Hinüberdeuten, auch nicht Erinnert-Werden an drüben, es war kein Hüben und Drüben, überhaupt keine Zweiheit, die ich verspürte: es war eins ins andere. Indem die Dinge an meine Seele schlugen, so war mir, ich läse ein buntes Buch des Lebens, aber das Buch handelte immerfort von Deutschland. (282)

[Everything that had something honorable about it, in which there was an honest truthfulness, a true humanity, even in small and in the smallest things, seemed to me to point over there. No, my awkward language again fails to tell you the truth of my emotion: it was neither a pointing toward nor a being reminded of that place over there, it wasn't any here or there, it wasn't any duality that I felt: the one thoroughly informed the other. While such things struck my soul, it seemed to me as if I were reading a colorful book of life, but the book was always about Germany.]

Homecoming fails to inspire such sensations: "Da bin ich nun vier Monate in Deutschland, und kein Haus, kein Fleck Erde, kein geredetes Wort, kein menschliches Gesicht . . . hat mir dies kleine Zeichen gegeben" [So now I have been in Germany for four months, and no house, no piece of earth, no spoken word, no human face . . . has given me this small sign] ("Briefe" 284). This ironic reversal leads the returnee to ask the question: "Wo *war* ich jedesmal, wenn ich in dem Land zu sein meinte, das man durch den Spiegel der Erinnerung betritt . . . ? Nun da dies Deutschland ist, so war ich nicht in Deutschland. Und dennoch, ich nannte es in mir Deutschland" [Where *was* I every time I thought I was in the country one enters through the looking glass of memory . . . ? Now, if this is Germany, Germany is not where I was. And yet, inside of me, I called it Germany"] (284). "Deutschland," in this formulation, is the name the traveler gives to the landscape of memory, to the looking-glass world constructed in the absence of the reality principle and internalized as *Heimat* ("ich nannte es in mir Deutschland"). In order to account for the discrepancy between this internalized "Deutschland" and the outside world that confronts him upon repatriation, the traveler explains how intense foreign impressions activated and organized a chaotic internal archive of impressions, ideals, memories, images, and cultural clichés into a sensation to which his longing gave the name "Deutschland": "Ich war nur wie die Klaviatur, auf der eine fremde Hand spielte. Aber in mir lag etwas, ein Gewoge, ein Chaos, ein Ungeborenes, und daraus konnten Figuren entstehen, und das waren deutsche Figuren. . . . Deutsche Figuren waren es, die sich zu diesen Zauberbildern zusammenballten . . . und gleich wieder auseinanderflossen, deutsche sparsame Gebärden, ich weiß nicht vom innersten Wesen der Heimat." [It was as if I was only the keyboard upon which a foreign hand played. But there was something in me, a fluctuation, a chaos, something unborn, from which figures could rise, and these were German figures. . . .The figures piling up into such magical pictures and then quickly dissipating were German figures . . . frugal German gestures, something ineffable from the innermost nature of home.] (285). The integrity of *Heimat* turns out, however, to have been borrowed from a foreign gesture ("eine fremde Hand"); the same repertoire of "fluctuation, chaos, something unborn" fails to respond to the stimuli of Germany. If *Heimat* is a collection of preconscious, unstable, unbound, even unborn internal predispositions that, when organized—"played"—by the hand of culture, designate a local habitation and earn a name, its irony lies in the seeming dependence of its dynamics on the *difference* between the culture to which these predispositions are native and that foreign culture whose appearances organize them into the sensation of home. In other words, *Heimat* is always nostalgic, coming into focus only through principles of longing that homecoming renders inoperative.

In his practical guide for returning expatriates, *The Art of Coming Home*, Craig Storti attributes the severe difficulties that repatriates experience to the "notion of home itself" and "the expectations it sets up in us." This notion encompasses both the fairly straightforward identification of "home" as being "the place where you were born and raised, where people speak your native language and behave more or less the way you do," and also more inchoate assumptions about familiarity, loyalty, routine, and predictability that the experience of homecoming is likely to baffle and disappoint (3). The returnee often finds that the native language and geography make homecoming more mystifying than arriving in a foreign country, since, on the one hand, the foreignness of home is entirely unexpected and, on the other hand, one's tools for dealing with the more conventionally foreign seem inadequate to the task of deciphering the ostensibly familiar. For this reason, the perspective from which the repatriate reconstructs the chain of events that connects departure and return is, perhaps unexpectedly, unstable. Iain Chambers suggests that homecoming makes it possible to regard expatriation as a detour from a life itinerary reconceived in terms of the geographical, national, social, racial, familial, and class determinants into which an individual was born, and to recast the future in terms of these determinants.[13] Yet, as Biddy Martin and Chanda Mohanty point out, if "'being home' refers to the place where one lives within familiar, safe, protected boundaries," experiences of "not being home," such as expatriation, tend to foster the realization "that home was an illusion of coherence and safety based on the exclusion of specific histories of oppression and resistance, the repression of differences even within oneself" (196). Thus, the reconception of the life trajectory that accompanies homecoming must come to terms both with the contradictions and incommensurabilities that absence has forged and with those of which distance and return have made the individual aware. As James Clifford writes, "Perhaps there's no return for anyone to a native land—only field notes for its reinvention" (173).

The change of perspective that results from expatriation ensures that the returnee never entirely coincides with the world that he or she rejoins.[14] In her "Meditations on being about to visit my native land," Gertrude Stein worries about the nature and possible sources of the "difference" she anticipates: "The cities do seem to have much less to do with my memories, they seem to be different, but I hope not. I hope they are not really different. One does not like to feel different and if one does not like to feel different then one hopes that things will not look different. It is alright for them to seem different but not to be different" (2). Is America different because it has changed, in which case things would "*be* different," or because Gertrude Stein has changed, and her changed perspective makes things that have remained the same "*seem* different"? Stein fears the change of the "things" to which she is planning to return but rejoices in the change of perspective she plans to bring to them. What, however, if both have changed? Have they moved together or apart? In *The Street I Know*, Harold Stearns recalls savoring the conundrum posed by this play of difference: "This was in reality a voyage of rediscovery for me—after all, nobody can stay away as long as I had from home, and then expect to step right into the new rhythm of things, especially in America. . . . I couldn't understand this lack of any feeling of strangeness, a kind of vague wonder and doubt as to whether or not you really have ever been away at all. What was happening to me, however, was really the simplest thing in the world, though I didn't know it until I experienced it—I was coming home" (373). The residual familiarity with and self-implication in the American scene that so excites Stearns exasperates Henry Miller, who considers them impediments to the true appreciation of what he takes to be America's grotesqueness: "I wish I were a foreigner and getting it from scratch" (5).

Miller's desire to get it "from scratch" is a particularly radical response to the crisis of estrangement and belonging that afflicts all returnees. Most returnees are anxious to reestablish connection with their home countries, to hear and share in what Chris Offutt calls "the sounds of home, the language of the land" (39). Yet, as Offutt discovers, the other languages he's learned to speak and understand during his time away from home distance him from the intimacies he seeks, and his fluency with "the sounds of home" distances him from the intimacies he's forged abroad. In his account of his return to teach at the "high school with ashtrays" that is the rural Kentucky college from which he graduated, he tells of meeting an old friend on the way to his job interview:

"What are you doing back? Going to court?"
"No, why?" . . .
"You're dressed for it."
"These are my job-hunting clothes." . . .
"You coming back?" he said.
"Trying to. I got an interview today."
"Where at?"
"The college."
"They're hiring," Otis said. "I don't know if you can get on with the painters, but they need movers. You go in there and talk to Amos Riddle. You know any Riddles? They live up on Redbird."
"It's not for maintenance, Otis."
"It's not."
"No," I said. "It's for teaching. You know, to be a teacher."
Otis and Billy erupted with laughter, bellowing as if their lives lacked mirth and they were grateful for the joke. When the sound trailed away, they looked at me and I knew they were waiting for the truth.
"I swear, boys, I took it up out west." (23–24)

Offutt finds that his time "away" has put him on the wrong side of the boundary he hoped to have put behind him by returning home. Although he revels in his renewed communion with the world into which he was born, he also rediscovers—in new and unexpected forms—the reasons why he left it, and finds that what he brings back with him— most tangibly, his Jewish wife and worldly sons—can find no place there. In the memoir's penultimate words, spoken by Offutt's father-in-law, an Auschwitz survivor whose story is presented in counterpoint to Offutt's, we hear echoes of the author's own disillusion: "Home is a feeling, nothing more. Home is illusory, like love, then it disappears. Once you leave, you become a stranger. I lost my home and that's forever. I wouldn't go back to Poland. It breaks my heart. They don't want me there. All my memories are shadows, lousy shadows. That country is forsaken. Home is where I hang my head" (266).

Repatriation is a lonely experience. Those who have remained at home are not necessarily interested in the experiences of the returnee, who is expected to do all the work of reaccommodation. In Milan Kundera's novel of repatriation, *Ignorance*, the protagonist, Irena, returns to Prague after twenty years of exile in Paris to confront first her old friends' "total uninterest in her experience abroad" and then, a more insidious interrogation that serves to "check whether she knows what they know, whether she remembers what they remember." With this interrogation, she realizes, "they are trying to stitch her old past life onto her present life. As if they were amputating her forearm and attaching the hand directly to the elbow; as if they were amputating her calves and joining her feet to her knees" (43). The particularity of Irena's life threatens to be obliterated by the stereotypes that determine others' perception of her. Irena's French friends are incapable of regarding her as anything but an émigrée, and they wrongly assume that she would want to return to Prague to share in the drama of rebuilding her liberated homeland; her Czech friends accept her only at the price of the repression of the experiences abroad that have constituted her adulthood. And while these projections and interdictions help Irena to admit to the contours of the personal motivations that guided both her emigration and her return, they further alienate her from the worlds she inhabits. If homecoming is a mirror in which the individual confronts with brutal clarity the partiality of the myths that have sustained him or her abroad, it is a mirror invisible to the denizens of home, whose own agenda has to do with issues and passions that expatriation has relegated to the past: "The life we've left behind us has a bad habit of stepping out of the shadows, of bringing complaints against us, of taking us to court" (90).

"Strange *man*": Penelope's first words to the man who claims to be Odysseus articulate the gulf that separates the returnee from the reality of home (Homer 461). The narrative of return is written both in defiance and in the context of this "strangeness." The returnee insists upon the authority of the experience that separates him or her from those who have remained at home and, however anxious he or she may be to rejoin the community, remains suspicious of even the best-intentioned attempts at domestication. As André Gide's rewriting of the biblical parable of the Prodigal Son dramatizes, that it is right to return does not mean that it was wrong to leave. In the biblical parable, the son, by repenting, repudiates his experience abroad ("Father, I have sinned against God and against you; I am no longer fit to be called your son" [Luke 15:21]); the parable closes with the reintegration of the son into the closed circle of the father's love ("Your brother here was dead and has come back to life, was lost and is found" [15:32]). By expanding the context in which we read the biblical parable and recording the Prodigal Son's inner monologue as well as his conversations with his father, mother, and brothers, Gide's text insists upon the substance, authority, and contagion of the son's experience even within the context of repentance and return. The desires that initiated the Prodigal Son's journey have been neither quenched nor invalidated; they have been exhausted. What remains is the desire for reconciliation that he describes to his mother:

—Mon seul soin désormais c'est de ressembler à vous tous.
—Tu dis cela avec resignation.
—Rien n'est plus fatigant que de réaliser sa dissemblance. Ce voyage à la fin m'a lassé. (Gide 194)

["My only aim from now on is to be like all of you."
"You say this as if with resignation."
"Nothing is more exhausting than to realize one's difference. In the end, this journey has worn me out."]

Yet this desire to come to "be like" the rest of his family is as doomed as the desire to "realize his difference," not only because the returnee cannot forget the desires that sent him away in the first place but also because the family is already different from itself; the returnee's younger brother is on the verge of setting out on his own quest to "realize his difference." Whatever needs and motivations determine the Prodigal Son's return to the parental fold, this return is neither an argument against his younger brother's setting out nor necessarily a model for the futility of the younger brother's quest. Rather, the change in perspective that is the result of living abroad has so altered the returnee's perspective that he sees beyond the apparent failure of his own quest to the potential success of his brother's. Because he is not like the rest of his family, he can both encourage his brother to leave and find in his brother's departure his own reason to stay on at home: "pour consoler notre mère" [to comfort our mother] (Gide 207).

IV

The[y] were also trying to escape something more subtle, some
quality of American civilization that they carried within themselves.

—MALCOLM COWLEY, Exile's Return

Thus far, I have foregrounded the general issues surrounding any expatriate's return home, even though my discussions have suggested how the characteristics of a specific country or community shape and color the experience of return. This study addresses the ways in which America determines the returns that are the central events in *The American Scene*, *The Street I Know*, *Exile's Return*, and *Everybody's Autobiography*. For James, Stearns, Cowley, and Stein, the reencounter with America involves coming to terms both with a country they felt they had to leave in order to realize themselves as writers and with a self that has experimented, through expatriation, with the notion that it is properly native to a country or culture other than its native one. Expatriation and, more specifically, the migration to Europe of American artists and intellectuals in the early twentieth century are commonplaces of United States cultural history and have been amply documented, both by scholars and by the expatriates themselves.[15] The litany of America's lacks with which Henry James explains why Nathaniel Hawthorne never wrote a truly great novel is traditionally taken to explain more generally the sense of America's cultural poverty, which compelled James and generations of artists after him to settle, at least temporarily, in Europe:

> It takes so many things . . . it takes such an accumulation of history and custom, such a complexity of manners and types, to form a fund of suggestion for a novelist. . . . One might enumerate the items of high civilization, as it exists in other countries, which are absent from the texture of American life, until it should become a

wonder to know what was left. No State, in the European sense of the word, and indeed barely a specific national name. No sovereign, no court, no personal loyalty, no aristocracy, no church, no clergy, no army, no diplomatic service, no country gentlemen, no palaces, no castles, nor manors, nor old country-houses, nor parsonages, nor thatched cottages nor ivied ruins; no cathedrals, nor abbeys, nor little Norman churches; no great Universities nor public schools—no Oxford, nor Eton, nor Harrow; no literature, no novels, no museums, no pictures, no political society, no sporting class—no Epsom nor Ascot! (*Hawthorne* 351–52)

For James as well as for subsequent generations of writers, Europe represented a cultural alternative to an America in which, as Kenneth Burke wrote in a 1923 letter to Malcolm Cowley, "there is . . . not a trace of . . . the really dignified richness which makes for peasants, household gods, traditions. America has become the wonder of the world simply because America is the purest concentration point for the vices and vulgarities of the world" (Jay 131). Rather, however, than cementing the kinds of prejudices articulated by Burke, the experience of Europe has often led to a more distanced and nuanced—and often more generous—attitude toward one's native country. Responding from France to his stay-at-home friend's excoriation of America, Cowley objected:

> *That really dignified richness*—shit, Kenneth, since when have you been a furniture salesman. You seem to have the disease of the American lady I met in Giverny. "You know, in America the wallpaper hardly seems to last a minute, it fades or peels off so quickly, but heah the good European papuh dyed with European dyes and put on with *that good European glue* . . . it just seems to last forevuh." Let me assure you that the chiefest benefit of my two years in Europe was the fact that it freed me from the prejudices of that lady—whose European flour paste was so much better than the American product—and of Harold Stearns. America is just as Goddamned good as Europe—worse in some ways, better in others, just as appreciative, fresher material, inclined to stay at peace instead of marching into the Ruhr. I'm not ashamed to take off my coat anywhere and tell these cunt-lapping Europeans that I'm an American citizen. (134–35)[16]

The confrontation with a foreign culture initiates a process of self-scrutiny and reassessment of one's national identity. Cowley's defense of the culture he scorned as mercilessly as Burke before his European sojourn echoes a shift in perspective experienced by many expatriates. The newly won patriotism that he vents in the passage above is one, perhaps dubious, result of this process. As part, however, of his realization that things European are not by definition better than things American, it *can* represent a necessary first step toward a possibly more tolerant—although no less critical—and, hence, potentially more productive relation to the country to which he will return. Along the same lines, it can also represent an important first step toward a more productive acceptance of himself as an intellectual within the American context.

The expatriate's relation to America is thus marked by a double distancing: a first distancing that mandates expatriation and a second that is its product. These two acts of distancing appear, at first glance, to annul each other. The perspective on one's native land that deems it unlivable is at least offset by a more generous attitude borne of physical distance and the experience of cultural relativity. But instead of canceling each other out, the two perspectives tend to coexist. Expatriation is thus a liminal experience in which one inhabits and responds to two cultures simultaneously and does so from two distinct vantage points. When, for instance, I am at home among Americans, I often find the texture of my native culture as well as my ideological implication in it unbearable. The longer I live in a foreign country, the more abstract my involvement with my native country necessarily becomes. Since I no longer experience America on a daily basis and enjoy the foreigner's perspective on the country in which I live, I enjoy the tolerance born of distance vis-à-vis both. At the same time, because of my difference—in attitude, in status, in (dis)enfranchisement, even in physical appearance—from the "foreign" culture in which I live, I am more—and more constantly—aware of my national identity (or of my identity *as* a national one) than is the case when I am at home among Americans. Against the backdrop of a host culture in which, I recognize, I could never have become the person I am, I am forced to regard my native culture with more generosity. My defiant self-distancing from America is replaced by a national self-identification that is, however, dictated as much by the terms of the host culture as by those I generate myself. What might appear to be patriotism on my part is reactive: if I no longer inveigh against the aspects of America that made not living there an attractive possibility, it is in response to European myths of American philistinism, which I try to debunk through my own example, proving to Europeans that not all Americans chew gum and that, indeed, there are many Americans—most obviously, myself—who are fluent in foreign languages. I become—for the good of the country with which I am identified—an ambassador. In the process of becoming a "foreigner," I also become a representative American.

What happens to this representative American qua foreigner when she or he returns home? As soon as the airplane lands, being "home" makes claims and confers privileges that I may not have missed but whose presence changes entirely the texture of my relation to my world. Most palpably, when I speak English, I am no longer speaking a foreign language. However well I speak the language that is not my native one, it is always a relief not to have to and a joy to experience English—and more specifically, New York English—as background noise. After decades of transatlantic commuting, I still experience a frisson of something like pleasure and pride when, along with fellow Americans of all conceivable ethnic, racial, and social backgrounds, I can speed through the "American citizen" line at passport control, instead of waiting and being scrutinized with those predominantly white fellow passengers with whom, at the beginning of the trip, I shared a home town. It means a lot to me that my son, who was born abroad and has never spent more than eight consecutive weeks in the United States, has a passport like mine and can join me in this line. The almost euphoric feeling of arrival—of belonging, of enfranchisement—is tested as soon I confront—or even anticipate confronting—the airport's monumental welcoming photograph of whoever happens to be the current president. The iconography of the United States makes visceral, inescapable claims on me; even if I didn't vote for him, the president whose countenance greets me is my responsibility. Until recently, this man's face most often served to remind me that the majority of Americans who bothered to vote voted for him and that I belong to a minority—both because I voted and because I did not necessarily vote for him. The aggressive ubiquity of the American flag reminds me of my own lifelong refusal to salute it and of the FBI file that, I've been told, documents this and other, similar manifestations of my deficient patriotism. Before I have even passed through customs, I am anything but a representative American.

The critical national self-awareness that is a consequence of expatriation must stand up to the test of return. If, as James Baldwin points out, the "discovery of what it means to be an American" was the unexpected yield of his first sojourn in Paris, return is the logical consequence of this discovery:

> One day it begins to be borne in on the [American] writer, and with great force, that he is living in Europe as an American. . . . It may be the day on which someone asks him to explain Little Rock and he begins to feel that it would be simpler—and, corny as the words may sound, more honorable—to *go* to Little Rock than sit in Europe, on an American passport, trying to explain it.
>
> This is a personal day, a terrible day, the day to which his entire sojourn has been tending. It is the day he realizes that there are no untroubled countries in this fearfully troubled world; that if he has been preparing himself for anything in Europe, he has been preparing himself—for America. In short, the freedom that the American writer finds in Europe brings him, full circle, back to himself, with the responsibility for his development where it always was: in his own hands. ("Discovery" 174–75)

Although Baldwin considers voluntary repatriation to be the "honorable" response to the process of self-discovery undergone by the American expatriate writer, he warns that it is a "terrible" and complex experience. Both the documents of repatriation that we do have and the fact that there are so few of them suggest that what Baldwin called the "responsibility for his own development" that the American writer assumes is hard to bear and even harder to write about. That only a handful of the writers who have chronicled their expatriate adventures have been willing or able to write about their returns to America is not due to lack of opportunity; most expatriate writers return to the United States after several years, and even those who establish permanent residences abroad visit their native country at least occasionally. It seems, rather, to have to do with the difficulty and inescapability of the challenge that Lambert Strether sets himself vis-à-vis the "difference" he anticipates: "to come out right" in light of what one now "sees," to reconcile the radical changes wrought by expatriation with the claims of one's personal past and one's national identity. Moreover, scrutinizing oneself in the wake of repatriation not only involves coming to terms with such changes; one also runs the risk of recognizing the vulnerability of these changes and of blurring the line one has drawn between oneself and one's native country.

Return poses a serious challenge to the particular fictions of nationality and national identity, authority, and relation to culture granted by expatriation. The return of an intellectual or a writer to a country he or she had decided to leave raises a series of questions about the relations between national identity and individual creativity, alienation and enfranchisement, personal experience and the autobiographical rendering of this experience: How does someone who has become both more and less of an American through living abroad deal with the claims, both real and imagined, of America? What happens to a consciously and successfully constructed authorial "identity" when it is forced to confront those scenes it had to escape in order to construct itself? In which ways is the work of repatriation complicated by the constructs of citizenship, race, gender, and sexuality that structure American society (and thus, to some extent at least, the American "self") and from which the expatriate is at least provisionally or theoretically released? What happens to the persona self-consciously constructed in opposition to what it takes to be "American" when it is reclaimed by a native ideology of the self? What writing strategies do authors devise to deal with—or to avoid dealing with—these questions?

For all their differences and in their different ways, the texts of repatriation I discuss in this study make manifest what is at stake in the project of "writing back." Intentionally ambiguous, the phrase "writing back" suggests both the performative and conative aspects of repatriation memoirs. The text produced by the returning expatriate constitutes the official version of the return; the author writes him- or herself "back." This text stands in for—and can even obfuscate or compensate for—the actual experience. The effects of this process are particularly clear in the case of Henry James, who left four wildly different textual renditions of his return. James's letters give us a sense of what we take to be his ongoing experience of repatriation, while his journal entries reveal moments of emotional upheaval that he clearly kept to himself. The two texts written upon his return to England, *The American Scene* and "The Jolly Corner," represent two additional, and very different treatments of his journey home: *The American Scene* presents itself as a document of the absentee *writer's* reencounter with his native land, while "The Jolly Corner" examines the individual pathology of a return whose superficial circumstances resemble James's own but which cannot possibly be read as an account of his experience. In addition to its performative character, the text of repatriation is also both a response and an appeal. "Writing back" implies a reader or even an interlocutor whose critical attention is solicited by the text at the same time as it remains a source of some uneasiness. Addressing the sorts of questions enumerated in the preceding paragraph, the text of repatriation often also construes itself as a response to the implicit challenge to justify the necessity of expatriation. It is thus, simultaneously, an appeal for sympathy toward both the original decision to leave and the later decision to return. It is even possible, as in the case of Gertrude Stein, that the text of repatriation addresses itself "back" to Europe, becoming the vehicle of the authorial persona's renewed commitment to life abroad, of a return from return.

The act of "writing back" borrows something of its tension from the ocean voyage back to America, which, in the years before mass transatlantic air travel on which I focus here, represented a ceremonial buffer between the Old World and the New. During the week that it took to effect the transition from Europe to the United States, the past could be rehashed and the future rehearsed within the extraterritorial space and provisional society of the ocean liner. New friendships smoothed the transition back into American culture: Gertrude Stein writes of a Newark "throat doctor" whom she meets on the *Champlain* and whom she consults about the throat problems she anticipates having in America:

> I was beginning to have qualms, I had never bothered about my
> throat, in France when you say anything you say it very loudly
> and it is like standing, they can stand and stand but while they are
> standing they talk. In America they stand but as they stand they
> do not talk that is not much and never very loudly, but in France
> standing is always accompanied by violent conversation, and so
> I had never thought about my throat but now that I was going
> to lecture I at once was certain that my voice was failing me and

meeting Doctor Wood was perfect because I could tell him all my symptoms and he could console me. He did but even so I knew it would happen and it did. (*EA* 174)

The chance encounter with an otolaryngologist gives Stein the terms with which to name and work through her anxieties about the transition from France to America. Indeed, she continues, her voice did threaten to fail her on the eve of her first lecture. Doctor Wood was summoned, felt her pulse, "and he was there at the first lecture and so was my voice and we have never seen him again but we do not forget him. New York was coming nearer and we were nervous" (174).

Harold Stearns, too, writes of a shipboard acquaintance who helps him battle the anxieties of return: "There was a very agreeable fellow from Saint Louis or Cincinnati, who somehow made me realize that, when all was said and done, genuine human beings still lived in America,—I had been away a long time, but there was nothing to be frightened about. Things were bad, yes; but they would get better" (*Street* 371–72). The contagion of the midwesterner's American optimism is marked by the manner in which, in the indirect discourse of this essentially first-person narrative passage, Stearns's fellow-traveler's words of reassurance seem to be shared or taken on by the narrative voice. The companion whose attitude gave the penniless, friendless, decrepit Stearns the courage to dis-embark also accompanies him on his first sallies into this new old world: he invites him to share a taxicab and a hotel room, and, before disap-pearing forever from Stearns's life, presents him with a token of initiation into modern America, "a new trick form of safety-razor" (375).

Stearns's friend's gift of a razor—albeit a "safety-razor"—suggests that repatriation has its own dangers and can be a damaging experience if not handled well. If the text of return partakes of the liminal, transi-tional mood that James describes as "a kind of fluidity of appreciation—a mild, warm wave that broke over the succession of aspects and objects according to some odd inward rhythm . . . that carried me up into the subject, so to speak, and enabled me to step ashore" (*AS* 3), it also has its reality principle, figured in each of the texts I discuss here by New York. The reality of the New York he reencounters strikes Malcolm Cowley as "strange . . . the exhausting and dispiriting heat, the colors of the houses, the straightaway vistas, the girls on the sidewalk in their bright frocks, so different from the drab ones that French shopgirls wore, and most of all the lack of anything green to break the monotony of the square streets, the glass, brick and iron. The next year—the next three years, in fact—would be spent in readjusting myself to this once familiar environment" (*Exile's Return* 182). In these texts, New York represents both what is familiar and what is alien to the returnee. Stein writes, "It was foreign but also it was a memory and it was exciting" (*EA* 179). The sublime arrogance of its self-assertion, what James, thrilled and ambivalent, calls New York's "dauntless power," challenges the returnee to negotiate a future that is both a personal and a national one (*AS* 74). If, as James suggests throughout *The American Scene*, America is a master-text that threatens to overwhelm—or overwrite—the individual life trajectory, in the very act of claiming its legitimacy, the text of return places itself in defiance of this hegemonic narrative. To be sure, the persona honed abroad submits itself to the test of home; but the narrative of return submits "home" to the test of the returnee's experience, exploring to what extent the personal and national can be reconciled with each other and be figured as occupying a common trajectory.

V

I knew the dream couldn't go on forever, yet I couldn't see what
the awakening would be. And I didn't care. Paris is like that. Only
there, I think, is possible such a complete mood of each day and
hour for itself, without regrets about the past or plans concerning
the future—a sort of soft, animal contentment at just being alive.
It is a very dangerous mood for an American of my New England
temperament, the strong and beguiling reaction from a tradition of
purposefulness and moral integrity. Even as an experience I don't
recommend it.

—HAROLD STEARNS, *The Street I Know*

Expatriation needs to be set in relation to and distinguished from two related phenomena about which far more has been written: travel and exile. While expatriation in general and the writing it generates borrow many of their topoi and much of their emotional repertoire from exile and the literary tradition of exile writing, American expatriation in particular must be also be understood in the context and as an outgrowth of the European travel and travel writing that figured so prominently in American society and culture in the nineteenth century. Extensive European travel was a mainstay for earlier generations of American writers and intellectuals; writing about these travels represented a source of income and renown and evolved into a genre through which, as Larzer Ziff argues, Americans, "defensively conscious of their want of national traditions yet aggressively proud of their new ways," were able to "measur[e] those ways against the manner in which other societies met the problems of living the daily life" (7). The beginnings of Henry James's European career followed the model set by such illustrious "travelers" as Benjamin Franklin, Thomas Jefferson, Washington Irving, George Ticknor, James Fenimore Cooper, Henry Wadsworth Longfellow, Ralph Waldo Emerson, Nathaniel Hawthorne, Mark Twain, and Margaret Fuller. James's early fictional chronicles of American travelers confronting Europe's "traditions, glamour, polish, and culture" as well as its languor and corruption recall, at least in part, the writings of nineteenth-century travelers, for whom, William W. Stowe argues, "Europe served as a stage for independent self-definition, for establishing personal relations with culture and society that did not necessarily fit the conventional patterns prescribed by hometown and family standards" (5). Both Stowe and Ziff emphasize how travel abroad afforded Americans the opportunity both to contextualize and to evaluate what was taken for granted in American culture and society and to project alternative modes of thought and behavior. Mary Suzanne Schriber extends this argument by exploring the gender inflections of travel writing, arguing that if "writing home from abroad entails seeing 'home' in a new light and writing *about* home from a new vantage point," then "travel writing by women carries a special relationship to 'home' because by cultural assignment, women are 'about' home in a particular way" (9).

Traveling gives the American a new perspective on home; writing about one's travels, communicating the foreign to a domestic audience, serves both to challenge and to affirm the home to which, it is assumed, each traveler will return. Not only is America openly compared with the countries the traveler visits; the cultural skills gleaned from an American education are tested in foreign contexts. Yet none of the critics I have mentioned considers how the critical project of the traveler and the cultural skills gleaned from his or her adventures hold up to the actual experience of returning home. Certainly, this omission is due in part to the scant attention paid to return in the works they examine, although it is hard to understand how a book that is called *Return Passages* and that includes a substantial discussion of James's *The American Scene* can ignore the issue to the extent it does. If, as my epigraph from *Lord Jim* suggests, "going home must be like going to render an account," the failure to render an account, in the sense of chronicling, the experience of going home might represent an unwillingness to render an account of it, in the sense of taking stock and evaluating. However revealing the experience of travel might be, the experience of homecoming is more—and perhaps more frighteningly—so, for it brings the foreign to bear on the formerly familiar and vice versa, forcing both the traveler-writer and the critic to perform a task of evaluation in which the stability of home as a touchstone for comparison and evaluation is called into question by the gesture that ostensibly affirms it.

For the travel writer, return can conceivably be ignored, preempted by the activity of "writing home," or glossed over as one of the givens of the genre of travel writing. For the exile, whose sojourn abroad is involuntary, return, however complicated it might become, would seem to be the experience for which she or he has been yearning, the restitution of a wholeness that the ordeal of exile has sundered. For the expatriate who has chosen to stay abroad and claimed another country as "home," return is a highly ambivalent experience, since it remobilizes all the conscious and unconscious factors that contributed to the decision to abandon his or her native country.

There is a fine line between travel and expatriation in late nineteenth- and early twentieth-century America—how many expatriates simply stopped "traveling" abroad and settled down? The distinction between *expatriation* and *exile*, two terms that are often used interchangeably, is both a far more important and a more difficult one to draw. Many discussions of expatriation—not to mention a substantial number of expatriates themselves—have overlooked this distinction, and tended to apply the experiences and emotions associated with exile—expulsion from one's homeland, the pathos of homelessness, unquenchable nostalgia—to a phenomenon that has very different coordinates and a very different repertoire of affect. Exile, as Mary McCarthy points out, is essentially political, "a punishment . . . from above" that decrees that an individual be expelled from and prevented from returning to his or her home country (50). Although I think McCarthy goes too far in her distinction between exiles and expatriates when she calls the expatriate a "hedonist," whose goal is "never to go back to his native land or, failing that, to stay away as long as possible" (51), she is right in emphasizing that expatriation represents a "voluntary departure" that may or may not have a directly political component: the individual seeks in a new country conditions of self-realization not available at home. While the expatriate makes the decision to leave home, the exile is forced to do so, and typically yearns to return home. The exile measures the world into which he or she has been expelled against a home that comes to be perceived as essential to a sense of identity when—or even, to the extent that—it is no longer available. This involuntary banishment thus amounts to a "condition of waiting" in which "the exile's whole being is concentrated on the land he left behind, in memories and hopes" (49). The particular pathos that distinguishes exile from expatriation arises from the feeling that, in being estranged from home, the exile is involuntarily estranged from what she or he most essentially is.[17] In order not entirely to lose this "essential" component of the self, the exile must create and sustain an imaginary connection to the lost home that strains and compromises any accommodation to his or her new surroundings. The exile, Edward Said writes, "lives in a median state, neither completely at one with the new setting nor fully disencumbered of the old, beset with half-involvements and half-detachments, nostalgic and sentimental on one level, an adept mimic or a secret outcast on another" (*Representations* 49).

The expatriate, too, may live in a "median state" similar to that described by Said, but he or she does so by choice. While the exile mourns a "wholeness" that cannot be realized outside of the lost homeland (and that, at least theoretically, could be recaptured through return), the expatriate often leaves home in pursuit of a wholeness denied or impeded there. American intellectual expatriates have traditionally sought this wholeness in a foreign, often European, cultural environment that they perceive as being more responsive—or at least less hostile—to their concerns, and hence more conducive to creativity. Although there are as many modifications of this stereotype as there are individual expatriate artists, what Matthew Josephson described as "the emigration of talent to countries of an older civilization where some quantum of individual liberty is still to be enjoyed" has been a constant in the history of American culture (*Portrait* xi).

Sometimes, indeed, the fact of escape is more important than its destination; many individuals have considered being in America a more profound form of exile than expatriation.[18] James Baldwin, one of the most astute thinkers about what he called "the uses and hazards of expatriation," wrote, "I left America because I doubted my ability to survive the fury of the color problem here" and ultimately concluded that "my journey, or my flight, had not been *to* Paris, but simply *away* from America" ("Alas" 280–81; "Discovery" 171; "No Name" 469). Other writers, such as Henry James, were as conscientious in choosing their destinations as they were in plotting their escapes. Recalling his decision to settle permanently in London, James articulated what he considered the perfect match between his person and his adopted home: "*J'y suis absolument comme chez moi.* . . . For one who takes it as I take it, London is on the whole the most possible form of life. I take it as an artist and as a bachelor; as one who has the passion of observation and whose business is the study of human life" (*Complete Notebooks* 217–18). James's formulation "*J'y suis absolument comme chez moi*" ["I am absolutely *as if* at home"; "it is absolutely *like* home"] articulates the expatriate "median state": conscious of—and conscientious about—being *not* at home, the expatriate thrives on the difference between where he or she is and where he or she is no longer, but might be.

Unlike the exile, then, the expatriate chooses to live in a new country, one perhaps more congenial to self-fulfillment than the one she or he has chosen to leave, and most often continues to pursue a life trajectory that antedates the decision to leave home.[19] Thus, while the transposition to a new culture and society might represent a new phase in an individual's life and certainly presents a plethora of unforeseen and life-altering challenges, it is not necessarily a break—certainly not a break with what is considered essential about the "self"—and is not irreversible. Expatriation thus plays with exile's repertoire without being bound by its exigencies. In this sense expatriation is, perhaps, to recall Mary McCarthy's term, "hedonistic." Yet—and here I think I differ with McCarthy—expatriation is serious play, and the critique that expatriates level by leaving home is a radical one. They undertake to live in a foreign country, experience the freedoms, challenges, and humiliations of foreignness, learn a new language or learn to live without the perquisites of linguistic fluency, experiment with assimilation, try on the notion of not returning home, and even resist the temptation to do so. But expatriates are not prevented by home from returning there. However powerful any individual's personal aversions to home and resistances to return, they remain options that color and temper whatever experiences would otherwise be common to expatriation and exile.

VI

My choice is the old world—my choice, my need, my life. . . . My work lies there—and with this vast new world, *je n'ai que faire.* One can't do both—one must choose.

—HENRY JAMES, *Complete Notebooks*

In contemporary critical discourse, *exile* has come to be a general term designating a vast number of forms of alienation. In the introduction to her anthology, *Exile and Creativity*, Susan Rubin Suleiman identifies this "broad" semantic field in which contemporary examinations of exile are conducted: "In its narrow sense a political banishment, exile in its broad sense designates every kind of estrangement or displacement, from the physical and geographical to the spiritual. . . . Seen in broad terms, exile appears not only as a (or even *the*) major historical phenomenon of our century, affecting millions of people, but as a focal point for theoretical reflections about individual and cultural identity . . . which in turn are intimately bound up with problems of nationalism, racism, and war" (2). For Suleiman, the dislocations called "exile" initiate not only the true suffering and homelessness of people whose contact with their home has been violently severed but also the tantalizingly productive reflections that, as Edward Said maintains, are coeval with true intellectual work. In an essay entitled "Intellectual Exile: Expatriates and Marginals" (1994), Said invokes "those different arrangements of living and eccentric angles of vision that [exile] can sometimes afford, which enliven the intellectual's vocation, without perhaps alleviating every last anxiety or feeling of bitter solitude," and equates the exile's point of view with that of the true intellectual (*Representations* 59):

While it is an *actual* condition, exile is also . . . a *metaphorical* condition. By that I mean that my diagnosis of the intellectual in exile derives from the social and political history of dislocation and migration . . . but is not limited to it. Even intellectuals who are lifelong members of a society can, in a manner of speaking, be divided into insiders and outsiders: those on the one hand who belong fully to the society as it is, who flourish in it without an overwhelming sense of dissonance or dissent, those who can be called yea-sayers; and on the other hand, the nay-sayers, the individuals at odds with their society and therefore outsiders and exiles so far as privileges, power, and honors are concerned. The pattern that sets the course for the intellectual as outsider is best exemplified by the condition of exile, the state of never being fully adjusted, always feeling outside the chatty, familiar world inhabited by natives, so to speak, tending to avoid and even dislike the trappings of accommodation and national well-being. Exile for the intellectual in this metaphysical sense is restlessness, movement, constantly being unsettled, and unsettling others. You cannot go back to some earlier and perhaps more stable condition of being at home; and, alas, you can never fully arrive, be at one with your new home or situation. (52–53)

It is hard to take issue with Said's portrait of the "intellectual as outsider," but his blurring of the distinction between real exile and the metaphoric sense that he foregrounds is both troubling and misleading. There *is* a difference between a restless, unsettling, unaccommodating exile and a restless, unsettling, unaccommodating intellectual misfit.[20] Even those intellectuals who are "at odds with their society and therefore outsiders and exiles as far as privileges, power, and honors are concerned" have a *claim* to enfranchisement and authority of which the exile, regardless of the worldliness with which she or he compensates for homelessness, has been divested. Said himself is a prime example of a class of intellectuals "at odds with their society" whose personal history and political convictions cause them to feel like "outsiders and exiles," but who, nevertheless, enjoy considerable "privileges, power, and honors." The kind of dissident he describes here speaks from within the society to which he or she feels marginal and speaks to a society in which he or she claims membership. The exile, on the other hand, speaks from the elsewhere of banishment to whoever will listen, with an authority born of disenfranchisement.

In order, it seems, to heighten the pathos of his own debatable marginality, Said blurs the distinction between the experience of exile and experiences that are registered as being "like" exile.[21] It is worth noting that Said himself argues elsewhere against using exile as a metaphor for general alienation and estrangement. In "Reflections on Exile" (1984), he writes that "exile is strangely compelling to think about but terrible to experience" and insists that "exile cannot be made to serve notions of humanism. On the twentieth-century scale, exile is neither aesthetically nor humanistically comprehensible: at most the literature about exile objectifies an anguish and a predicament most people rarely experience at first hand; but to think of the exile informing this literature as beneficially humanistic is to banalize its mutilations, the losses it inflicts on those who suffer them, the muteness with which it responds to any attempt to understand it as 'good for us'" (138). Here, Said distinguishes between the possible knowledge to be gained from the actual experience of exile and the application of the name "exile" to experiences that communicate or make use of such knowledge. The exile's experience forces him or her to confront the fact that "homes are provisional. . . . Borders and barriers, which enclose us within the safety of familiar territory, can also become prisons and are often defended beyond reason or necessity"; an intellectual whose observations, reading, conversations, and processes of thought teach him or her the same lesson is not, however, therefore an exile. Rather he or she is someone who, having become aware of disjunctions similar to those experienced by the exile, "cultivate[s the] scrupulous . . . subjectivity" that, Said argues, is also the intellectual attitude of the exile (147). Here, the distinction between being an exile and feeling or thinking like an exile remains in place as a kind of bulwark against what Said terms the "pallid notion that non-exiles can share in the benefits of exile as a redemptive motif" (145).

While Said warns against a conflation of exile and intellectual attitudes derived from its lessons, his own practice is evidence of the seductiveness of such blurred distinctions. Even where he is most intolerant even of well-meaning domestications of what is "neither aesthetically nor humanistically comprehensible" ("Reflections on Exile" 138), he excuses such appropriations if the exile-by-choice is an artist or an intellectual. Said writes of James Joyce, for instance, that although he "*chose* to be an exile, . . . [he] perfectly understood its trials" (145). Said is capable of recognizing that Joyce's exile was voluntary and even briefly wonders whether it might indeed be of "a more benign variety," but he fails to see that what we read in Joyce's works is less the "perfect understanding" of exile than a perfect performance of an existential alienation that the expatriate Joyce insists on calling and staging as "exile."[22] In a massive study entitled *The Exile of James Joyce*, Hélène Cixous insists that we understand Joyce's "exile" to be a "metaphor" and reflects upon what is at stake in his deployment of this metaphor: "Exile [for Joyce] is no longer simply a separation from a world which he finds intolerable and which will not tolerate him, but becomes over the years an *absolute exile* mindful of its origins, though quite detached from them. . . . In fact the exile is effective even if he happens by chance to find himself again in the country he has denied" (438). Although the word *exile* expresses the pathos with which Joyce adorns his alienation, it does not describe his situation. *Expatriation* rather than exile is the gesture through which the individual plays out his or her alienation, be it founded or unfounded, by choosing to leave his or her native country. By resisting this distinction, Said perpetuates a romantic appropriation of the pathos of exile for forms of intellectual alienation that might better be examined in their particularity.

As the allusion to Joyce suggests, Said is not alone in his performance of this appropriation. In fact, he is in the formidable company of poets and thinkers who have called their alienation "exile" and staked their claims to a homeland of the intellect through their mastery of language. One important way in which the intellectual self-exile I insist on calling expatriation distinguishes itself from exile is the way it negotiates its relation to home and language. Svetlana Boym distinguishes between "restorative nostalgia," which focuses on the recovery in reality of a home really lost, and "reflective nostalgia," which "thrives in *algia*, the longing itself, and delays the homecoming—wistfully, ironically, desperately" (xviii). If "restorative nostalgia" is the mode of longing from which the exile would derive both sustenance and melancholy, "reflective nostalgia" describes and organizes the ambivalences of the expatriate. It selects and sustains the ties to home that the expatriate chooses to cultivate at the same time as it enforces (and even requires) his or her distance. More often than not, the medium in and through which this longing is negotiated is the expatriate's mother tongue: "Die Sprache," Hugo von Hofmannsthal writes, "ist alles, was einem bleibt, der seine Heimat entbehren muss. Aber sie enthält auch alles" [Language . . . is all that remains for a person deprived of his homeland. And yet it contains everything"] ("Französische Redensarten" 136). The mother tongue that is all that remains of home to the expatriate is also his or her cultural capital: In "Französische Redensarten," Hofmannsthal writes of a motley crew of exiles and expatriates who make their livings teaching their native languages in foreign countries, recreating and reliving through language the distinction life has denied them:[23] "Sie [waren] früher etwas anderes . . . nämlich wirkliche Menschen. . . . Es sind solche unter ihnen, die vom Leben noch sehr viel erwarten, und solche, die schon zuviel erlebt haben: verjagte Prinzen, abgedankte Offiziere, verkannte Dichter, enttäuschte Schauspieler, junge Mädchen, die zu viele Geschwister haben, Studenten, Erfinder, Verbannte." [They once (were) something else . . . real people. . . . Among them are those who still expect a lot from life and those who have already been through too much; exiled princes, decommissioned officers, misjudged poets, disappointed actors, young girls with too many siblings, students, inventors, outcasts.] (135).

These "banished people," who were once—and we must conclude are no longer—"real people" ("wirkliche Menschen"), have made their native language into their *Heimat*. No one, Hofmannsthal maintains, "loves his native language as much as these outcasts, not even the poets": "Ich glaube, dass niemand seine Sprache so sehr liebt, nicht einmal die Dichter, wie diese Verbannten" ("Französische Redensarten" 139). But, as Denis Hollier has pointed out, the native tongue that these teachers of language "profess" constitutes a distilled and idealized version of a culture whose reality would disappoint. It is this illusion in which they live that makes these people no longer "real." What Hollier here calls exile thus precipitates and maintains a poetic relation to one's own language, a "troubadour linguistics which organizes the many versions of the heart in love with its language . . . seductive because abandoned, a mother tongue is never more beautiful than when one has left it; never more alive in us than when we no longer live in it" (100). This poetics of exile is, as Hollier points out, actually a poetics of a certain form of expatriation, one that needs to call itself exile in order to generate its own drama. This drama involves the maintenance of an ambivalent relation to home: at once the source of the loved language and the reality that precludes the consummation of this love, the construction of home on which the exile grounds his alienation is his most precious and most fragile creation.

If, as Hofmannsthal reminds us, "language is all that remains for the person deprived of his homeland," is it not also true that the loss of homeland justifies a passionate attachment to language that might otherwise seem precious, effete, or simply insignificant? In other words, does the persona of the exile not dramatize and legitimize the persona of the artist? Stephen Daedelus's famous *non serviam* clearly articulates this transaction: "I will not serve that in which I no longer believe whether it call itself my home, my fatherland or my church: and I will try to express myself in some mode of life or art as freely as I can and as wholly as I can, using for my defence the only arms I allow myself to use—silence, exile, and cunning" (Joyce 246–47). The artist whose vocation is not recognized, valued, or supported by his world "uses" exile as "arms" in the struggle for legitimation, but like "silence . . . and cunning," this kind of self-exile is a reactive strategy that cannot afford to lose sight of what it rejects. Home must always be visible to, but just beyond the reach of, the exile whose banishment is self-proclaimed, since, outside of its shadow, he is no longer an exile. It follows that any return home threatens the structure of the love affair between the expatriate and his language that makes him both an exile and a poet.

VII

America is alone: many together,
Many of one mouth, of one breath,
Dressed as one—and none brothers among them:
Only the taught speech and the aped tongue.
America is alone and the gulls calling.

It is a strange thing to be an American.
— ARCHIBALD MACLEISH, "American Letter"

The specific critique of Germany launched by "Briefe eines Zurückgekehrten" is historically plausible and largely confirmed by the literary legacy of the turn of the century. Yet one suspects—and I think Hofmannsthal wants one to suspect—that any confrontation of any expatriate with his or her home country would have a comparable structure, however much it differed in substance. Much, that is, as Hofmannsthal's text is both about homecoming in general and turn-of-the-century Germany in particular, the accounts of repatriation I examine in this study need to be read as texts within a tradition of homecoming narrative and as documents that address the particularities of American culture in the modern period and the particular circumstances that confront American ex- and repatriates.

For most of the American writers who have chosen to live and work abroad, expatriation is a response to an experience of alienation which is seen as bound to the experience of America, on the one hand, and to creativity, on the other hand.[24] Although, of course, a good number of American writers, thinkers, and artists managed to thrive without leaving home, there is no doubt that late nineteenth- and early twentieth-century America failed to nurture the creative and intellectual life such as James, Stearns, Cowley, Stein, and many others imagined it. None of these writers wastes much ink on the kind of expatriate nostalgia or homesickness I discuss above.[25] Yet the shadow of home looms large during their expatriate years. In the same notebook entry in which James commits himself to expatriation ("My choice is the old world—my choice, my need, my life"), he describes the "terrible burden" of the American writer: "No European writer is called upon to assume that terrible burden [of choosing between the Old World and the new], and it seems hard that I should be. The burden is necessarily greater for an American—for he *must* deal, more or less, even if only by implication, with Europe; whereas no European is obliged to deal in the least with America" (*Complete Notebooks* 214). James, of course, turns this double consciousness into one of the structuring principles of his work. Stein's articulation of the necessity for her of the expatriate's double consciousness is even more pragmatic and far less elegiac than James's. In her famous formulation, "Writers have to have two countries, the one where they belong and the one in which they live really" (*Paris, France* 2), she describes the dual self-location that enables her to write an American literature that is not distracted from its project by the realities of America. Rather than manifesting an expatriate aesthetic, Cowley's and Stearns's works chronicle a cultural crisis addressed through the experience of expatriation. In their portrayals of an expatriate community and in their ruminations about the American culture they fled, their autobiographical narratives more nearly resemble those "romantic," reactive texts of expatriation described above.

All these texts have in common that a voluntary exile from America is the precondition for a self-construction that is then further explored through the narrative of return. To be sure, "America" has a very different significance for each expatriate, and to the extent that America is figured as the root of an individual's alienation, it remains, precisely, a figure, and as such, subject to refiguration. Put another way, America is a fiction necessary to the artist's self-construction, but this fiction is not necessarily—or not always—about America. As often as not, the America projected as the author's incentive to expatriate is the name given to other issues that she or he works out in and through expatriation. Repatriation occasions a revival of these issues and the opportunity for a new figuration of the relationship between the artist and America; the text of repatriation is the ambivalent record of this process.

CHAPTER ONE

Framing the Un-Scene/
Writing the Wrongs

Henry James's Text of America

> Everything was somehow a surprise; and that might be natural when
> one had so long and so consistently neglected everything, taken pains
> to give surprises so much margin for play. He had given them more
> than thirty years—thirty-three, to be exact; and they now seemed to
> him to have organised their performance quite on the scale of that
> licence.
>
> —"THE JOLLY CORNER"

> He knew what he meant and what he wanted; it was as clear as the
> figure on a cheque presented in demand for cash.
>
> —"THE JOLLY CORNER"

H ENRY JAMES'S EXPATRIATION, his explorations of the "international theme," and the way in which he conducted and documented
his eventual journey home represent a touchstone for the writers who
followed his example—or attempted to—in the early twentieth century.[1]
For James, return was implicit in both travel and expatriation. Even before the 1880s, when he finalized his decision to live as an expatriate in
England and decades before he embarked on the journey chronicled in
The American Scene, he began to explore the potential drama of "ship-
ping" his Europeanized compatriots back to America. *The Europeans*
(1878) recounts the first encounter with America of two American citizens born and raised in Europe. While *The Europeans* cannot be regarded
as a text of return—the novel's conceit depends on the two "European"
Americans' being as entirely innocent of American innocence as their
American relatives are of their sophistication—the "European" couple's

vague sense of entitlement to "their" country already raises the issue of what being American means. In fact, because it deals with figures whose Americanness is totally without content, *The Europeans* could be read as a kind of zero-degree study of the claims of American identity that the reality of America repeatedly challenges and complicates. In James's later novels and stories, as well as in *The American Scene*, the Europeanized American's encounter with America is complicated not only by such refinements (or corruptions) as those of Felix Young and Eugenia but also by the inescapability of an individual American past that colors both the experience of Europe and that of return. The palimpsest of identity that every returning expatriate needs to negotiate lends particular pathos to the end of *The Ambassadors*. It also promises to determine the "queer future" awaiting Charlotte and Adam Verver at the end of James's last completed novel, *The Golden Bowl*, as they prepare to return to the United States to "represent . . . the arts and graces to a people languishing afar off and in ignorance" (564, 572). And "The Jolly Corner," written after James's year-long sojourn in the United States, relates the uncanny events surrounding the return to New York of an expatriate who has been in Europe for thirty-three years and who becomes obsessed with the question of what kind of person he would have become had he not left home.

Although—or perhaps because—James realized that, as regards his own return to America, it would be "grotesque to treat the molehill of a 'run'" as a "mountain of repatriation" (*Letters* 4: 259), he kept his distance from America for more than twenty years. He began toying with the idea of returning to the United States himself during the years in which he wrote *The Ambassadors* and *The Golden Bowl*. The prospect filled him with a combination of apprehension and exhilaration. Like Lambert Strether, he sensed that the "logic" of his life trajectory demanded a return to America, although his aim was, at least superficially, the obverse of Strether's: to take the measure of and to celebrate the yield of his European experience rather than to pay its price. Yet, this celebration turned out to have its price; the return to the country that he'd left in order to realize himself as a writer promised to be ambivalent from the outset. If James had written, during a US sojourn in 1881, "my choice is the old world—my choice, my need, my life. . . . My work lies there—and with this vast new world, *je n'ai que faire*" (*Complete Notebooks* 214), twenty-three years later he saw "this vast new world" as "the one chance that remains to me in life of anything that can be called a *movement*: my one little ewe-lamb of possible exotic experience, such experience as may convert itself, through the senses, through observation, imagination and reflection now at their maturity, into vivid and solid *material*, into a general renovation of one's too monotonised grabbag" (*Letters* 4: 271). Whereas in 1881, James dismissed the "impressions" he gathered in America as "exactly what I expected they would be," in 1904, he was tantalized by the strangeness the country would have amassed during his twenty-year absence, and he hoped that what he later called "the differences, the newnesses, the queernesses, above all the bignesses, for the better or the worse" ("Jolly Corner" 697) would jumpstart a fatigued imagination—and a depleted bank account.

In the 1903 letter cited above, in which James tries to persuade his brother of the viability—indeed, the desperate necessity—of his first trip to America in over twenty years, he wrote:

> My native land, which time, absence and change have, in a funny
> sort of way, made almost as romantic to me as "Europe," in
> dreams or in my earlier time here, used to be—the actual bristling
> (as fearfully bristling as you like) U.S.A. have the merit and the
> precious property that they meet and fit into my ("creative") pre-
> occupations; and that the period there which should represent the
> poetry of motion, the one big taste of travel not supremely missed,
> would carry with it also possibilities of the prose of *production*
> (that is the production of prose) such as no other mere bought,
> paid for, sceptically and half-heartedly worried-through adventure,
> by land or sea, would be able to give me. (*Letters* 4: 272)

The voyage home as a voyage into the romantic: on the threshold of his sixties and fixed by the life of sociability and creativity he had constructed around the persona of the expatriate, anglophile "artist and . . . bachelor" (*Complete Notebooks* 216), James contemplates what travel, what adventure he should undertake before he loses the taste for "movement" entirely, clearly anticipating and counting on America's providing him with unexpected impressions, a version of the exotic relevant to his "mature" creative agenda.

James's ruminations on repatriation are haunted by the ambivalent acceptance that the "choice," the "need," the "life" of the "old world" might require the supplement of the "vast new world" he had so self-affirmingly left behind him more than two decades earlier. Even if he could argue that his cultural past—indeed, the culture that treasures and preserves the past in a manner he considers crucial to art—is in Europe, his personal past—that past that made him the author who "needs" the European ambience—is in America. The "exotic," "new" world is also his old home, populated by the "tramping *ghosts* of other years" (*Letters* 4: 259). The newness of the old, the unfamiliarity of the familiar, the difference of the same—what Gertrude Stein would later call the "shocks of recognition and nonrecognition" (*Everybody's Autobiography* 180) that await the returning expatriate—render the prospect even of temporary repatriation "somehow, absurdly, indescribably difficult" (*Letters* 4: 259). Would the America that James now confronted actually deliver "exotic experience" in such a way that his "observation, imagination and reflection" could find in them the kind of material he needed, or would "the differences, newnesses, queernesses, and bignesses" turn out to be nothing more than new and spectacular trappings of the old monotony? Could America both satisfy his creative needs and confirm the solemn decision never again to live there that he had made twenty years earlier? Would the "ghosts" hold their peace, or would their demands complicate his agenda and itinerary? Would the citizen, son, and brother, Henry James, react differently than the artist? Would home be—positively as well as negatively—what James needed it to be? Did James know what he needed home to be? Does anyone?

A projection of home as romantic and unfamiliar is the privilege of the expatriate and stands in stark contrast to the sentiment of nostalgia that traditionally binds the exile to his or her native land. The commonplace about exile would have it that the further away from home one is, the more one misses what is familiar, comfortable, and predictable about it. In 1880, James flew in the face of this commonplace by complaining that the America to which he then returned was exactly as he'd expected it to be; the *heimlich*, in this case, is dismissed as redundant and uninteresting. Two decades later, James explicitly courted the "shocks" whose possibility he'd formerly denied: "My native land, in my old age, has become, becomes more and more, romantic to me altogether: *this* one, on the other hand has, hugely and ingeniously ceased to be" (*Letters* 4: 259). In the interim, England had become for him a familiar, comfortable, and predictable home, in contrast to which the barbarities of American manners and speech about which William James had warned his brother were bound to seem exotic. But this is not, I think, the major reason for the relative absence of nostalgia in James's anticipatory writings. This absence seems better explained by the terms in which James had always figured his decision not to live in America. He was not an exile; there was nothing keeping him from living in America except his own disinclination to do so, and to express or even entertain a longing for the country he had officially rejected would have dangerously challenged his life decision. To the extent that he plotted his return to America as a journey of self-affirmation, he could not afford to cultivate any nostalgia more comprehensive than that wistful anticipation of the ghosts of the dead I cited above.

Yet James's actual confrontation with the United States is saturated with the kind of nostalgia that Svetlana Boym terms "a longing for a home that no longer exists or has never existed . . . a romance with one's own fantasy" (xiii).[2] This nostalgia represents one of the greatest shocks the returnee will experience and constitutes both a powerful, uncanny subtext to his journey home and a powerful representational challenge.[3] The discovery that the home from which he so stridently and self-affirmingly distanced himself "no longer exists or has never existed" causes James to reevaluate the distinctions and identifications upon which he had based his self-definition as an expatriate and as a writer. Not only does repatriation deconstruct the terms in which James had figured his personal and artistic calling, it seems to deny him the tools he would need to (re)construct a persona anything like as stable as the one he had sought to affirm. Yet, as we shall see, in setting out for an America he figured as the "romantic" antidote to an "oscillation from here [Lamb House] to London and from London here" whose prospect seemed "thin, starved, lonely, defeated, *beaten*," James risked precisely such a self-destabilization (*Letters* 4: 272). *The American Scene* is the record of the "romantic" undertaking of this writer so wary of the "romantic," of his attempt "to picture . . . to embroider . . . at one's ease—to tangle . . . up in retrospect and make the real romantic claim for" what he found in America (*AS* 228).

I

The house, as the case stood, admirably lent itself [to hallucina-
tion]; he might wonder at the taste, the native architecture of the
particular time, which could rejoice so in the multiplication of
doors—the opposite extreme to the modern, the actual almost complete proscription of them; but it had fairly contributed to provoke
this obsession of the presence encountered telescopically, as he
might say, focussed and studied in diminishing perspective.

—"THE JOLLY CORNER"

The confrontation with America and the transformation of the anticipated material into *The American Scene* posed problems that baffled
precisely those representational faculties James had hoped to indulge.
If, as he wrote to his brother, he wanted to immerse himself in American "Shocks in general," to "see them, . . . to see everything, . . . to see
the Country . . . in *cadres* as complete, and immeasurably more mature
than those of the celebrated Taine" (*Letters* 4: 273), it was the country's antagonism to cadres of any sort that he confronted at every turn.
This antagonism seemed to thwart his own ability to frame what he
saw, to arrange the spectacle of America in a manner that would enable him to do it full literary justice. Critical discussion of *The American
Scene* long focused on the justice of James's portrayal of the America he
(re)discovered after more than twenty years of expatriation and on comparisons between his fictional and nonfictional representations of his native country.[4] The particularly avid attention the text has solicited in the
past decades addresses the political positions James is seen to assume
in this difficult text; in such readings, *The American Scene* serves as a
touchstone for interrogations of what are taken to be—and often seem
to be—anti-Semitic and racist tendencies as well as a general ambivalence to modernity in his oeuvre as a whole.[5] Yet *The American Scene* is
consummately a record of his attempts—and failures—to see, and more
particularly, to transcribe the America he confronts and of the corre-
sponding difficulty of making the definitive statement that critics seem
to be seeking. I'll even go so far as to claim that James's attitude toward
anything in America is first and foremost a matter of its representability,
or rather, of his ability or inability to represent it. This representability,

in turn, depends upon his ability to frame the phenomena he encounters, that is, to place them within a context that renders intelligible what would otherwise seem random or arbitrary.

James's concern with framing and its ideological implications anticipates contemporary critical discussions of the ways borders, boundaries, and frames are deployed in negotiations between the claims of individuals, groups, and nations.[6] A frame, like a border or boundary, is an index of coherence, albeit a purely arbitrary one; by designating a set of limits (of a painting, a photographic image, even a temporal period, as in the expression "time frame"), a frame marks the structure, unity, and intelligibility of a phenomenon, determining at what point and in what terms it begins to signify. Much as a border designates the inside and outside of a geographical—and, by extension—political space, separating what is proper to this space from everything it will construe and deploy as its Other, a frame signals that the items it encloses cohere according to laws other than those governing what lies outside its confines. James's letters prior to his American sojourn suggest that he anticipated that "Americanness" would represent for him and for his creative enterprise an exotic but unambiguous frame in which his efforts of representation would be duly rewarded. This project's straightforwardness, however, was doomed both by the constitution of the country he reconfronted and that of the "returning absentee" himself.

The series of titles James records having entertained and rejected before settling on *The American Scene* documents how the experience of America transformed his relation both to his material and to his project. In a letter to George Harvey written from Edith Wharton's Lenox estate, James reiterated his ambition to write not only "the best book (of social and pictorial and, as it were, human observation) ever devoted to this country, but one of the best—or why 'drag in' one *of*, why not say frankly *the* Best?—ever devoted to any country at all" (*Letters* 4: 327). Had Thomas Hardy not already called his 1878 novel *The Return of the Native*, it would have been James's title of choice. But "as that's out of the question I have found myself thinking of, and even liking better—*The Return of the Novelist*": "It *describes* really my point of view—the current of observation, feeling etc., that can float me further than any other. I'm so much more of a Novelist than of anything else and see all things *as* such" (328). The transcribed confrontation with America was to represent a *prise de position*, a text in which the "native" was to affirm his novelistic vocation by using the tools ("my necessary kind of form and tone and feeling absolutely personal to myself and proper to my situation") honed in more than two decades of the exile he had always seen as crucial to his writing at all. More a novelist than a native, James set out to exert his birthright through his mastery of the craft whose exigencies had demanded his expatriation and whose continued demands, it turns out, seriously trouble the novelist's sense of himself as "native."

The title James ultimately chose for the volume, *The American Scene*, gestures away from the self-definition, indeed self-affirmation, of the native-become-novelist toward those "scenic" techniques of representation traditionally associated with authorial self-effacement that James invoked throughout his discussions of the art of fiction. In order, it would seem, to stage his return under any guise, be it native or novelist, James had first to situate a place to which this figure—the "I" of his narrative—could return. The optimism with which he anticipated the transformation of the "poetry of motion" into the "prose of production" and "the production of prose" yielded to other, more equivocal sentiments. While still in America, he wrote to Edmund Gosse:

> Alas . . . with perpetual movement and perpetual people and very few concrete objects of nature or art to make use of for assimilation, my brilliant chapters don't yet get themselves written—so little can they be notes of the current picturesque—like one's European notes. They can be only notes on a social order, of vast extent, and I see with a kind of despair that I shall be able to do here little more than get my saturation, soak my intellectual sponge—reserving the squeezing-out for the subsequent deep, ah, the so yearned-for peace of Lamb House. (*Letters* 4: 351)

This statement reveals more than the busy traveler's frustration at not having time to write. James complains of the lack of those "concrete objects of nature and art," which, re-presented in prose, would amount to an account of America as he sees it. More to the point, however, what he does see fails to consolidate itself into "notes of the . . . picturesque," since, he suggests, the conventions for representation that arrange random impressions into an aesthetic category, the picturesque, in "one's European notes" fail to do the transformational work required of them.

"Assimilation," for James, is always a matter of "seeing," and his comparison of himself to a "sponge," insensate and uncritical, in relation to the American medium, betokens an inability to confront the matter before him in the manner to which he is accustomed. It is, he promises, with the perspective of England and the "peace of Lamb House" that he will get his America seen in the proper focus.

The "peace of Lamb House" was, however, to present further obstacles to representation. When James sat down to "wring out the sponge," he discovered that the "impressions" he had absorbed defied expression: "I am very busy 'in my poor way,' trying to make my ten months in America, the subject of as many *Sensations d'Italie* as possible and finding, strangely, that I have more impressions than I know what to do with or can account for—and this in spite of finding that, also, they tend exceedingly to melt and fade and pass away, flicker off like the shadows from firelight on the wall" (*Letters* 4: 375). If proximity brought him too close to his material, distance, James finds, renders him impossibly far away. American excess is, for representation, insufficient; "the effort of *holding rather factitiously on* to its (after all virtual) insubstantiality . . . is a very great tension and effort. It would all so melt away, of itself, were it not for this artificial clutch!" (381).

In order to maintain his "factitious hold," his "artificial clutch" on the insubstantiality he is under contract to render, James invokes the "complete analogy" he draws elsewhere "between the art of the painter and the art of the writer" ("Art of Fiction" 5). His description of the American "canvas" recalls an evocation in "The Lesson of Balzac"—one of the two lectures with which he financed his stay in America—of his great predecessor's "thick and rich and heavy" world, "a mixture richer and thicker, and representing an absolutely greater quantity of 'atmosphere,' than we shall find prevailing within the compass of any other suspended frame" (125–26). According to these criteria, America is an unsatisfactory object of representation because it is an unsatisfactory "permitting medium" (*AS* 54). In a passage that seems to be a negative echo of his description of Balzac's world, James writes: "Thin and clear and colorless, what would it ever say 'no' to? or what would it ever paint thick, indeed, with sympathy and sanction? With so little, accordingly, within the great frame of the picture, to prevent or to prescribe, it was as if anything might be done there that any sufficient number of subscribers to any sufficient number of sufficiently noisy newspapers might want" (54). Unlike Balzac's France, "all picturesque and all workable, full . . . with the revelation of the lingering earlier world . . . in which places and people still had their queerness, their strong marks, their sharp type" ("Honoré de Balzac, 1902" 101–2), America is a "concert of the expensively provisional" (*AS* 77), a medium in which everything exists in a state of undifferentiated potential that it is willing to relinquish to the highest bidder.[7]

As James bemoans the absence in America of the circumscribed "permitting medium" that would make America available to representation as he understands it, he begins to develop a rhetorical strategy for dealing with its challenge. "Thin and clear and colorless," attenuated by the "ands," deprives these negative attributes of the cumulative, mutually complicating effect that a closer syntactical juxtaposition ("thin, clear, and colourless") would have created. As this string of equally weighted adjectives threatens to go on forever, James's "no" stops the invisible parade, as if to see whether thinness, clearness, and colorlessness, forced to stop and stumble over each other as if they had all bumped into the same wall, would overlap, complicate, and "paint thick" the otherwise empty canvas "within the great frame of the picture." With the question, "What would it ever say 'no' to?" James interposes the interdiction whose lack he bemoans and initiates a dialogue of provocation and response in which the undifferentiated spectacle is forced into a form, a mode of self-justification. If nothing "within the frame of the picture" causes its elements to organize themselves into anything like a scene, James must ensure that his text provide the frame, the structural interface between perceiver and perceived, in terms of which the American material can become available to critical perception.

The ambivalence of James's impressions of the country to which he returned and his doubts about its representability compromised his stated ambition to represent America in "*cadres* as complete" as those in which Hippolyte Taine had rendered his impressions of Italy. The terms in which, as early as 1868, he described Taine's travel writing make it clear why he could not proceed in the manner of his predecessor. James emphasizes two related aspects of Taine's attitude toward his subject: his utter detachment, on the one hand, and his "arrogant, insolent . . . dogmatism," on the other hand ("Italy" 826–27). Taine's cadres, the frames he can posit before he describes with such bravado and assurance what is inside of them, are a product of a pose both of national, cultural, and class self-knowledge and of epistemological certainty:

> The truth for M. Taine lies stored up, as one may say, in great lumps and blocks, to be released and detached by a few lively hammer-blows. . . . His errors and misjudgments arise . . . from his passionate desire to simplify his conception and reduce it to the limits, not merely of the distinctly knowable, but of the symmetrically and neatly presentable. The leading trait of his mind, and its great defect, is an inordinate haste to conclude, combined with a passion for a sort of largely pictorial and splendidly comprehensive expression. ("English Literature" 844–45)

It follows that Taine's "powerful, though arbitrary unity of composition" (847) and the "picturesque" of which James deems him a master are produced at the expense of "truth in so far as truth resides in fine shades and degrees" (846)—any truth, that is, that may not be in kind or in substance the truth that Taine set out to find.

Crucial to Taine's ability to frame his subject and extract from it what he wants is his assumption of a "distant external standpoint" ("Italy" 828); throughout his remarks on Taine, James emphasizes the observer's willful divorce from the material he is rendering—a practice so consistent that when Taine writes about Paris, he constructs a narrator who, although a Frenchman, has spent most of his life abroad and who writes about his native land as a returning stranger. This persona, however, is "a decidedly ineffective creation, and it was hardly worth while to be at so much labor to construct him. But the point was that M. Taine desired full license to be sceptical and cynical, to prove that he had no prejudices; that he judged things not sentimentally but rationally; that he saw the workings of the *machine humaine* completely *à nu*, and he could do all this under cover of a fictitious M. Graindorge more gracefully than in his own person" ("Notes on Paris" 851). In *The American Scene*, James, too, adopts the persona of someone he calls the "restored absentee" or even the "repentant absentee." But this figure, who, for all his epithets never ceases to be James himself, is also—and more often—the "restless analyst," the "story seeker," and even "the observer on whose behalf I more particularly write" (*AS* 12, 125).

II

For, with all his resolution, or more exactly with all his dread, he did stop short—he hung back from really seeing. The risk was too great and his fear too definite: it took at this moment an awful specific form.

— "THE JOLLY CORNER"

The troubled, "restless," self-divided authorial figure produced by the scene of America James confronts produces an *American Scene* in which the search for cadres complicates the self-confident rendering of their contents. For instance, in his encounters with the immigrant world that has all but eradicated the New York scene of his childhood, James must evaluate the challenge of the "alien" in relation to the framework in which he conceives of his own national identity. In the course of his meditations on Ellis Island, James remarks, "One's supreme relation, as one had always put it, was one's relation to one's country—a conception made up so largely of one's countrymen and one's countrywomen" (*AS* 85). Yet a relation so articulated depends on a framework of certainties—what constitutes one's own national identity, what criteria have determined who one's countrypeople are, what the country's boundaries mean—that the confrontation with America has eroded. If, throughout his expatriation, James considered himself in control of this "supreme relation" (for what, if not rejection, is the ultimate articulation of control?), his experience of the immigrants whose equal claim to Americanness he is forced to accept severely challenges this control:

> This affirmed claim of the alien, however immeasurably alien, to share in one's supreme relation was everywhere the fixed element, the reminder not to be dodged. One's supreme relation, as one had always put it, was one's relation to one's country—a conception made up so largely of one's countrymen and one's countrywomen. Thus it was as if, all the while, with such a fond tradition of what these products predominantly were, the idea of the country itself underwent something of that profane overhauling through which it appears to suffer the indignity of change. (85–86)

If the "idea of the country itself" seems to undergo "the indignity of change," how can James, who has discovered his "supreme relation" to be "his relation to his country," not suffer comparable upheavals? "What meaning, in the presence of such impressions, can continue to attach to such a term as the 'American' character?—what type, as the result of such a prodigious amalgam, such a hotch-potch of racial ingredients, is to be conceived as shaping itself?" (121). And several pages later: "Who and what is an alien . . . in a country peopled from the first under the jealous eye of history?—peopled, that is, by migrations at once extremely recent, perfectly traceable and urgently required. . . . Which is the American, by these scant measures?—which is *not* the alien . . . and where does one put a finger on the dividing line, or, for that matter, 'spot' and identify any particular phase of the conversion, any one of its successive moments?" (124). James's meditations on immigration have led him to recognize himself as an alien at home.[8]

So, however, according to James's logic, are all Americans. I continue this discussion of James's complicated identification with the "alien" and its implications later. Here, I want to examine how this structural identification with the subjects of his alarmed curiosity affects James's ability to represent America in the manner he projected at the outset of his sojourn, when he saw his perspective as particularly conducive to the kind of account he wanted to write: "I was to return with much of the freshness of eye, outward and inward, which, with the further contribution of a state of desire, is commonly held a precious agent of perception. I felt no doubt, I confess, of my great advantage on that score; since if I had had time to become almost as 'fresh' as an inquiring stranger, I had not on the other hand had enough to cease to be, or at least to feel, as acute as an initiated native" (*AS* 1). James recognizes, however, that the binary oppositions ("stranger"/"native"; insider/outsider; "fresh"/"initiated") with which he constructs his point of view do not yield the coherent advantage he anticipated. The associations fail to line up: his "strangeness" leads to identifications with other "strangers" and not simply to clear, unprejudiced perceptions; far from finding his advantage in his "native" knowledge, James repeatedly mourns the absences of things he associated with his "birthright," is scandalized by the sacrifice to commercial concerns of those aspects of his native country that he remembers as valuable, beautiful, and worthy of cultivation; and, in his resistance to the homogenizing commercial ethos, imagines himself in league with the uninitiated immigrant and the dispossessed native par excellence, the American Indian.

On the one hand, James experiences America as resisting the faculties he brings to it, while on the other hand, he finds himself subject to precipitate and unexpected identifications with aspects of his native country toward which he would have seemed least predisposed. Instead of being able to take easy artistic advantage of his situation as returning absentee, he finds himself negotiating and renegotiating the "artificial clutch" with which he attempts to establish a relation to a country he experiences as simultaneously over- and underdetermined. James's "hold" on America is a matter of the artifice with which he accommodates the country to his powers of representation. Instead of being able to "paint thick" with "sympathy and sanction" what he discovers within the frame of an American scene, he sets the scene himself, invoking the binary oppositions whose juxtaposition designate the outside and the inside of a frame of his own making. But the willful self-exile from the inside of the American frame that this strategy entails fails to accommodate and is challenged by a dynamics of identification and personal investment that is occasioned by repatriation and that gives *The American Scene* its authority and its pathos.

Again and again, the frame collapses under the weight of James's self-implication, as in the passage early in the text where he attributes the "ugliness" of rural New England to the absence there of the kind of physical evidence of a social order that makes it possible to read a society's history, structure, and values out of its "appearances":

The ugliness—one pounced, indeed, on this as on a talisman for the future—was the so complete abolition of *forms*; if, with so little reference to their past, present or future possibility, they could be said to have been even so much honoured as to be abolished.

The pounce at any rate was, for a guiding light, effectual; the guiding light worked to the degree of seeming at times positively to save the restless analyst from madness. He could make the absence of forms responsible, and he could thus react without bitterness—react absolutely with pity; he could judge without cruelty and condemn without despair; he could think of the case as perfectly definite and say to himself that, could forms only *be*, as a recognized accessory to manners, introduced and developed, the ugliness might begin scarcely to know itself. He could play with the fancy that the people might at last grow fairly to like them. (*AS* 25)

As soon as he attributes America's "ugliness" to the "absence of forms," he is able to imagine this ugliness redressed by the imposition of such "forms" as are necessary not only for his own relation to America but also in order that the country itself achieve self-consciousness and aspire to beauty. But James ends up talking "to himself" about alternatives to what he sees rather than engaging the scene on its own terms. The malaise for which the "absence of forms" is "responsible" is evident only to him, and the line of reasoning that holds America innocent of the "forms" that it might learn to "like" if it could be beguiled into adopting them leads him to consider that it might just be *he* who is innocent of *its* forms. When he asks, "What 'form' . . . *could* there be in the almost sophisticated dinginess of the present destitution?" he also suggests the answer to this only apparently rhetorical question: what James terms "dinginess" is a matter of system and "sophistication" rather than of blundering naïveté (25).

In his search for what would constitute "standards" in his own system of values, James willfully overlooks those sophistications of capitalist democracy whose appearance is so different from the "forms" he is accustomed to associating with sophistication. Once, however, he acknowledges the one, homogenizing "wage standard" that determines the forms and values of American society, he recognizes that the social interactions that seem "formless" to him are organized according to the ideology of this "standard": "After [the wage standard] there was the standard, ah! the very high standard, of sensibility and propriety, so far as tribute on this ground was not owed by the parties themselves, but owed *to* them, not to be rendered, but to be received, and with a stiff, a warningly stiff, account kept of it. Didn't it appear at moments a theme for endless study, this queer range of the finer irritability in the breasts of those whose fastidiousness was compatible with the violation of almost every grace in life *but* that one?" (*AS* 25–26). Traditionally, "forms" determine the gestures through which an individual invests in a community by deferring to its laws of cohesion. In America, James finds a reversal of this logic: the forms that govern intercourse are determined by the taker rather than the giver, by the individual rather than by the community. Translated into *The American Scene*'s discourse of representation: instead of the frame determining the terms of coherence of the painting, the contents determine the frame; instead of the force of the past determining the present, the present determines the extent to which the past is permitted to have any force at all.

This reversal of the traditional relation of forms to the matter they organize determines that the country to which James returns is simultaneously "thin" and noisily overdetermined, passive in its acquiescence to the "democratic consistency" and aggressive in its enforcement of it, governed not by checks and balances but, rather, by *"the will to grow"* (*AS* 54).

> That . . . was but another name for the largest and straightest perception the restless analyst had yet risen to—the perception that awaits the returning absentee from this great country, on the wharf of disembarkation, with an embodied intensity that no superficial confusion, no extremity of chaos any more than any brief mercy of accident, avails to mitigate. The waiting observer need be little enough of an analyst, in truth, to arrive at that consciousness, for the phenomenon is vivid in direct proportion as the ship draws near. The great presence that bristles for him on the sounding dock, and that shakes the planks, the loose boards of its theatric stage to an inordinate, unprecedented rumble, is the monstrous form of Democracy, which is thereafter to project its shifting, angular shadow, at one time and another, across every inch of the field of his vision. It is the huge democratic broom that has made the clearance and that one seems to see brandished in the empty sky. (54–55)

From the moment of disembarkation, the "restless analyst" is challenged by a spectacle that aggressively resists, and perhaps even disenables, his canon of discrimination; democracy's "form" is "monstrous"—protean and ubiquitous. Simultaneously everywhere and nowhere, it enforces a consistency whose terms and contours remain baffling. How, then, can one capture and record the life lived under its aegis? How, James wonders, does such "democratic consistency . . . determine and qualify manners, feelings, communications, modes of contact and conceptions of life"—all those aspects of the human spectacle that, at least in his understanding, require the kinds of forms with which democracy seems to have dispensed? If this "monstrous form" is determined by the "wage standard" and the "will to grow"—the "'business' field" in whose workings James confesses himself to be "fatally uninitiated"—is there a place here for the student of the "'social' field" of the American scene? Is there a "social field" that he can distinguish from and interrogate independent of the "business field"? James concedes readily that "the condition [of democracy], notoriously, represents an immense boon," but he is unsure "what . . . the enjoyment of the boon represent[s]" (55).

III

He circulated, talked, renewed, loosely and pleasantly, old relations—met indeed, so far as he could, new expectations and seemed
to make out on the whole that in spite of the career, of such different contacts . . . he was positively rather liked than not. He was a
dim secondary social success—and all with people who had truly
not an idea of him. It was all mere surface sound, this murmur of
their welcome, this popping of their corks—just as his gestures of
response were the extravagant shadows, emphatic in proportion as
they meant little, of some game of *ombres chinoises*.
                                        — "THE JOLLY CORNER"

Here, James seems less antidemocratic than truly perplexed by the question of what the positive cultural yield of the democratic "boon" looks
like.[9] In order to have anything to represent beyond the deficiencies and
absences prepared by the "democratic broom," James sets himself the
challenge of rendering "the aching void . . . (as an aching void) striking and interesting" by imposing form where it is absent and focusing
on the quality he fails to encounter, the occasion for nuance, appreciation, reflection that he repeatedly calls *manners*: "The *manners*, the manners: where and what are they, and what have they to tell?" (*AS* 56, 35).
Manners, those codes of sociable behavior whose subtleties have both

charmed and exasperated readers of James's novels, are not simply the obsession of the old, Europeanized snob James is often accused of having been; they are the organizing principle of his art. Although by the time he wrote *The American Scene*, James's deployment of manners in his novels was deliberately anachronistic and arbitrary, manners continue to perform the function of circumscribing an arena of interest, imposing laws of composition upon this arena, and governing the way in which the unspeakable in the human drama can be represented.[10] And when, as James discovers, "there [are no] manners to speak of" (10), the search for manners compensates for their absence. Since he cannot "introduce forms" to America "as a recognized accessory to manners," he introduces the issue of manners in order to give his text a writeable form.

Manners perform this function of framing by designating the inside and outside of a social boundary that James has turned into the organizing principle of his art.[11] What one "does" or "doesn't do" implies a social group whose standards one aspires to meet—or, seen from another perspective, the criteria an elite maintains in order to remain an elite: "Old societies, old and even new, aristocracies, are arranged exactly to supply functions, forms, the whole element of custom and perpetuity, to any massiveness of private ease, however great" (*AS* 159). Yet even the interrogation of American manners brings James back to the pecuniary considerations he had hoped to circumvent or defer: the new American society seems to have acknowledged as its purpose the prosperity that traditional manners leave unspoken and for which they construct a discourse of social and cultural purpose. In America, the unobscured prominence of the money question as an end in itself rather than as a means to an end is, at best, quaint and, at worst, vulgar:

> I have had occasion to speak—and one can only speak with sympathy—of the really human, the communicative, side of that vivid show of a society trying to build itself, with every elaboration, into some coherent sense *of* itself, and literally putting forth interrogative feelers, as it goes, into the ambient air; literally reaching out (to the charmed beholder, say) for some measure and some test of its success. This effect of certain of the manifestations of wealth in New York is, so far as I know, unique; nowhere else does pecuniary power so beat its wings in the void, and so look

round it for the charity of some hint as to the possible awkward-
ness or possible grace of its motion, some sign of whether it be
flying, for good taste, too high or too low. (159)

James illustrates the dilemma of American manners in his account of
a sumptuous New York soiree whose superficial resemblance to the rituals of European high society highlights the disconnection between the
"forms" and the social continuum to which such forms traditionally refer:

> It was impossible not to ask one's self with what, in the wide
> American frame, such great matters might be supposed to consort
> or rhyme. The material pitch was so high that it carried with it
> really no social sequence, no application, and that, as a tribute to
> the ideal, the exquisite, it wanted company, support, some sort
> of consecration. The difficulty, the irony, of the hour was that so
> many implications of completeness, that is, of a sustaining so-
> cial order, were absent. There was nothing for us to do at eleven
> o'clock—or for the ladies at least—but to scatter and go to bed.
> (*AS* 163)

High society has the material resources to give a good party, but it seems
not to know why it is doing so. Unless the object of the party is the display of wealth (in which case it is again only James who is at a loss for its
significance), American society finds itself at a dead end when it attempts
to emulate the "European" manners James would want it to adopt. It is
stuck in the "foredoomed *grope* of wealth, in the conquest of the amenities—the strange necessity under which the social interest labours of
finding out for itself, as a preliminary, what civilization really *is*" (164).
It assumes forms foreign and irrelevant to American institutions, and any
idea it might glean of "what civilization really is" refers it to models that,
for all their familiarity to James, have no referent on native soil.

James ends his vignette of New York sociability with his "tiara-ed
ladies" curtsying perforce only to each other, and comments that "in
worlds otherwise arranged, besides there being plenty of subjects for
genuflection, the occasion itself, with its character fully turned on, produces the tiara. In New York this symbol has, by an arduous extension of
its virtue, to produce the occasion" (*AS* 165). This episode summarizes

the different relation between manners and money in America and in the societies on which James honed his representational and narrative skills: if the traditional dilemma of European elites involves the quest for financial backing commensurate with their pretensions, the American elite faces the opposite challenge of counteracting its prosperous vulgarity through a truly interested and interesting myth of purpose. If the American elite could learn to take its money for granted, it could begin cultivating its self-consciousness and fulfilling a definite cultural role. The country would gain a goal beyond the merely pecuniary, and the Europeanized "foredoomed student of manners" (5) would assume the role of consultant and supervisor to the project of civilization: "If old societies are interesting . . . I am far from thinking that young ones may not be more so—with their collective countenance so much more presented, precisely, to observation, as by their artless need to get themselves explained. The American world produces almost everywhere the impression of appealing to any attested interest for the word, the *fin mot*, of what it may mean; but I somehow see those parts of it most at a loss that are already explained not a little by the ample possession of money" (114–15). It certainly presents a problem to the student of cultural elites when the only elite available is obviously the part of the American world that is exactly explained "by the ample possession of money," and James tries repeatedly to see America as pleading for a more interesting explanation. One saving feature of American society is its curious openness to the kind of scrutiny that would, anywhere else, be called criticism: "My point is, at all events, that you cannot be 'hard,' really, with any society that affects you as ready to learn from you, and from this resource for it of your detachment combining with your proximity, what in the name of all its possessions and all its destitutions it would honestly be 'at' " (115).

Yet America's amiability seems both wantonly promiscuous and dangerously naive; there seems to be no guarantee that the *fin mot* provided by the critical observer will not immediately be superseded by definitions from other quarters. Nor is there any sign that the culture would know what to do with the definition bestowed upon it. The role James imagines for himself—as student, observer, or even adviser—is limited. His attempt to accommodate American raw material to the frame of a fiction of continental manners is one way of limiting his participation. As long as the frame serves his purposes, he is blessed with understanding at a distance, with vision without its expense. But might not his method also imperil his understanding and blur his vision? James's well-mannered account of America threatens to recapitulate the folly of the New York socialites whose trappings fail to correspond to any reality of the world in which they live—except, perhaps, their fortunes. Since his criteria are extrinsic to the material, his reading of America runs the risk of remaining a conspicuously willful misreading that protects against the immediacy of untenable impressions. James remains acutely conscious of the incommensurability of his perceptual and representational strategies and the American material: "And as it is the restored absentee, with his acquired habit of nearer limits and shorter journeys and more muffled concussions, who is doubtless most subject to flat fatigue, so it is this same personage who most avails himself of the liberty of waiting to see" (*AS* 122).

IV

He had found the place, just as it stood and beyond what he could
express, an interest and a joy. There were values other than the
beastly rent-values, and in short, in short—! But it was thus Miss
Staverton took him up. "In short you're to make so good a thing of
your sky-scraper that, living in luxury on *those* ill-gotten gains, you
can afford for a while to be sentimental here!"

— "THE JOLLY CORNER"

At the end of *The American Scene*, James is still "waiting to see." The text ends with a gesture toward a sequel rather than with a conclusion. It is tempting to blame the book's lack of definitive closure on a failure of the referent, in which case James would have demonstrated in the form of the book the formlessness for which he has excoriated America. And indeed, James's complaint, in a 1905 letter to Paul Bourget, that "victim in all ways to the immense incoherence of American things," he had "failed to arrive at a single conclusion, or to find [himself] entertaining a single *opinion*" places the blame on the country for providing him with the wrong kind of stimuli (*Letters* 4: 388). But it is equally James's resolution to remain well-mannered, "to avail himself of the liberty of waiting to see," and the ensuing need to meet the demands of discretion by limiting both the nature of his responses and the nature of the stimuli to which he will respond that make America unwriteable for him. The book's lack of resolution is substantially due to James's own lack of resolution—that is, his ambivalence toward his conclusions about America.

But such a deferral is only half the story of *The American Scene*. James writes of his "distance combined with proximity," and it is only as long as he is able to maintain the distance from the American spectacle afforded him by his framing techniques that he can maintain his critical equanimity and forestall the fits of identification and self-implication that punctuate the text. The longer James defers the *fin mot* that would make democracy and American capitalism directly responsible for what he sees as America's "unwriteability," the more pressing the question becomes whether his self-proclaimed elite of one can maintain its fiction about itself in good faith. For nothing he confronts in America seems to measure up to his standards, and it becomes increasingly difficult to find anything that rewards the patience he is willing to muster. The answer to all the questions he asks seems to be the same, and the pronouncement of the dreaded *fin mot* therefore inevitable: "Money in fact *is* the short-cut—or the short-cut money" (*AS* 11). The shortest route between desire and fulfillment is the exchange of cash for the object of desire and the display of the object, which, in turn, is perceived as a sign of wealth, the highest standard of society. This is not a very interesting story. It is also a frightening one, whose redundancy allows for none of the shading, secrets, and developments that are so crucial to James. In a society where everything that is not money stands directly for it, there can be none of the play of the signifier that is, ultimately, the adventure of culture. But James does not give up on finding an experience of America that offers more than this ubiquitous *fin mot* and where he can elaborate upon what *is* rather than what is not or what should be.

James's meditation on Harvard Yard gives us a sense both of the conditions under which the transmogrification of money into manners that he imagines might transpire and of the forces that would challenge this project. Harvard Yard is one of the few landmarks of James's personal past that has not only survived but thrived and improved in the twenty years of his absence. The improvement consists of a fence; like the "frame" that James has been superimposing on the American spectacle, the formal "enclosure" of Harvard Yard may appear, in spots, extemporized and thin; but that signifies little in presence of the precious idea on the side of which, in the land of the "open door," the all-abstract outline, the timid term and the general concession, [the high, decorated, recurrent gates and the still insufficiently high iron palings] bravely range themselves. The open door—as it figures here in respect to everything but trade—may make a magnificent place, but it makes poor places; and in places, despite our large mistrust of privacy, and until the national ingenuity shall have invented a substitute for them, we must content ourselves with living. This especial drawing of the belt at Harvard is an admirably interesting example *of the way in which the formal enclosure of objects at all interesting immediately refines upon their interest, immediately establishes values.* The enclosure may be impressive from without, but from within it is sovereign; nothing is more curious than to trace in the aspects so controlled the effect of their established relation to it. This resembles, in the human or social order, the improved situation of the foundling who has discovered his family or of the actor who has mastered his part. (*AS* 62, emphasis added)

As James contemplates the process through which formal enclosure transforms value to values, he subtly shifts his ground from the sociological to the literary; the yard is a "place" whose constitution allows James to describe social processes in aesthetic terms. However dissimilar the origins of the students, their futures promise to be governed by the spirit of the enclosure that "refines upon their interests, immediately establishing values." James sees "their established relation" to this enclosure as changing, quite literally—and also literarily—the plot of the "human or social order," and he supports this contention with examples of closure that are very much of the literary order.

Literary conventions of closure are always inadequate to the material they are called upon to accommodate. The fence around Harvard Yard is similarly taxed. The enclosure that so charms James remains in places "extemporized and thin"; it assumes its great value in relation to the absence elsewhere of anything comparable. "Impressive from without but from within . . . sovereign," it exists in neglect and probably at the expense of its surroundings. Not only is this "insufficiently high [and] complete" structure asserting itself against the society whose "monstrosity" James has been documenting, but it is naive to assume that the young people it nurtures will reenter American society at large with permanently refined, durable, and established values.

Yet much as the fence around Harvard Yard has the effect on "objects at all interesting" of "refin[ing] upon their interest, immediately establish[ing] values," it provides James with a "place" where he can organize and refine reflections that take both sides of the fence into account. The metaphors of the family and the stage James chooses to suggest the boon of enclosure ("the improved situation of the foundling who has discovered his family or of the actor who has mastered his part") are both figures that complicate the relation between inside and outside; the rediscovered family might represent the occasion for belonging and self-affirmation or for disappointment and conflict. Similarly, that the actor "has mastered his part" says nothing about his mastery of the arts required offstage and even less about his ability to negotiate the boundary between the stage and the street. But if such figures do not resolve the issues they raise, they do enable James to consider what he sees in terms of conventional determinants and suggest possible narratives and conceivable outcomes. Within the constraints of "formal enclosure," James enjoys the freedom to frame and analyze important aspects of the American conundrum: here, for instance, he is able to dwell at length on the mysterious relation between the one-dimensional American male and his mismatched female counterpart.[12] Imaginatively juxtaposing the "open door" of Ellis Island and the "enclosure" of Harvard Yard, James tries to imagine a plot of acculturation for the "swarming ingenious youths," wondering "what might be becoming of us all, 'typically,' ethnically, and thereby physiognomically, linguistically, *personally*" (*AS* 64). Here, furthermore, he is able to articulate the attitude toward his material that makes *The American Scene* more than a jeremiad against the blight of "unredeemed commercialism" (66). The circumstances of Harvard Yard remind James that there are no such "pleasure-giving accidents"

> for the mind, as violations of the usual in conditions that make
> them really precarious and rare. As the usual, in our vast crude de-
> mocracy of trade, is the new, the simple, the cheap, the common,
> the commercial, the immediate, and, all too often, the ugly, so any

human product that those elements fail conspicuously to involve or to explain, any creature, or even any feature, not turned out to pattern, any form of suggested rarity, subtlety, ancientry, or other pleasant perversity, prepares for us a recognition akin to rapture. (67)

V

Proportions and values were upside-down; the ugly things he had expected, the ugly things of his far-away youth, when he had too promptly waked up to a sense of the ugly—these uncanny phenomena placed him rather, as it happened, under the charm; whereas the "swagger" things, the modern, the monstrous, the famous things, those he had more particularly, like thousands of ingenuous enquirers every year, come over to see, were exactly the sources of his dismay.

— "THE JOLLY CORNER"

James finds such "lonely ecstasies of the truly open sense . . . in the hustling, bustling desert" (*AS* 67) when he can locate and isolate social phenomena circumscribed by something he can identify as manners. His attempt to represent America through the frame of manners yields two surprising and diametrically opposed gratifications, which reveal both the aesthetic implications of his representational strategy and the dimensions of the personal stakes of repatriation as he experienced it. His discovery, in Philadelphia, of "a much nearer approach to the representation of an 'old order,' an *ancien régime*, socially speaking, than any the field of American manners had seemed likely to regale him with" (286) demonstrates how the strategies he devises to make the invisibilities visible and the absences present and to prolong fruitfully his deferrals often make it difficult for him to render the kinds of places he is looking for when he finally does find them. On the other hand, and at the other end of the social continuum, the issue of manners enables James to consider and articulate the profound and ambivalent identification with the "alien" that shatters the notion of the "supreme relation . . . to his country" with which he disembarked and which reshapes the entire experience of repatriation. James recognizes in the tightly knit and highly regulated

New York Jewish community a self-knowledge and a purposive cultural energy that, although they baffle him and challenge the linguistic canons that are the hallmark of culture as he conceives it, represent the kind of positive force he finds missing elsewhere in America. Since both Philadelphia and the Jewish immigrant scene in New York exclude him to the extent that they attract him, it would seem that they would make it possible for him to deploy positively the framing strategies that, elsewhere in America, he can only invoke negatively. The difficulties James encounters when he attempts to represent those aspects of America that seem best to conform to his expectations as well as to his manner of writing testify to the way repatriation complicates both James's quest for the romantic and the "romance with one's own fantasy" that is nostalgia.

Although James discovers in Philadelphia a society that fulfills the criteria he misses elsewhere in America, he never gets around to discussing what this society does or looks like. Philadelphia society seems to be governed by a code different from that of the other communities he has encountered—so different, indeed, that it is exactly what he had set out to find.[13] Philadelphia's apparent conformity to James's notion of manners presents a surprising problem: the writer who has no trouble engaging skyscrapers in polite and witty conversation reaches an impasse when it comes to representing Americans who do so. Instead of penetrating what he calls Philadelphia's conspicuous *"cadre,"* he dwells on the existence there of exclusiveness and enclosure; instead of describing Philadelphia, he celebrates its conformity to the criteria he has sought elsewhere in vain. This inability to take representational advantage of Philadelphia's unique closure is due to the way James has adapted his modes of representation to America's formlessness. By the time he arrives in Philadelphia, he has devised a descriptive strategy in which the nonpresence of the qualities he is seeking allows him to frame and paint the American scene. It would seem that a new principle of difference must be devised to represent the original criteria; in order to represent Philadelphia (the locus of what he has championed as "real" values), he now develops a system of relation based on the "reality" of everything he has hitherto excoriated. In other words, he is now in a position of having to describe presence by the nonabsence of its absence: "She couldn't not be perfect" (*AS* 279).

James compares his enjoyment of the "style and allure" of the Pennsylvania Railroad that takes him to Philadelphia to "living, all sublimely, up in a balloon" (*AS* 277). This phrase echoes the passage in the "Preface" to *The American*, written at about the same time (1907), in which the metaphor of the "balloon of experience" is associated with the quality of "romance" revealed in the rereading of the early novel: "The only *general* attribute of projected romance . . . is the fact of the kind of experience with which it deals—experience liberated, so to speak; experience disengaged, disembroiled, disencumbered, exempt from the conditions that we usually know to attach to it and, if we wish so to put the matter, drag upon it, and operating in a medium which relieves it, in a particular interest, of the inconvenience of a *related*, a measurable state, a state subject to all our vulgar communities" (*Art of the Novel* 33). He qualifies this notion of dissociation by noting that the "greatest intensity may be arrived at evidently—when the sacrifice of community, of the 'related' sides of situations, has not been too rash" (33). The situation romantically portrayed appears to be free of the reality principle at the same time as it seems to be composed of the most real, most familiar of materials. This illusion of contiguity between the mundane and the extraordinary is rendered all the more effective through the imperceptibility of the borderline between and the resemblance of the real and the romantic. The romantic can never fully dissociate itself from the real; its effect is a product of the apparent suspension of the relatedness toward which all signs would point. But James seems to want to push this notion of dissociation even further. He writes: "The balloon of experience is in fact of course tied to the earth, and under that necessity we swing, thanks to a rope of remarkable length, in the more or less commodious car of the imagination; but it is by the rope we know where we are, and from the moment that cable is cut we are at large and unrelated: we only swing apart from the globe" (33–34). Since James proceeds to say that the "art of the romancer is, 'for the fun of it,' insidiously to cut the cable, to cut it without our detecting him," we are tempted to draw the simple conclusion that this "rope" can indeed be cut and that romance would be this "unrelated" flight of the imagination. But the *apparent* abolition of "relation" and this abolition itself are two very different things. The art of romance involves using the same language used to represent the real to represent *new* relations that can often seem like *no* relations.

James's comparison of his experience of the passage from New York to Philadelphia to "living, all sublimely, up in a balloon" invites us to read his encounter with Philadelphia in the context of his discussion of romance.[14] In his description of the train that carries him from New York to Philadelphia, James stresses the fantastic nature of the vehicle and gives the long-sought exception to the American rule an aspect romantic both in the popular sense and in the sense he has ascribed to the term:

> [The Pennsylvania Railroad] affected me as better and higher than its office or function. . . . It ought really to be on its way to much grander and more charming places than any that happen to mark its course—as if indeed, should one persistently keep one's seat, not getting out anywhere, it would in the end carry one to some such ideal city. One might under this extravagant spell . . . have fancied the train, disvulgarized of passengers, steaming away, in disinterested empty form, to some terminus too noble to be marked in *our* poor schedules. The consciousness of this devotion would have been thus like that of living, all sublimely, up in a balloon. (*AS* 276–77)

James first states that the train should be on its way to an "ideal city too noble to be marked in our poor schedules" and then presents us with an impression of Philadelphia so noble and apparently ideal that the two places, the fantasy city and the real one, seem to coincide. Philadelphia thus becomes associated with romance, although it represents everything James has set in opposition to America's failure elsewhere to correspond to his manner of representation. Given both James's association of the "romantic" with the "shocks" of the new he anticipated before sailing for America and the strategy of representation with which he undertook to render America once he arrived, stodgy Philadelphia should barely have registered in his search for sensation and should have figured, if at all, as the "real . . . [one of the] things we cannot possibly *not* know, sooner or later, in one way or another" (*Art of the Novel* 31). Yet "with all the faculties in the world, all the wealth and all the courage and all the wit and all the adventure," James can render Philadelphia "only through the beautiful circuit and subterfuge of [his] thought and [his] desire" (31–32). The inversion of the terms of representation here seriously challenges the authority and viability of the distinctions that are at the heart of James's representational strategies.

Instead of representing directly what he "reads out" of Philadelphia's cadres, James needs to invoke his entire "chemistry of criticism"; the one place in America where James might have found the proper application for his frame of manners, Philadelphia is described not in terms of what it is but, rather, in terms of what it is not; the significance of its being as it is can be expressed only in double negatives: "The afternoon blandness, for a fugitive from Madison Avenue in January snow, *didn't mean nothing*; the little marble steps and lintels and cornices and copings, all the so clear, so placed accents in the good prose text of the mildly purple houses across the Square . . . *didn't mean nothing*" (AS 276, emphasis added). Philadelphia is, most obviously, not New York. After dwelling in New York on sparkling tiaras in search of their occasions, garrulous skyscrapers celebrating their built-in obsolescence, and full-fledged Americans for whom English is a foreign language, James has only to say that Philadelphia is everything New York is not to give us an idea of its "admirable comprehensive flatness" (275). The city's failure to "bristle," the lack of "incoherence . . . with which he had been mainly occupied in New York" (273) is its distinctive feature: "New York . . . had appeared to me then not a society at all . . . [not] as a human group, having been able to discriminate in its own favour with anything like such success. The proof of that would be, obviously, in one's so easily imputing to them alteration, extension, development; a change somehow unimaginable in the case of Philadelphia, which was a fixed quantity and had filled to the brim . . . the measure of her possibility" (277–78). In New York, James sees foreigners losing their foreignness but is unable to predict what Americanization will do to them. The thousands of immigrants who flock to America lose whatever it is (their national color, their manners) that distinguished them in the Old World. But there exists no norm to which they are assimilated, no equally conspicuous set of manners to describe or regulate what they have and will become. In addition, the influx of immigrants is such that any outlook for the future based upon the present changes with every boatload from the Old World. This instability, this game of Ellis Island roulette with the future, is the painful excitement of New York. Philadelphia, on the other hand, represents an "absolute final condition" (278) that it had arrived at long ago: "The social equilibrium, forestalling so that of the other cities, had begun early, had had plenty of time on its side, and thus had history behind it" (280).

Instead of forcing disorder to respond to the challenge of manners, in Philadelphia James ferrets out the disorder subtending the kind of facade of manners whose order, stasis, and invulnerability is what he has sought elsewhere in America in vain. If Philadelphia is a closed book, the revised process of reading involves reopening the finished story, rediscovering "an heroic or romantic association" (AS 290) in the stodgy consanguinity at the foundation of Philadelphia's stability. James attributes Philadelphia's attractive, mannerly quiescence to its "innocent beatitude of consanguinity" (286). The Philadelphia atmosphere is characterized by intermarried families and shared, inherited knowledge so codified that only the hush of mutual understanding meets an outsider's ears:

> What makes a society was thus, more than anything else, the number of organic social relations it represents; by which logic Philadelphia would represent nothing *but* organic social relations. The degrees of consanguinity were their *cadres*; every one of them was full; it was a society in which every individual was as many times over cousin, uncle, aunt, niece, and so on through the list, as poor human nature is susceptible of being. These degrees are, when one reflects, the only real organic social relations. . . . Consanguinity provides the marks and the features, the type and tone and ease, the common knowledge and the common consciousness. (278–79)

Philadelphia's cadre is constituted by the borderline between membership and nonmembership in an ancient extended family. But even James's discussion of the phenomenon of unbroken relatedness seems inexact, as if consanguinity were only a name for a quality even less communicable than itself. James says that Philadelphia "*represents* nothing but organic social relations" (278, emphasis added), and the cadres he invokes to frame Philadelphia's spiritual isolation emphasize the extent to which he is re-presenting a condition that itself seems to figure something resistant to representation. While insiders take these cadres for granted, the outsider who struggles to get an angle on what they enclose violates the quality he is extolling by calling attention to them.

James's observation about Philadelphia consanguinity tells us very little about the members of the society except that they are all related and that this makes them different from anyone else; and indeed, when we think of what families—and especially Jamesian families—do, James's decision to represent "innocent beatitude" and "natural relation" through the figure of the family seems rather perverse. For the author of *What Maisie Knew*, *The Awkward Age*, and *The Golden Bowl* to have associated the family with quiescence, something else must have been at stake. In order to make the scene visible at all, he needed a phenomenon—like the family—whose relation is both absolute and unstable enough to be narratable.

Much as James has to suggest familial disruption in order to write about Philadelphia's cohesiveness, he is able to represent Philadelphia Society only at the expense of the myth of its stability:

> The essence of old orders, as history lights them, is just that innocent beatitude of consanguinity, of the multiplication of the assured felicities, to which I have already alluded. From this, in Philadelphia, didn't the rest follow?—the sense, for every one, of being in the same boat with every one else, a closed circle that would find itself happy enough if only it would remain closed enough. The boat might considerably pitch, but its occupants would either float merrily together or (almost as merrily) go down together, and meanwhile the risk, the vague danger, the jokes to be made about it, the general quickened sociability and intimacy, were the very music of the excursion. (*AS* 286)

It is only through a process of representational make-believe that James associates with romance that he is able to represent the real. The "happy circle" must remain closed in order to be what James wants to describe, but the value of closure can only be emphasized in relation to its precariousness. Once the circle is opened even hypothetically, its closure can no longer be absolute, and if the closure is no longer absolute, then the whole case James is making for Philadelphia is lost. In order to describe his *bateau ivre* of sociability, James had to narrate its demise; Philadelphia becomes visible at all only through a process that undermines the quality it wishes to express. James's narrative suggests two possible outcomes for Philadelphia's adventure of sociability: the boat may indeed survive intact and retain its curious, mute existence, but it may also sink. In either case, the possibility of something happening remains the basis of representation. "The risk, the danger, the jokes" imply an awareness of inside and outside and even of internal discord anathema to the innocent beatitude James wishes to convey. "Quickened sociability and intimacy" have to do not with mute consanguinity, but rather with the bristling family romance that is so often the subject of James's novels.

Even as Philadelphia bristles within its cadre, it still represents to James romance's welcome exception to the American rule, but the city first becomes visible when James deploys the strategies of relation that romance, in his own definition, abjures. The "Happy Family" can be located only in terms of an "Infernal Machine," an outland lurking "parallel to this, and not within it, nor quite altogether above it, but beside it and beneath it, behind it and before it, enclosing it as in a frame of fire in which it still had the secret of keeping cool" (AS 283). The perils of immolation, invasion, engulfment, and temporality are necessary in order to frame this phenomenon, to establish it in relation to a background that renders it visible.

Before closing the Philadelphia chapter, James examines one final way in which Philadelphia differs from the rest of America:

> If . . . signs of a slightly congested, but still practically self-sufficing, little world were all there, they were perhaps there most, to my ear, in the fact of the little world's proper intimate idiom and accent . . . representing the common things of association, the things easily understood and felt, and charged as no other vehicle could be with the fund of local reference. . . . It contains itself, colloquially, a notable element of the academic and the classic. It struck me even, truly, as, with a certain hardness in it, *constituting* the society that employed it—very much as the egg is made oval by its shell. (AS 286–87)

Instead of providing the reader with an example of Philadelphia's language—which would have been, one assumes, a matter of mere citation—James again chooses to represent the dialect in terms of its difference both from less cultivated American dialects, on the one hand, and from his own "English," on the other. As he describes it, Philadelphia's language serves the purpose of discrimination as much as it does that of communication, constituting the society much as his own language has, all along, constituted the boundary between his standards and a world that fails to meet them. James's analogy between the "misdeed from the point of view of manners" of speaking "English" in Philadelphia and that of speaking Russian in Warsaw suggests the limitations implicit in the elitist idiom. First, this linguistic isolation prevents communication, prevents Philadelphia's values from being available to the country as a model. In light of James's descriptions of loud, cacophonous America, it is hard to believe that Philadelphia could ever amount to a civilizing force (even if it wanted to be one); its voice would not be heard. Second, it implies, as have James's other descriptive strategies, that the city is not as well protected as it might seem; the comparison of Philadelphia's language to an eggshell does denote closure, but it carries with it other obvious facts about eggs. Eggs break, and it is altogether possible that the brittle protection of an elitist idiom will not be enough to guard society against dangers less subtle and less forgettable than the occasional social faux pas. Snobbery alone does not explain why Russian is not spoken in Warsaw, and the dangers to which a precious society is vulnerable may be more than its hushed local language can deal with.

James's satisfaction with Philadelphia has to do with its ability to "discriminate in its own favour"; this American city is uniquely capable of establishing for itself the differentiations that frame it. Philadelphia shares this distinction with another American enclave whose kinship it would most certainly disavow: New York's Jewish immigrants. Although the denizens of the Lower East Side "bristle" with all the intensity that Philadelphia eschews, this intensity is evidence of a self-knowledge—indeed, of a history of forced discrimination "in its own favor"—that sets it, like Philadelphia, apart from most of homogeneous and homogenizing America. Unlike Philadelphia, New York Jewry, at least in James's rendition of it, is anything but silent, anything but refined, tending to exhibit an excess of the sensual stimulation that Philadelphia withholds. And where James has had to "frame" Philadelphia by invoking its unruly, energetic outland in order to bring it to the threshold of representability, in the case of the "swarming" New York "Jewry that had burst all bounds," he invokes conventional framing devices to tame and domesticate a scene that insists so loudly on its own terms that it seriously challenges his terms of representation, and, in turn, the way he (re)figures himself as an American.[15]

In his plans to record the "shocks" of America, James took for granted certain conventions of framing that would serve the function of a shock absorber, putting the unsettling into a context that would interpret it, transforming the random "human subject" first into an issue of "the appreciation of life itself" and ultimately into a "question of literary representation" (*AS* 2). A comparison of James's account of a visit to the Lower East Side to his description, several chapters later, of Jews in Central Park, demonstrates how conventionalizing and aestheticizing his distance from the reality he confronts determines the attitude he can articulate toward the immigrant culture. While the Central Park encounter resolves itself into a series of conventional vistas that lead James to conclude that he "was seeing New York at its best" (176), his confrontation with Jewish immigrant life in its own context yields far more disturbing reflections. During his visit to the "New Jerusalem," James loses sight of the borders of his spectacle; in the absence of the "formal enclosure of objects at all interesting" that "immediately refines upon their interest, immediately establishes values," James falls back upon conventional "values," a repertoire of cultural stereotypes that not only fails to do justice to his material but also casts the spectacle in an ominously racist frame.

At the beginning of his account of his visit to the Lower East Side, James remarks on the density of the spectacle and wonders that "the thick growth all round him . . . [has] not forestalled" (130) his writing about it. In fact, in rendering this density, James suspends the perspectival control that has enabled him, elsewhere in *The American Scene*, to do the work of framing that America fails to perform. The scene here impinges on him, denies him evaluative distance; more than anywhere else in the text, the reader is given a palpable sense of James's physical experience of traveling from "a comparatively conventional neighborhood" into a "great swarming" that stretches as far as the eyes and imagination can reach:

> There is no swarming like that of Israel when once Israel has got
> a start, and the scene here bristled, at every step, with the signs
> and sounds, immitigable, unmistakable, of a Jewry that had burst
> all bounds. That it has burst all bounds in New York, almost any
> combination of figures or of objects taken at hazard sufficiently
> proclaims; but I remember how the rising waters, on this sum-
> mer night, rose, to the imagination, even above the housetops and
> seemed to sound their murmur to the pale distant stars. It was

as if we had been, thus, in the crowded, hustled, roadway, where multiplication, multiplication of everything, was the dominant note, at the bottom of some vast sallow aquarium in which innumerable fish, of over-developed proboscis, were to bump together, for ever, amid heaped spoils of the sea. (131)

"Overflow," James remarks, "is the main fact of life" of the district. And "overflow" dictates as well James's rhetorical practice as, caught up in a "human presence beyond any I had ever faced," he risks his authority and his political correctness for the sake of the impression. In a passage that has deservingly received its share of agonized attention, he writes:

The intensity of the Jewish aspect . . . makes the individual Jew more of a concentrated person, savingly possessed of everything that is in him, than any other human, noted at random—or is it simply, rather, that the unsurpassed strength of the race permits of the chopping into myriads of fine fragments without loss of race-quality? There are small strange animals, known to natural history, snakes or worms, I believe, who, when cut into pieces, wriggle away contentedly and live in the snippet as completely as in the whole. So the denizens of the New York Ghetto, heaped as thick as the splinters on the table of a glass-blower, had each, like the fine glass particle, his or her individual share of the whole hard glitter of Israel. This diffused intensity, as I have called it, causes any array of Jews to resemble (if I may be allowed another image) some long nocturnal street where every window in every house shows a maintained light. The advanced age of so many of the figures, the ubiquity of the children, carried out in fact this analogy; they were all there for race, and not, as it were, for reason: that excess of lurid meaning, in some of the old men's and old women's faces in particular, would have been absurd, in the conditions, as a really directed attention—it could only be the gathered past of Israel mechanically pushing through. (132)

Here, James is overwhelmed by the kind of self-confident ethnicity whose absence in America he had bemoaned several pages earlier. Unlike those immigrants who, under the spell of assimilation, divest themselves—or are divested—of what constituted their local color in their native countries, the Jews retain and perpetuate their Old World manners and language. Yet the pressure of this "gathered past of Israel mechanically passing through" arouses dismay as well as relief: if the Jews conform to James's notions of what immigrants should be, it is less certain that they represent an altogether comfortable example of what Americans should be. Several pages earlier James writes that the immigrants "were *at home*, really more at home, at the end of their few weeks or months or their year or two, than they had ever in their lives been before" and continues that "the observer on whose behalf I write"—that is, James himself—"was at home too, quite with the same intensity" (*AS* 125). If, then, both immigrants saturated with Jewish tradition and James himself claim, and hence, define this "home" to an equal extent, with what "intensity" analogous to that of the immigrants does James manifest his Americanness? How much do the European immigrant and the Europeanized returnee have in common? Are they both marginalized by bland, commercialized America, or do they constitute a critical margin whence the promise of a satisfying notion of American culture might originate? Can the supersubtle James bear his identification with the hyperbolic Jew? What is the price of this identification?

James's identification with the immigrants deprives him of the "margin" that has hitherto enabled him to frame the American scene: "The study of the innumerable ways in which this sense of being at home, on the part of all the types . . . took on that last disinterestedness which consists of one's getting away from one's subject by plunging into it, for sweet truth's sake, still deeper" (*AS* 126). The price of immersion is, however, a new form of self-distancing that sounds disturbingly like racism. By representing himself as "[hanging] over the prospect from the windows of [his host]" (134), James sacrifices to the impression of immediacy the compositional conveniences the window frame would afford if he placed it between himself and the spectacle it enclosed. Instead of organizing the scene compositionally—that is, organizing it in terms of the "frame" of the window that separates him from the world outside—James organizes it according to "type," thus intensifying the impact of his representation at the same time as he reasserts his distance from the spectacle that threatens to engulf him. But the boundary between type and stereotype turns out to be a subtle one, and James's less-than-subtle formulations threaten to cross it. The "over-developed proboscis" becomes the sign not simply of any particular individual's membership in the tribe but of the Jewish (stereo)type. Despite the positive intent of James's claim that "the individual Jew" is "more of a concentrated person, savingly possessed of everything that is in him, than any other human, noted at random" (132), it cannot avoid invoking and, hence, unwittingly participating in, a discursive history of anti-Semitic rhetoric. Figures have their own logic: working the intensity of this impression, James concludes that "they were all there for race, and not, as it were, for reason." This assertion redoubles the force of the "excess of lurid meaning" James reads into the countenance of each figure in his scenario without pinning down what this meaning might be. Since this meaning, encrypted in every face, remains a "racial" secret, James is able to assert the distance from the spectacle that he had suspended in order to render its impact: "Who can ever tell . . . in any conditions and in presence of any apparent anomaly, what the genius of Israel may, or may not, really be 'up to'?" Is, finally, this self-distancing purely a matter of representational necessity? Or does James's flirtation with the representational conveniences of stereotype also put him in contact with the conventional repertoire of anti-Semitism?

James finds himself far more able to provide himself with a comforting answer to the question of the intentions of the "genius of Israel" when he surveys the immigrant spectacle within the context of Central Park, the "mere narrow oblong, much *too* narrow and very much too short [that] had directly prescribed to it, from its origin, to 'do' officially, on behalf of the City, the publicly amiable, and *all* the publicly amiable" (AS 174–75). Singularly capable, in New York, of satisfying the "aesthetic appetite," the park transforms the "Jewry that had burst all bounds" into a framed spectacle that has, "for what it is, none but the mildest action on the nerves": "The nerves are too grateful, the intention of beauty everywhere too insistent; it 'places' the superfluous figures with an art of its own, even when placing them in heavy masses" (177). The discipline of the park, the fact of its "inevitably too self-conscious" composition within arbitrary and fixed boundaries, enables James to render this New York spectacle in the tradition of his European impressions. Even when James's language recalls that of his Lower East Side impressions, it does so to the opposite effect. He recalls "a splendid Sunday afternoon of early summer, when, during a couple of hours spent in the mingled medium, the variety of accents with which the air swarmed seemed to make it a question whether the Park itself or its visitors were most polyglot. The condensed geographical range, the number of kinds of scenery in a given space, competed with the number of languages heard, and the whole impression was of one's having . . . in the most agreeable manner possible, the tour of the little globe" (177).

Despite the "enormous . . . number of persons in circulation," despite the sounds, from outside the park, of the streetcars that connect this bucolic moment with the very different landscapes of the tenements, the park delivers the immigrants to James as a spectacle that, however potentially challenging in its implications, is totally manageable. If the effect of Ellis Island on "the questionably privileged person who has had an apparition, seen a ghost in his supposedly safe old house" is "that he comes back from his visit not at all the same person that he went" (*AS* 85), Central Park transforms the "taste of the [tree of knowledge]" into "the benediction of the future"—and the affirmation of the writer's stance:

> I left the Park steeped in the rose-colour of such a brightness of
> Sunday and of summer as had given me . . . exactly what I de-
> sired—a simplified attention, namely, and the power to rest for the
> time in the appearance that the awful aliens were flourishing there
> in perfections of costume and contentment. One had only to take
> them in as more completely, conveniently and expensively *endi-
> manchés* than one had ever, on the whole, seen any other people,
> in order to feel that one was calling down upon all the elements
> involved the benediction of the future—and calling it down most
> of all on one's embraced permission not to worry any more. (282)

VI

It had turned altogether to a different admonition; to a supreme
hint, for him, of the value of Discretion! . . . It was the strangest of
all things that now when . . . all the hunger of his prime need might
have been met, his high curiosity crowned, his unrest assuaged—it
was amazing, but it was also exquisite and rare, that insistence

should have, at a touch, quite dropped from him. Discretion—he jumped at that; and not yet, verily, at such a pitch, because it saved his nerves or his skin, but because, much more valuably, it saved the situation.

— "THE JOLLY CORNER"

The park's tonic effect on James's nerves wears off in time for him to continue to experience and register the continued "shocks" of repatriation. Without closure such as that represented by "places" like Central Park or Harvard Yard, the America James confronts remains raw, unprocessed, menacing in its insistence on challenging "the safe . . . [instinct] of keeping the idea [of America] simple and strong and continuous, so that it should be perfectly sound" but also forcing him to acknowledge the "sense of dispossession [that] haunted me so, I was to feel, in the New York streets" (AS 86).

There is an important difference, however, between the "sense of dispossession" provoked by the immigrants and the alienation James experiences when confronted by things more officially American. The challenge to the "supreme" relation to his country posed by the New York streets is a productive one. Confronted with the Jewish immigrants, he envisions a cultural progress that might render the language and concerns of Henry James precious relics of a bygone time without annihilating the notion of culture as he understands it. Such totems of American progress as the hotel and the Pullman car represent a far more dismaying dispossession, since they seem directly to challenge everything he understands culture to be and do. For James, hotels "stand" for America's failure to become a "place" whose "multitudinous, complicated life" would entice people for whom hotels—like their successors, the theme parks—represent "the richest form of existence" to explore the world "behind and beyond the hotel"; Americans, he laments, live "at hotels" rather than "from them" (AS 406). Even more disturbing is the "hotel-like chain of Pullman cars," which "carries almost all the facts of American life" as it plows through the perpetual change of scenery, homogenizing all potential difference. Its arrogance lies in the smug certainty, the "few remarkably plain and direct words" with which it takes it upon itself to simplify and summarize the complexities—by which James means America's untoward beauties as well as the immense cultural possibilities and yet-unmet social challenges of democracy—that would interfere with its dominion:

> The Pullmans . . . in their way, were eloquent; they affected me ever . . . as carrying . . . at least almost *all* the facts of American life. . . . What it comes back to is that in such conditions the elements of the situation show with all possible, though quite un-noted, intensity; they tell you all about . . . the situation . . . in a few remarkably plain and distinct words; they make you feel in short how its significance is written upon it. It is as if the figures before you and all round you, less different from each other, less different, too, I think, from the objects about them, whatever these in any case may be, than any equal mass of appearances under the sun—it is as if every one and everything said to you straight: "Yes, this is how we are; this is what it is to enjoy our advantages; this moreover is all there is of us; we give it all out. Make what you can of it!" (406–7)

"Its significance" is precisely that it means what it would say, were it able to speak. No amount of interpretation, no sounding of a collective unconscious, no rearranging of objects reveals any meaning beyond that asserted by the distressingly tautological, promiscuous surface. James feels compelled to resist this juggernaut and to turn the tables on the challenge he has the scene offer him. Again he does so by turning tautology into dialogue, by apostrophizing America's "extraordinary . . . enormous," passive-aggressive consistency, grasping "behind and beyond" appearances for a last-ditch sense of its "meaning": "Yes, I see how you are, God knows . . . for nothing in the world is easier to see, even in all the particulars. But what does it *mean* to be as you are?—since I suppose it means something; something more than your mere one universal type with its small deflections but never a departure" (407).

While James is able to infuse drama into his encounter with America, his attempt to penetrate "behind and beyond" its self-satisfied surface in order to discern and represent what "it would mean to be as you are" remains frustrated. This failure, despite the rhetorical gymnastics of his framing strategies, to organize the American scene in such a way that it tells the kind of story he wants to tell, confirms that the real trauma of repatriation is a trauma of representation. The triumphant "Return of the Novelist" that James envisioned is doomed in a country whose conditions defy and even scorn the novelist's tools. Hence, when James deplores America's "one universal type," he does more than lament a monotonous parade of redundant "particulars"; he is bemoaning America's resistance to representation as he understands it. Here, the allusion to type points nostalgically to the vast repertoire of human types on which Honoré de Balzac could draw to populate his novelistic world. In his "Avant-propos" to *La Comédie humaine*, Balzac argued for a comprehensive novelistic rendering of society that—along the lines of nineteenth-century taxonomies of the natural world—would reproduce the variety and density of the human world ("un plan qui embrasse à la fois l'histoire et la critique de la société, l'analyse de ses maux et la discussion de ces principes" [a project that comprehends the history and the criticism of society, the analysis of its faults, and the discussion of its principles] [20]). For Balzac, the social, cultural, religious, and political institutions of nineteenth-century France were the "cadres that organized "the infinite variety of human nature" into a myriad of "social types" ("Espèces Sociales") whose interactions provided a drama that the novelist needed merely to transcribe (11, 8):

> Le hasard est le plus grand romancier du monde: pour être fécond, il n'y a qu'à l'étudier. *La société française allait être l'historien, je ne devais être que le secrétaire.* En dressant l'inventaire des vices et des vertus, en rassemblant les principaux faits des passions, en peignant les caractères, en choisissant les événements principaux de la société, en composant des types par la réunion des traits de plusieurs caractères homogènes, *peut-être pouvais-je arriver à écrire l'histoire oubliée par tant d'historiens, celle des moeurs.* (11, emphasis added)

> [Chance is the world's greatest romancer; to be productive, one has only to study it. *French society would be the real author; I didn't have to be anything but the secretary.* By drawing up an inventory of vices and virtues, by collecting the chief facts of the passions, by depicting characters, by choosing the principal incidents of social life, by combining the characteristics of homoge-

nous characters in order to create types, *I might perhaps succeed in writing the history that so many historians have neglected: that of manners.*]

The nature of the American scene frustrates James's attempt to follow the example of the writer he considered "the father of us all" ("Lesson of Balzac" 120) and to write the definitive account of the manners ("moeurs") of his country. As early as 1879, James had registered the deficits that, in his opinion, had kept Nathaniel Hawthorne from writing great novels; his expatriation and his apprenticeship to Balzac and the great European novelists of the nineteenth century were direct responses to this sense of an inadequate novelistic patrimony. Twenty-five years later, James continues to see America as depriving the writer of the kind of cadres that it was Balzac's "striking good fortune" to find in "the great garden of France" ("Honoré de Balzac, 1902" 92).[16] But he now recognizes that America's lacks are not accidental, not a matter of the country's not having had enough time to develop institutions and cadres. Instead, they are intentional and programmatic, part and parcel of, on the one hand, democracy's repudiation of the kinds of hierarchies that structure both European societies and European novels, and, on the other hand, a capitalistic "will to grow" that knows exactly what it is doing and for whom the question of "what it means to be as you are" must remain unuttered lest it impede the juggernaut of progress.

Balzac could "read the universe, as hard and as loud as he could, *into* the France of his time" ("Honoré de Balzac, 1902" 92) because he saw his France as both tightly circumscribed and connected both historically and geographically to other moments and other places; for Balzac, drawing distinctions was a matter of hypothesizing connections. The America that James encounters disavows both its circumscription and its connections; it is both seemingly boundless and, to the extent that it regards itself as a universe unto itself, unrelated to anything generally taken to be the "universe." Thus, instead of relating random details and aperçus to some—even hypothetical—universal, James finds himself repeating the particulars, at a loss for the vaguest sense of what "universal" other than money would be the *ultima ratio mundi* and of what universe America would be a related part.[17]

Although Balzac declares money the *ultima ratio mundi* of French society in the Restoration, it is not his society's *fin mot*; he shows it to be the kind of "permitting medium" James has sought in vain. In Balzac's fictional world, money makes interesting and significant things happen, and even if it ultimately does reduce everything to its measure, it participates in a dense, polysemous, significant system of exchange and sequence. In Balzac's novels, money corrupts, to be sure, but as it does so, it plays a decisive role in the moral history of a society that claims at least to have higher values. James does not see American money as representing or even complicating any values except those of the market. In fact, James is impatient even with Balzac's obsession with money. Although the "particular avidity of his interest" in "the terms of the market" is vindicated in Balzac's case by the specific circumstances of his novelistic success, James sees in "the general money question" both a moral and an aesthetic challenge to good literary manners: "The imagination, as we all know, may be employed up to a certain point in inventing uses for money; but its office beyond that point is surely to make us forget that anything so odious exists" ("Honoré de Balzac, 1902" 98). Isabel Archer's inheritance, Milly Theale's fortune, the unknown object manufactured by the Newsome family, and Adam Verver's millions are responsible for there being plots and plotting in James's novels, but the money question remains unspoken, hovering "behind" the scene, for as long as James and his characters can manage.

Throughout James's oeuvre, the moment when money is shown to stand for itself is a dreadful one; when the imagination finds itself betrayed by its own fictions, its most terrible truths are revealed. In this light, it is interesting to recall how early in *The American Scene* James began obsessing about money, and how he then had to defer equating his ominous *fin mot* with the currency of his entire discourse. But it returns repeatedly, is covered up and modified, in the name of a "beneath and behind" that James is ultimately unable to discover. Thus, the governing metaphor not only of America but also of *The American Scene* is money. And the redundant face America presents to this traveler can finally only be construed as "an installment, a current number, like that of the morning paper, a specimen of a type in the course of serialization—like the hero of the magazine novel, by the highly-successful author, the climax of which is still far off" (*AS* 407–8). The "social, the readable page, with its more or less complete report of the conditions" (408) is this most ephemeral and market-governed commodity. Its plot, like that of the cheapest feuilleton novel, is predictable and vulgar, but without the suspense, the consciousness of the "risk, the vague danger, the jokes to be made about it, the general quickened sociability and intimacy" that are the music of the better exemplars of the genre.

The risk James runs in writing America is that, in his zeal for verisimilitude, he will accede to America's own terms, sacrifice his critical margin, and write something cheap, bad, or vulgar. As I have noted, his strategies for avoiding this pitfall involve discretion and deferral. In the section of *The American Scene* that deals with New York's immigrant population, James tries to make sense of the process of Americanization and asks: "What meaning, in the presence of such impressions, can continue to attach to such a term as the 'American' character?—what type, as the result of such a prodigious amalgam, such a hotch-potch of racial ingredients, is to be conceived as shaping itself?" (121). He comforts himself by observing that "you find your relief not in the least in any direct satisfaction or solution, but absolutely in that blest general drop of the immediate need of conclusions, or rather in that blest general feeling for the impossibility of them, to which the philosophy of any really fine observation of the American spectacle must reduce itself, and the large intellectual, quite even the large aesthetic, margin supplied by which accompanies the spectator as his one positively complete comfort" (121). Much as James's prose here just barely scans, his comfort with the strategy of deferral is an uneasy one. For James is aware that the license to defer some conclusions that he has truly not yet made has also enabled him to postpone articulating others that he has. His deferral, most importantly, of the "*fin mot* . . . money" allows him to read, according to a fiction acceptable to him, what he can out of the situation without prematurely foreclosing his project. But this deferral also calls into question the verisimilitude of his representation. He cannot be, like Balzac, the secretary of his culture, but remains an interpreter whose achieved distance is not only important to his understanding, but, finally, constitutive of it. He avoids reproducing what he excoriates in America by valorizing a code of manners which has only very limited applicability in this context, and which does, as we have seen in the example of Philadelphia, prevent him from representing the familiar as successfully as he does the strange.

James's willingness to defer has two sources: patience and a reluctance to conclude. For all the patience James is willing to bring to those aspects of the American project for which he has genuine sympathy, his reluctance to conclude has its source in the America with which he has no patience. And as he prepares to end *The American Scene*, James stops equivocating and pronounces the *fin mot* with a vengeance. In his final diatribe against the epidemic "irresponsibility" (465) of the American project, James addresses the Pullman car, whose ravages epitomize the way in which the "will to grow" has devastated America's promise:

> I see what you are *not* making, oh, what you are so vividly not;
> and how can I help it if I am subject to that lucidity?—which
> appears never so welcome to you, for its measure of truth, as it
> ought to be! If I were one of the painted savages you have dispos-
> sessed, or even some tough reactionary trying to emulate him,
> what you are making would doubtless impress me more than what
> you are leaving unmade; for in that case it wouldn't be to *you* I
> should be looking in any degree for beauty or for charm. Beauty
> and charm would be for me in the solitude you have ravaged, and
> I should owe you my grudge for every disfigurement and every
> violence, for every wound with which you have caused the face of
> the land to bleed. No, since I accept your ravage, what strikes me
> is the long list of the arrears of your undone; and so constantly,
> right and left, that your pretended message of civilization is but a
> colossal recipe for the *creation* of arrears, and of such as can but
> remain forever out of hand. (463)

What America is making and what it is leaving unmade: while what it is making has wreaked havoc with the "beauty" and "charm" of nature, it leaves unmade the compensatory "beauty" and "charm" of civiliza-tion. The "painted savage" and the repatriated "reactionary," two unas-similated representatives of the American birthright, are united in their alienation in a country that insists upon "thin and clear and colourless" homogenization.

This frightening homogenization wipes out both the distinctions that make a society interesting and those that make it available to critical speculation and representation. It recalls James's description of assimila-tion, in which the immigrant's Old World "colour of that pleasant sort" is "washed out" in a magical process in which the "stuff loses its brightness" without even "more or less agreeably" dying the "water of the tub" (*AS* 128). This chemistry of assimilation is thus the opposite of the "chemistry of criticism"; the critical observer who persists in framing the distinctions that have been washed out of the national fiber writes himself out of the American scene. But James is committed to rescuing his motley group of outsiders—the Indian, the *mondain*, the "restless analyst," and the immigrant, who insist upon codetermining the terms of their assimilation—from the text of national amnesia, and wonders:

> What *does* become of the various positive properties, on the part of certain of the installed tribes, the good manners, say, among them, as to which the process of shedding and the fact of eclipse come so promptly into play? It has taken long ages of history, in the other world, to produce them, and you ask yourself, with independent curiosity, if they may really be thus extinguished in an hour. And if they are not extinguished, into what pathless tracts of the native atmosphere do they virtually, do they provisionally, and so all undiscoverably, melt? Do they burrow underground, to await their day again?—or in what strange secret places are they held in deposit and in trust? The "American" identity that has profited by their sacrifice has meanwhile acquired (in the happiest cases) all apparent confidence and consistency; but may not the doubt remain of whether the extinction of qualities ingrained in generations is to be taken for quite complete? Isn't it conceivable that, for something like a final efflorescence, the business of slow comminglings and makings-over at last ended, they may rise again to the surface, affirming their vitality and value and playing their part? It would be for them, of course, in this event, to attest that they had been worth waiting so long for. (129)

James's apocalyptic rhetoric figures the return of the American repressed. Unlike a Freudian repressed, which is constituted by the antisocial, self-aggrandizing, and destructive urges that the constraints of civilization, relation, and coming of age have forced into the "pathless tracts" of the individual unconscious, the American repressed would seem to be composed of precisely those constraints—systems of manners, relations, and tribal codes that channel and control antisocial, self-aggrandizing, and destructive energies—that it has "taken long ages in the other world to produce" and that seem to have vanished into the thin American air. The alternative to the frighteningly endless serial novel of American growth is the return to a social text of manners that would reward both his discretion and his patience and affirm that "it had been worth waiting so long for."

VII

. . . for the bared identity was too hideous as *his*, and his glare was the passion of his protest. The face, *that* face, Spencer Brydon's?— he searched it still, but looking away from it in dismay and denial, falling straight from his height of sublimity. It was unknown, inconceivable, awful, disconnected from any possibility—! He had been "sold," he inwardly moaned, stalking such game as this: the presence before him was a presence, the horror within him a horror, but the waste of his nights had been only grotesque and the success of his adventure an irony. Such an identity fitted his at *no* point, made its alternative monstrous. A thousand times, yes, as it came upon him nearer now—the face was the face of a stranger.

—"THE JOLLY CORNER"

In his biography of the expatriate sculptor William Wetmore Story, James writes of the "change in the value, proportion, dignity, decency, interest, whatever it might be called, of objects and aspects once agreeably, once innocently enough familiar" experienced by the "repatriated American" who has been accustomed "to other conditions and appearances" (*Story* 2: 173–74). The yield of this "drama of repatriation" is the heightened awareness "that a man always pays, in one way or another, for expatriation, for detachment from his plain primary heritage, and that this tax is levied in an amusing diversity of ways" (*Story* 1: 333). However high a personal price he might have paid for his expatriation, *The American Scene* suggests that for Henry James, the novelist, the cost of having stayed home would have been greater. His notebook entries suggest, however, that, for Henry James, the man, repatriation proved to have been "priceless," "worth waiting so long for"; his solicitation of the ghosts of the past delivered the exquisite pain of nostalgia and belated grief as well as a bittersweet affirmation of his commitment to Europe—an affirmation that takes the form of the renunciations he had rehearsed in his fiction.[18] James's account of his visit to the graves of his parents and sister in Mount Auburn Cemetery documents an overwhelming, private experience that more than justifies and even consecrates the journey home: "It was the moment; it was the hour, it was the blessed flood of emotion that broke out at the touch of one's sudden *vision* and carried me away. I seemed then to know why I had done this; I seemed then to know why I had *come*—and to feel how not to have come would have been miserably, horribly to miss it. It made everything right—it made everything priceless" (*Complete Notebooks* 240).

The American Scene alludes to this November day in words that echo the notebook entry, but it suppresses the personal experience in favor of reflections precisely on the processes that necessitate and accomplish this suppression. In *The American Scene*, James stages a deliberate writerly negotiation between the requirements of the present and the ghosts of the past. The emotional geography of the notebook entry is refigured as a series of literary challenges: he writes of "looking down, if one would, over the flood of the real, but much more occupied with the sight of the old Cambridge ghosts, who seemed to advance one by one, even at the precarious eminence, to meet me" (68). In the *Notebooks*, long-suppressed memories and a sense of tragedy well up into a flood of tears, while in *The American Scene*, the "old . . . ghosts" who vie for James's attention must contend with the "flood of the real," of which he admonishes himself not to lose sight. In the *Notebooks*, the "empty Soldiers' Field" Stadium joins the "early, white, young" moon in a tableau that opens the cathartic floodgates of mourning: "the recognition, stillness, the strangeness, the pity and the sanctity and the terror, the breath-catching passion and the divine relief of tears" (240). In its refiguring in *The American Scene*, the stadium represents the occasion, not for tragic emotions, but for the representation of the occasion of such emotions: the "white face of the great empty Stadium stared at me, as blank as a rising moon—with Soldiers' Field squaring itself like some flat memorial slab that waits to be inscribed" (69). While the source of the inscription on Alice James's urn that James records in the *Notebooks* is Dante's *Paradiso*,[19] the passage in *The American Scene* recalls Odysseus's visit to Hades in book 11 of *The Odyssey* and his struggle to negotiate between the claims of memory and the demands of his mission: "My small story would gain infinitely in richness if I were able to name [the old Cambridge ghosts, who seemed to advance one by one . . . to meet me], but they swarmed all the while too thick, and of but two or three of them alone it is true that they push their way, of themselves, through any silence" (68).[20] While, however, Odysseus is finally frightened off by the hordes of the dead "surging round me,/hordes of them raising unearthly cries" (Homer 270), in James's notation, the voices of the dead are drowned out by "the many-mouthed uproar . . . the more multitudinous modern hum through which one listened almost in vain for the sound of the old names" (69). The "fantastic lettering of a great intercollegiate game of football" turns out to be the "memorial inscription" that Soldiers' Field Park—the Soldier's Field Park of "documentary" rather than of personal reality—has written for itself.

In other words, the bane of the "restless analyst" turns out to be the satisfaction of "the son and brother." Even the experience that reconciles James most dramatically with his personal past raises strong doubts about America's cultural future; his sojourn in Cambridge is less a homecoming than a stopover in the Underworld. While America inspires the work of personal memory, its ruthless disregard of cultural memory compromises the "permitting medium" in which the voice of the past resonates in the present and helps to determine the future. As James attempts to speak the name of James Russell Lowell ("J.R.L") amidst the din of the "multitudinous modern hum" and remembers Lowell's role in Harvard's "literary consecration without which even the most charming seats of civilization go through life awkwardly and ruefully, after the manner of unchristened children" (AS 69), he is forced to the recognition that "titles embodied in literary form are less and less likely, in the Harvard air, to be asked for. That is clearly not the way the wind sets" (69).

However mixed his feelings about America remained, James seems to have grown certain that it was uncongenial to the business of representation as he practiced it. America's boundlessness and rampant growth, its practices of assimilation, and even the forms assumed by its forces of reaction demanded technologies of representation foreign to those he had spent a lifetime honing. Like the ghostly alter ego who confronts Spencer Brydon in the 1907 fable of repatriation, "The Jolly Corner," a Henry James who had remained in America would have to be "unknown, inconceivable, awful, disconnected from any possibility" (725) precisely to the extent that James becomes aware of the conditions of that "possibility." In "The Jolly Corner," Spencer Brydon's attempt to curtail his pursuit of his alter ego in the name of "Discretion" is thwarted by the "awful" persistence of his adversary, to whom such self-limitation would have to be foreign. The writer who "chose" Europe because it held him at the threshold of "Discretion" recognized that the alternative, "American" Henry James would have possessed—or have been possessed by—the crude will to power that is "framed" and kept at bay by his construction of "Europe."[21]

Much as, at the end of "The Jolly Corner," Spencer Brydon recovers from his swoon in the arms of the "discrete," well-mannered Alice Staverton, James retreats to the Old World "peace of Lamb House" to transform the America he encountered into the text of manners of *The American Scene*.[22] As he wrote to Paul Bourget, "I went to America saddled with the engagement, the inevitable, to produce a book of Impressions; but if the Impressions didn't fail to assault me, nor I (as I think), to catch them on the wing, it proved a very different matter to pluck them of their feathers and truss them up properly and serve them at table. I came back, in short, victim in all ways to the immense incoherence of American things" (*Letters* 4: 388). In a letter to Paul Harvey, he reported, "I found my native land, after so many years, interesting, formidable, fearsome and fatiguing, and much more difficult to see and deal with in any extended and various way than I had supposed" (397).[23] Both letters testify to the difficulty of turning the "poetry of motion" into "the prose of production (that is, the production of prose)." In its attempt to render an America in which "there couldn't *be* any manners to speak of," James's prose becomes the deliberately anachronistic, studiedly inappropriate "permitting medium" in which a texture of manners is recuperated (*AS* 10). A project of representing America in its own terms would have required resources of temperament as well as technique that were not at James's disposal.[24] As willing as James is to contemplate new conceptualizations of citizenship and national identity, he is not ready to explore—or capable of exploring—new representational modes. What has variously been termed his racism, anti-Semitism, jingoism, or high-cultural snobbery has everything to do with his *formal* refusal—or inability—to abandon the representational strategies that characterize his career.

James's failure to find the America to which he returns organized in tableaux that would enable him merely to transcribe what he finds is redressed by his framing and reframing phenomena in order then to represent them. That these frames are always inadequate to the material is something James stresses again and again. Comparing, for instance, the challenge of representing the New York business world to the Paris captured by Zola, he writes:

> Zola's huge reflector got itself formed, after all, in a far other air; it had hung there, in essence, awaiting the scene that was to play over it, long before the scene really approached it in scale. The reflecting surfaces, of the ironic, of the epic order, suspended in the New York atmosphere, have yet to show symptoms of shining out, and the monstrous phenomena themselves, meanwhile, strike me as having, with their immense momentum, got the start, got ahead of, in proper parlance, any possibility of poetic, of dramatic capture. (*AS* 82–83)

As long as the technology of representation is rendered obsolete by the phenomena it undertakes to render, writing America is doomed to be a reactionary enterprise. James sees the American spectacle as presenting "too much . . . for the personal relation with it" (122). His return is marked by this inability to establish a "personal"—that is, writerly—relation to his native land. The account of his attempt to force the "*il*legible [American] word" into a Jamesian sentence bears the scars of this painful transaction.

In the notebook entry in which James documents the return to Cambridge discussed above, he anticipates the transformation of intensely personal experience into what will become *The American Scene*: "The word about Elmwood—that is all it can, at the very most, come back to; with the word about Longfellow's house, and about poor W.W. Story's early one—and the reminiscence of that evening—late afternoon—walk with William, while the earlier autumn still hung on, through all the umbrageous 'new' part of Cambridge; up to where Fresh Pond, where I used to walk on Sunday afternoon with Howells, once *was*! (Give a word if possible, to *that* mild memory—yet without going to smash on the rock of autobiography.)" (*Complete Notebooks* 240–41). *The American Scene* grants us few glimpses—and certainly no "unauthorized" ones—of the man in his early sixties whose letters from America describe experiences ranging from walks and visits with friends and family to the tortures of state-of-the-art American dentistry. Since James did not risk "going to smash on the rock of autobiography," we can only adduce the quotidian "feel" of repatriation from those rare occasions I have discussed when personal shock temporarily overwhelms his masterly persona.

Harold E. Stearns, the subject of Chapter 2, had so totally and so publicly gone to "smash" by the time he returned to the United States after more than a decade of expatriation that he risked nothing by making his readers privy to the personal details of repatriation. Unlike *The American Scene*, *The Street I Know* adheres to the conventions of traditional autobiography, tracing Stearns's life from his birth ("Accidently I Get Born"), student days at Harvard and early professional life in New York, through both the vicissitudes of his sojourn in Paris in the 1920s and his return to the United States ("Home Once More"), to the moment in the present when he brings retrospection to bear on his hopes for the future ("Can Life Begin Again at 44?").

Stearns's and James's curricula vitae would seem to yield few points of comparison. Stearns was born into neither wealth nor culture and pursued with the tenacity of the disenfranchised everything that James's citizenship in the James family entitled him to take for granted. Nothing could be further from the magisterial persona that James projected in his years of expatriation than the abject self-portrait that emerges from Stearns's thirteen years in Paris, and the James who returned to America "to see just what I want in just the way I want" (*Letters* 4: 259) was a far cry from the penniless Stearns, who returned to America because he had nowhere else to go. Yet the two men shared many of the same concerns: both were attracted to the fine arts at the same time as they were troubled by what they took to be the feminization of what Stearns called the "purely literary view towards life" (*Street* 81). Both of these white, Anglo-Saxon male intellectuals worried about identifying with America's women and found themselves identifying with America's most recent immigrants. For both James and Stearns the project of "writing back" turned out to involve accounting not only for the changes that had transpired in America in their absence but also for the changes wrought by expatriation and the dual perspective on their homeland that is the yield of the expatriate experience. While James tried, and often managed, to sublimate personal shocks into sublime Jamesian prose, Stearns had no interest in sparing himself or his reader the visceral experiences of dislocation and belonging that accompany repatriation. What we find in Stearns's narrative is both the register of quotidian texture of the experience of repatriation that James's text generally "sublimates" and a powerful reflection on this experience that echoes—often in terms recalling James's—many of the concerns of *The American Scene*.

CHAPTER TWO

An Intellectual Is Being Beaten

The Escape and Return of Harold E. Stearns

I N *EXILE'S RETURN*, his classic 1934 chronicle of what is known as the Lost Generation, Malcolm Cowley describes the effect on Americans living abroad of the Great Depression, and more specifically, of Franklin D. Roosevelt's decision on 19 April 1933 to take the United States off the gold standard. The precipitous fall of the dollar signaled the end of the expatriate culture that had flourished in Europe, and particularly in Paris, during the twenties:

> The whole tide of middle-class migration turned backwards over the Atlantic. Those of brief culture and unsteady fortunes went first, then the richer ones, then the bank clerks and portrait paint-ers and reporters for American newspapers abroad who had depended on the presence of expatriated wealth. . . . Majorca, Bali, Capri and the Riviera were emptied of Americans. People reappeared in Manhattan who hadn't been there since the days of issues and arguments that everybody had forgotten; even Harold Stearns, the Young Intellectual of 1922, was back in New York. (285)

When Cowley reevaluated this period in his 1980 memoir, *Dream of the Golden Mountains: Remembering the 1930s*, he again invoked the example of Harold Stearns as a sort of *cas limite*, an index of the pro-fundity of the "crisis for the Americans [he] had known in Paris" and the comprehensiveness of the movement of repatriation it set in motion:

> Most of them came trooping home, even those who had thought of living in France for the rest of their lives. . . . Even prosperous writers no longer felt at home in France. . . . As for impecunious

or unpublished writers, those who had clustered in the Montparnasse cafes, many of them had already been driven homeward when the flow of American tourists stopped in the depression years, and with it the supply of small jobs and borrowable money. Only a few stayed on like Henry Miller, always on the nether edge of destitution.

Harold Stearns was one of those who surrendered. Long before, at the beginning of the 1920s, he had become famous as the editor of *Civilization in the United States*, a big volume of essays on our cultural poverty. In another book, *America and the Young Intellectual*, he had asked the famous question "What Should a Young Man Do?" and had answered it on July 4, 1921, by taking ship to Europe as a refuge from Babbittry and Prohibition (Cowley, *Dream* 185)

Cowley's synopsis of his slightly older contemporary's curriculum vitae represents this "Young Intellectual" as an Elpenor to his Odysseus, a figure who has succumbed to all the pitfalls and temptations that he, himself, has successfully navigated in what he has called his "literary odyssey" of the 1920s:

[Stearns] had soon become a tottering monument of the Quarter, famous for the piles of saucers that he accumulated night after night at café tables. Hemingway had depicted him in *The Sun Also Rises* under the name of Harvey Stone. . . . But he worked too, though he no longer wrote books of challenging essays. Almost every afternoon he went to the races, won or lost a few bets, and selected his favorites for the next day. His choices, signed "Peter Pickem," appeared in that zany newspaper, the European edition of *The Chicago Tribune*. Then suddenly he found that during eleven years in France he had lost everything: his job, his girl, his room, his clothes, his talent, and every tooth in his head. There were nights when he dozed on a bench beside the boulevard Montparnasse, waiting for a church to open at four in the morning. The American Aid Society bought him passage on a freighter bound for Hoboken. He arrived in February 1932 without money or luggage or a typewriter. (185–86)

But, then, not quite Elpenor, since Stearns was not entirely undone by his Paris sojourn. Like Cowley, he returned to New York, where, like Cowley, he proceeded to document his experience as a witness-participant-returnee of the great expatriate decade, publishing a volume of impressions entitled *Rediscovering America* in March 1934 and, a year later, an autobiography, *The Street I Know*.

Although Cowley would have known about—and probably read—*Rediscovering America* in the two months between its publication and the completion of *Exile's Return* on 1 May 1934, he didn't acknowledge Stearns's rehabilitation until he reissued *Exile's Return* in 1951, and appended the following footnote to the passage I cited at the beginning of this chapter:

> Stearns had come back for good in 1932. On an earlier visit to this country he had landed in Baltimore and had wired me to meet him at the Pennsylvania Station in New York. My wife didn't think that his return should go uncelebrated, considering the sensation caused by his departure, and she made a big badge for me, a paper sunflower with "Harold Stearns Welcoming Committee" printed across the face of it. The Pennsylvania Station was crowded with radicals meeting a delegation they had sent to Washington; there were all sorts of badges and nobody noticed mine. Stearns didn't notice it either, but then he was never very observant. In the subway—we weren't rich enough for taxis—two women stared at the badge and whispered to each other. After a while I unpinned it shamefacedly and slipped it into my pocket while Stearns went on talking about Paris.
>
> In New York he became a reformed character. He wrote the story of his exile and his rediscovery of America (*The Street I Knew* [sic], 1935) and later he edited a big symposium (*America Now*, 1938) as a companion volume to his famous *Civilization in the United States*. He died in 1943.[1] (*Exile's Return* [1951] 285)

The footnote Cowley appends to his 1980 portrayal of Stearns's repatriation is even more patronizing and less generous: "It is pleasant to record that he was sheltered for some weeks at the house of the poet and trotting-horse pundit Evan Shipman (though Evan was in Europe) and that the correspondent Walter Duranty paid a good dentist to make him a set of choppers. Stearns became a reformed character. In 1935 he published his candid memoirs, *The Street I Know*, and in 1938 he edited another big symposium, *America Now*, as a reaffirmation of American values. It lacked the freshness of his earlier work" (*Dream* 186). In 1951, Cowley acknowledges Stearns's "reform" and records his death; three decades later, he feels compelled to up the ante on death itself, striking one more blow at Stearns's postreform oeuvre. While the 1951 footnote documents Stearns's "reform" and his productivity, its 1980 counterpart stresses Stearns's dependence upon the largesse of others and discounts his productivity: although Cowley never had anything good to say about Stearns's "earlier work," he now invokes its "freshness," but only in order to discredit the four books Stearns produced between 1934 and 1938.

Although Cowley is incapable of finding anything good to say about Harold Stearns, he seems incapable of ignoring him. He takes a patronizing and gossipy pleasure in recording Stearns's loss of teeth and typewriter—as complete a symbolic castration as any man and journalist could imagine. What Cowley does not mention, however, is that he is not spreading any gossip that Stearns has not perpetrated himself in the "candid memoirs" to which the footnote alludes, although Stearns's confessions retain a dignity—in tone if not always in substance—about his abjection and rehabilitation that disappears in Cowley's rehearsal of it. Nor, it turns out, had Cowley waited until the 1930s to turn Stearns's misfortune into his own literary capital; as early as 1922, in the figure of "Young Mr. Elkins," Cowley represented Stearns as epitomizing everything wrong with dissident intellectual culture in America. Later the same year, in the poetic triptych "Three Americans in Paris," Cowley contrasts the expatriate Stearns seated at a cafe table and "hiding his glances in a glass of beer" with the "sophisticated demon" who "told us to go to Europe and Be Bad." While many of Cowley's contemporaries responded with alarm and dismay to the Parisian fortunes of the former enfant terrible of the New York intellectual and journalistic scene, only Cowley publicly accused Stearns of hypocrisy.

Cowley's preoccupation with the man whom Carl van Doren later termed "a legend almost as soon as he was a name" ("Life after Legend" 574), and his apparent need actively and repeatedly to topple this already "tottering monument" set him apart from the majority of his contemporaries and merit critical examination. What is at stake in Cowley's scape-goating of a figure who seems to have made few of the claims implicit in this series of particularly unflattering portraits? I doubt whether Cowley was entirely conscious—or in control—of the virulence of his own aversion to Stearns, and I suspect that for him, the figure of Stearns seriously threatened something fundamental to but not articulated in his project of representing and speaking for the Lost Generation. As I hope to demonstrate, there exists a fundamental antagonism between the profile of and agenda for the American male intellectual that Stearns projects and then embodies and the official portrait of this figure that has come down to us through Cowley. Both men tell their stories of expatriation and return in order to situate—and resituate—themselves as men, as Americans, and as intellectuals vis-à-vis a culture in which what it was to be an intellectual, a man, and an American was in crisis. Both use the motif of expatriation and return in order to delineate what aspects of American life they found unlivable, to suggest the change of perspective that comes with living in a foreign culture, and to reassess both the country to which they return and the role of the American intellectual.

In this chapter, I introduce the largely forgotten figure of Harold E. Stearns and trace his career as represented in the two autobiographical texts he wrote upon returning to America, *Rediscovering America* and *The Street I Know*. In Chapter 3, I return to Malcolm Cowley to read *Exile's Return* in light of the critical portrait of the twentieth-century male intellectual I have derived from my reading of Stearns. Cowley and Stearns stand for two antagonistic versions of the story of ex- and repatriation which are, as I hope to demonstrate, very much part of the same story. Cowley's *Exile's Return*—and to a substantial extent, his entire oeuvre—present the emigration of the 1920s as a moment in the saga of a generation of a new kind of intellectual, whose return initiates a new kind of intellectual life in the United States. Stearns, the figure Cowley insists on associating with the institution of the "Young Intellectual" of the late teens and early 1920s, resolutely resists this association, presenting the adventure of ex- and repatriation for which Cowley makes his cultural historical claims as irreducibly personal and idiosyncratic. The irreducibility of this personal, idiosyncratic life as Stearns records it to the kinds of cultural generalizations that are Cowley's stock in trade must have disturbed Cowley. Moreover, Stearns's self-representation raises questions about the male intellectual in America that remain un-addressed—although not, I argue, unarticulated—in Cowley's work. In fact, many of the most curious and disturbing aspects of Cowley's work—its gratuitous and seemingly unmotivated misogyny; its exclusive attention to male lives and concerns in a period characterized by the prominence and excellence of its women; its particular and by no means unidiosyncratic appropriation of European culture; its naturalization of an intellectual geography that is not as self-evident as it is made to seem; its sentimentalization of deracination and homelessness—achieve a kind of critical highlighting in juxtaposition with Stearns's renditions of the same times, places, and concerns. If we read Cowley's account through and against the portrait of the ex- and repatriate sketched by Stearns, we see *Exile's Return* as constructing the canonical returned exile it claims to represent, and we are given a perspective from which to assess what is at stake in this construction.

Unlike Malcolm Cowley, Harold Stearns is all but unknown today; if he is mentioned at all in discussions of the expatriate decade, he appears in a footnote or in a particularly scurrilous anecdote. In order to retrieve Stearns from his posthumous obscurity and before discussing the texts in which he documents his return to the United States after more than ten years abroad, I offer a brief biographical sketch and then survey the notoriety he enjoyed during his life.

Harold E. Stearns was born in Barre, Massachusetts, on 7 May 1891 to a single woman who worked as a nurse to support her family. After a childhood spent in relative poverty and punctuated by frequent moves and changes of school, Stearns passed the Harvard entrance examinations and secured himself financial support, graduated with honors after three years, and left Boston for New York, where he quickly established himself as a journalist and intellectual. After stints at the *Evening Sun*, the *Dramatic Mirror*, and the *Press*, Stearns contributed to such journals as the *New Republic*, *Harper's Weekly*, *Collier's*, *Seven Arts*, and the *Freeman*, and served as editor of the *Dial*, first in Chicago and later in New York.[2] In addition to his journalistic work, between 1919 and 1922 Stearns published *Liberalism in America* (1919) and a collection of essays entitled *America and the Young Intellectual* (1921). Stearns was—and remains—best known for *Civilization in the United States* (1922), a controversial symposium he conceived and edited in which thirty-odd writers and intellectuals profoundly critical of American society undertook to articulate "the truth about American civilization as we saw it, in order to do our share in making a real civilization possible" (*Civilization* iii). After the death in childbirth of his wife, Alice MacDougal, Stearns left the United States for what was to be a "legendary" eleven-year expatriation in Paris.

During his early years in Paris, Stearns worked as a foreign correspondent for *Town and Country* and the *Baltimore Sun* and as reporter and copy editor for the Paris edition of the *New York Herald*. After a bittersweet sojourn in the United States at the end of 1925, during which he both visited with his son, Phillip, who was being raised by his maternal grandparents in California, and reestablished his professional contacts (in New York, he was greeted at Pennsylvania Station by Malcolm and Peggy Cowley), Stearns returned to Paris, where his life began seriously to veer out of control. For a time, he was able to reconcile his heavy drinking with gainful employment; in 1926 he became the horse-racing correspondent first of the European Edition of the *Chicago Tribune* and later of the *Daily Mail*. But mysterious attacks of blindness and general ill-health led to the loss of his job. By 1930, Stearns was sick, homeless, and derelict, sleeping on park benches and church pews, and begging from friends and strangers alike. His illness was finally diagnosed as blood poisoning caused by bad teeth. His Paris sojourn ended in a dental surgery; the American Aid Society furnished him passage back to New York, where he disembarked in February 1932, "with no teeth, few friends, no job, and no money" (*Street* 370).

Stearns put his life back together with astonishing alacrity. Friends rallied to his aid, and he vindicated their generosity by producing four books in the eleven years before his death. Two of these, *Rediscovering America* (1934) and *The Street I Know* (1935), deal specifically with Stearns's repatriation. *Rediscovering America* is the first and less conventionally autobiographical of the two, although Stearns makes the personal stakes of the project the book's title announces quite clear; reacquainting himself with a country he realizes he no longer knows, Stearns assesses the changes that have taken place since his departure and charts the adventure in self-knowledge represented by repatriation. *The Street I Know* is an autobiographical narrative, recounting Stearns's life up to the publication of *America Rediscovered*. His two last books, *America: A Re-appraisal* (1937) and *America Now: An Inquiry into Civilization in the United States* (1938), continue Stearns's project of reevaluating and even celebrating the country whose most notorious critic he had once been. If, in the 1920s, he had been regarded by many as the quintessential expatriate, in the 1930s, he became something of a professional repatriate. Although Stearns never regained the prominence or notoriety of either his pre-Paris years or his expatriate career, he did rehabilitate himself personally and professionally. His biographer reports that, in the last years of his life, Stearns married Elizabeth Chapin, "a wealthy socialite," and lived a "quiet existence" of "some self-contentment" (Orwoll 2–3).[3] He died in 1943.

I

Do I remember (it was in the *Freeman*,
A very brilliant article, begad)
Last March that some sophisticated demon
Told us to go to Europe and Be Bad?
"New York is ruled by preachers. Buy a ticket
For irreligious France, and there be wicked."
— MALCOLM COWLEY, "Three Americans in Paris"

In the eyes of many of his contemporaries, Stearns represented the temptations and pitfalls of expatriate life in Paris as well as the resourcefulness and tenacity of a certain kind of American man. In depictions ranging from Ernest Hemingway's distinctly shabby, although not altogether unsympathetic Harvey Stone in *The Sun Also Rises*, to Kay Boyle's down-and-out visionary Wiltshire Tobin, in *Monday Night*, to his cameo appearances in such memoirs as Robert McAlmon and Kay Boyle's *Being Geniuses Together*, Hemingway's *A Movable Feast*, John Dos Passos's *The Best Years*, Matthew Josephson's *Life among the Surrealists*, and William Shirer's *Twentieth-Century Journey*, Stearns emerges as both an entirely ambivalent figure and a figure of ambivalence.

Stearns's appearance in *A Movable Feast* illustrates something of his aura. "Hemingway" recounts how, after a good day's work, he strolls through the streets of his *quartier*, contemplating the pursuit of virtue and economy in Paris: "Coming back from the Select now *I had sheered off at the sight of Harold Stearns who I knew would want to talk horses, those animals I was thinking of righteously and light-heartedly as the beasts that I had just forsworn.* Full of my evening virtue I passed the collection of inmates at the Rotonde and, scorning vice and the collective instinct, crossed the boulevard to the Dôme. The Dôme was crowded too, but there were people who *had* worked" (*Feast* 90–91, emphasis added). Debunking the mythos that he is in the process of constructing, "Hemingway" seeks the company of those "who worked," only to admit that the virtue of work, too, is equivocal: "There were models who had worked and there were painters who had worked until the light was gone and there were writers who had finished a day's work for better or for worse, and there were drinkers and characters some of whom I knew and some that were only decoration" (91). Later that night, "Hemingway" has divested himself of his "evening virtue" and succumbed to a temptation neither more nor less ignoble than the one he forswore in avoiding Stearns. Here, as elsewhere in the writings of the expatriates, the figure of Stearns functions as a mirror in which both the protagonist's self-delusions and the strategies he devises to avoid acknowledging them are made available to the reader. "Hemingway" avoids Stearns because he is trying to avoid his own capacity for "vice" and clearly doesn't trust himself to withstand the temptation "to talk" with someone who has already realized a potential for abjection he recognizes in himself.

In *A Movable Feast*, the critical light that Stearns's mirror reflects back on "Hemingway's" virtue remains relatively gentle. In *The Sun Also Rises*, Hemingway uses the figure of Harvey Stone to organize a scathing critique of the novel's expatriate community. Like Stearns in *A Movable Feast*, Stone is a café sitter: "He had a pile of saucers in front of him, and he needed a shave" (*Sun* 37). But whereas "Hemingway" mentions Stearns in order then to avoid him, Jake Barnes approaches Stone and engages him in conversation. Their exchange reveals Stone to be a loner ("I tell you it's strange, Jake. When I'm like this I just want to be alone. I want to stay in my own room. I'm like a cat") and a something of a hanger-on ("I felt in my pocket. 'Would a hundred help you any, Harvey?' 'Yes.'") but also someone whose opinions are valued and shared, both by Jake, and, ultimately, by the novel:

"There comes Cohn," I said. Robert Cohn was crossing the street.

"That moron," said Harvey. Cohn came up to our table.

"Hello, you bums," he said.

"Hello, Robert," Harvey said. "I was just telling Jake here that you're a moron."

"What do you mean?"

"Tell us right off. Don't think. What would you rather do if you could do anything you wanted?" . . .

"I don't know," Cohn said. "I think I'd rather play football again with what I know about handling myself, now."

"I misjudged you," Harvey said. "You're not a moron. You're only a case of arrested development." (*Sun* 38)[4]

The fact that the novel will bear out Stone's evaluation of Cohn suggests something of Hemingway's evaluation of Stearns. The man he describes as "small, heavy, slowly sure of himself in the traffic" (*Sun* 39) is, in Jake Barnes's words "all right" (64).[5] However "daunted" he might be, he is never represented as being all that much further gone than his companions. Indeed, throughout the Stearns lore, those who describe this man with his "plump stomach glued to the bar as usual, while he sipped at a glass of port wine" (McAlmon and Boyle 222) are invariably habitués of the same bars and cafes. Unlike the others, however, Stearns—called the "Hippique Buddah" by his journalist colleagues[6]—is represented as manifesting an odd, lonely, self-sufficiency ("Doesn't eat any more. Just goes off like a cat" [*Sun* 64]). His apparent freedom—or alienation—from the affairs and entanglements of the other characters in the expatriate community invests him with a clarity of vision seemingly at odds with his chronic inebriation.

Like Hemingway, Kay Boyle tempers her reminiscence of Stearns with both affection and critical self-reflection:

There at the Sélect that night was Harold Stearns. . . . He was standing drinking at the bar, with a brown felt hat set, in a shabby parody of respectability, quite high on his head. McAlmon ordered drinks for the three of us, and I knew it must be nearly dawn, but my will was gone, sapped utterly by alcohol and the need for

sleep. The collar of Harold's black and white striped shirt was
frayed, and the ear that was turned towards me was dirty, and
the side of his face was in need of a shave. But under the brim of
his disreputable felt hat it could be seen that his eyelashes were
jet black and as luxuriant as an underbrush of fern. This was the
single mark of beauty Harold had; but beauty did not matter, for
once he began to talk you forgot the stubble-covered jowls packed
hard from drink, and the stains of food on his jacket lapels, and
the black-rimmed fingers holding his glass. As soon as he began to
speak that night, and on through all the nights and years that we
talked (or that I listened) in the Sélect together, I never questioned
the truth of every word he said. I knew if the things he described
had not happened in this lifetime they had happened sometime,
somewhere else, or else they should have happened; and if they
had not happened to him, he believed by this time that they had,
and one had no right by any word, or look, or gesture to take this
desperately accumulated fortune of belief away. (I wrote a book
about this man [*Monday Night*, 1938], and it is to me the most
satisfying book I ever wrote.) (McAlmon and Boyle 290–91)

Throughout the literature in which Stearns is mentioned, one discovers this mixture of revulsion and respect. William Shirer records his shock
upon meeting Stearns in Paris, remembering the sad difference between
the seedy visitor to the newspaper office where he'd just taken a job and
the iconoclastic, urbane journalistic "hero" of his youth. John Dos Passos writes of Stearns's "pathetic barfly life eking out a living selling tips
on the ponies to American tourists he picked up in the various ginmills
he frequented" but also recalls the "sallow charm" of this "entertaining talker" who "never charged his friends for his tips" (144–45). Boyle
substantiates Stearns's reputation as a mesmerizing raconteur, relating
his yarn about the "horse that had fallen in a steeplechase and broken
its leg": "He had persuaded them not to destroy it but to let them take it
home. He'd borrowed the money to get a horse van to haul it into Paris,
and he was taking care of it in the overgrown courtyard that his apartment opened on. The leg had been set, it was going to mend, he said, but
the horse was eating him into the poorhouse: oats, bran, alfalfa, not to
mention the rye straw for its bedding. . . . And then there was the veteri-

nary's fee. . . . 'So several times in the evening I have to take up a collection for him. I have no choice'" (McAlmon and Boyle 291).

Stearns's use of his booty ("Harold came back looking modest, and grave, and pious, both pockets of his jacket carelessly stuffed with all that had been given him for the horse whose pastern bone was going to mend . . . and he ordered drinks for everyone, and paid for them across the bar" [McAlmon and Boyle 291–92]) demonstrates something of the relation between his talents and his ability to put them to lasting, practical use. Unlike Cowley, who capitalized on and maximized the gains of his talent, Stearns seems to have been unable to sustain the success of which he was so obviously capable. The appeal of his writing lies partly in a modesty that seems to derive from his own deep understanding of limitations that even the sharpest intellect could not overcome. Stearns was brilliant—according to many contemporaries, the most brilliant of his coterie—but he lacked the driving ambition, protracted self-discipline, and, ultimately, self-conviction that brought his less-gifted contemporaries success and lasting renown. Stearns remained "notorious": for his intellectual brilliance and daring as well as for his profound capacity for abjection. In fact, as I shall demonstrate, these two aspects of his personality bear significantly upon each other; in the gap between his only partially realized potential and what he experienced in its stead we find a counternarrative to the canonical tale of expatriation and return epitomized by *Exile's Return*. Whereas Cowley fashions his tale of expatriation in order to authorize the persona he will assume upon return, Stearns tells the story of a return that has, and can have, no immediate agenda beyond a survival that has become impossible for him in France. The loss of direction and ensuing abjection that Stearns represents as his expatriate experience has its uncanny counterpart in a return that allows him to "rediscover" his native country with a combination of the naïveté and helplessness of the immigrant and the sophistication and entitlement of the native. His accommodation to America is a humble one, one that turns the self-willed humiliation of his last expatriate years into a reevaluation of many of the aspects of democracy he'd criticized in his early writings. He concludes: "I myself discovered that I was an American after all—only when I was brought by misfortune, ill-health, and no work to a realization that all this might or might not be inevitable in America, but that in any event it was unnatural to experience it abroad. . . . We are homeless enough in this world under the best of circumstances without going to any special effort to test our capacity to be more so" (*Street* 409).

II

Who wrote these lines? Could it be Harold Stearns?
Do I remember? No, I can't remember,
For that was March and now it is September.
　　　　　—MALCOLM COWLEY, "Three Americans in Paris"

The Street I Know must be read in light of Stearns's awareness of his own notoriety, first as what Eugène Jolas called the "*enfant terrible* of American journalism," then as the indigent café-sitter and racing pundit of the 1920s, and finally as the repatriated "reformed character" from whose point of view the story is told.[7] Without referring to the versions of his curriculum vitae that circulated in manifold and exaggerated forms, Stearns addresses them. His narrative confirms many of the sordid details relished by such contemporaries as Cowley at the same time as it offers a perspective on his life that robs these details of their power to ridicule or condemn. Stearns is masterful at engaging the reader's sympathies; without asserting a cause and effect relationship between his unusual boyhood and youth and the uneven fortunes of the lonely alcoholic who returned to New York in 1932, he presents a compelling argument for the integrity of the life he has led.

In an essay entitled "Where Are Our Intellectuals?" reprinted in *America and the Young Intellectual*, Stearns wrote, "the true and permanent influence of the intellectual is never so much the result of what he specifically advocates as of the example that he sets, and of the ideas that he clarifies and sets in motion" (50). *The Street I Know* reads as an ironic, almost tragic commentary on this "example," for, having clarified and set in motion the critique launched in *Civilization in the United States*, and apparently having heeded what was generally interpreted as his own call to the young intellectual to "get out," Stearns opted out of the world whose spokesman he had become. In *America and the Young Intellectual* he called for a civilization that "cherish[es] enough freedom to permit a man to go to hell in his own way" (164) or, put more positively, to take "disinterested," potentially "ineffective" intellectual and personal risks that are thoroughly anathema to the "gospel of accomplishment" crippling American intellectual life (49–50). His sojourn in Paris seems to have represented his personal assumption of this freedom, although the resistance to the American "gospel of accomplishment" he indulged there was of an entirely different order and magnitude. His life—and the understanding of it that he reveals in *The Street I Know*—illustrate that the personal freedom "to go to hell in [one's] own way" guarantees neither that the quality of the intellectual risks one takes nor that the risks one does end up taking will be intellectual ones at all. Stearns's autobiography documents a return from the "hell" to which he'd gone "in his own way"; *The Street I Know* demonstrates the power that personal imperatives wield over intellectual pretensions and suggests that the return from hell requires not simply the intellectual freedom Stearns demanded in his early essays but also the ability to confront one's personal situation with the same constructive disinterest, discipline, courage, and commitment one brings to one's intellectual tasks.

The texts he wrote upon his return to America put to the test of life many of the myths about the intellectual to which Stearns subscribed in the teens and 1920s and that still enjoyed considerable currency in the intellectual climate of the early and mid-1930s. In order fully to appreciate the way Stearns performs the work of repatriation, it is necessary to examine both the overt critique of American culture and society he leveled prior to his expatriation and the crisis of masculinity that emerges as the powerful subtext of this critique. Against the backdrop of a society that, as Stearns saw it, demands that the artist—and the intellectual in general—climb "on the national band wagon of moral idealism and see that a few gracious aesthetic roses are festooned around it as it hurries along the hard road of ethical and material progress" (*Young Intellectual* 13), Stearns defends a "younger generation . . . in revolt," which "*does* dislike, almost to the point of hatred and certainly to the point of contempt, the type of people dominant in our present civilisation, the people who actually 'run things'" (11–12).

In "The Intellectual Life," the essay he wrote for *Civilization in the United States*, Stearns rails against the "contempt for mere intellectual values" exhibited by the descendants of a Puritan, pioneer society for whom "the intellectual life is an instrument of moral reform" (144–45).

In an America where intellectual impulses have become "so fundamentally social in quality and mood," not only is "individualism in thought" frowned upon, but those thinkers that exist are both insufficiently nurtured and insufficiently disciplined: "Individualism in thought, unless mellowed by contact with institutions that assume and cherish it and thus can, without patronizing, correct its wildnesses, inevitably turns into eccentricity" (146). Because in America the kind of intellectual life Stearns advocates is inadequately anchored in any institutions or traditions, and hence, in any intellectually coherent system of values, it fosters its own parodies ("cranks, fanatics, mushroom religious enthusiasts, moral prigs with new schemes of perfectibility, inventors of perpetual motion, illiterate novelists, and oratorical cretins" [147]), thus contributing to its own discredit and demise. Those few who attempt to pursue genuine intellectual endeavor in this atmosphere have been, Stearns claims, crippled by their own isolation and preciosity: "The genteel tradition, which has stolen from the intellectual life its own proper possessions, gaiety and laughter, has left it sour and *déraciné*. It has lost its earthy roots, its sensuous fulness, its bodily *mise-en-scène*. One has the feeling, when one talks to our correct intellectuals, that they are somehow brittle and might be cracked with a pun, a low story, or an animal grotesquerie as an eggshell might be cracked" (148).

Yet Stearns sees hope for America in "the contempt of the younger people for their elders; they are restless, uneasy, disaffected." Although this nascent rebellion lacks direction, discipline, and disinterestedness, its refusal to conform either to goal-oriented mainstream society or to the "genteel tradition" signals a potentially effective challenge to "an authority that has lost all meaning, even to those who wield it" (*Civilization* 149). Stearns sees a raw and beautiful power in America's human energy and its physical magnitude, and he blames the failure to realize the "magic of America" on "those who never really loved it, who never knew our natural gaiety and high spirits and eagerness for knowledge." Stearns dreams of a struggle for the soul of America in which the rebellious and disaffected would prevail over the enforcers of "dull standardization," release "the flashing beauty of form, the rising step of confident animalism, the quick smile of fertile minds," and realize the country's joyful, creative, critical promise (150).

Stearns's dismay over the state of intellectual life in America remains, however, stronger than his prophetic hopes for its revitalization. In the final essay of *America and the Young Intellectual*, Stearns asks "What Can a Young Man Do?" in a society whose "institutional life . . . is a combination of the blackjacking of our youth into the acceptance of the *status quo* not of 1920, but of the late eighteenth century in government, of the early nineteenth century in morals and culture, and of the stone age in business" (166). Framed as a response to an English friend's bewilderment at the large number of young Americans embarking to seek their fortunes in Europe, the essay explains how the conditions of American prosperity have prevented "that small part of the younger American generation which regards its condition and quality as of something higher than a piece of animated lard" from participating in the "revolt . . . experiment . . . [and] general idealism that is eager for action" for which "youth is the natural time" (158–59): "Any civilisation which has the wisdom of self-preservation will allow a certain margin of freedom for the expression of this youthful mood. But the plain, unpalatable fact is that in America to-day that margin of freedom has been reduced to the vanishing point. Rebellious youth is not wanted here. In our environment there is nothing to challenge our young men; there is no flexibility, no colour, no possibility for adventure, no change to shape events more generously than is permitted under the rules of highly organized looting" (159).

Stearns is not at all programmatic about precisely in which intellectual direction a young person should move; his point is rather that the country needs to foster risk-taking and then to respond critically, tolerantly, and constructively to what comes of these risks. Yet, as he put it in "Where Are Our Intellectuals?," the problem is that the very people who should be taking risks and provoking the country to respond to them have themselves sold out: "Where in this present American environment of propaganda and counter-propaganda, of material triumphs and spiritual defeats, can [the intellectual] be found? He can not be found; he is too busy getting on the band-wagon. It is part of our national tradition that he should get on the band-wagon, and that he follows this tradition is the ultimate reason why he has such negligible influence. He wants to 'find' himself so eagerly and so quickly, that he only succeeds in losing himself in the crowd" (*Young Intellectual* 51). Here again, the American penchant for instant solutions and its tendency to value results over process doom the formation of a group that would effectively challenge this "national tradition." Whereas in the essay written for *Civilization in the United States*, Stearns nurtures the daydream that "the America of our natural affections . . . may some day snap the shackles of those who to-day keep it a spiritual prison" (150), in "What Can a Young Man Do?" there seem few alternatives to expatriation.

III

> But let us take his authorship for granted,
> And picture Harold Stearns arrived in France,
> Tasting the freedom that he so vaunted,
> Most gay, most wicked of the celebrants.
> Alas, I find that there is much disparity
> Between this fetching picture and the verity.
>   —MALCOLM COWLEY, "Three Americans in Paris"

When Stearns boarded the *Berengaria* for Europe on Independence Day 1921, his departure was hailed as the logical consequence of his social criticism. Cowley's description of it in *Exile's Return* set the tone for subsequent accounts of this moment in Stearns's life: "Early in July, 1921, just after finishing his Preface and delivering the completed manuscript to the publisher, Mr. Stearns left this country, perhaps forever. His was no ordinary departure: he was Alexander marching into Persia and Byron shaking the dust of England from his feet. Reporters came to the gangplank to jot down his last words. Everywhere young men were preparing to follow his example" (89–90).

This reading of Stearns's departure, which has become the canonical one, has more to do with the role Cowley needs it to play in his profile of the Lost Generation than with what seem to have been Stearns's motivations at the time.[8] Stearns's own writings give us a more complicated take on the event. In "What Can a Young Man Do?" Stearns seems to distinguish between himself and the generation of "young men" whose crisis he is addressing. He does not deploy the words "we" and "they" rhetorically—as Cowley will in 1934—to generalize his own story as that of his "generation"; Stearns is drawing a distinction between himself and his peers, on the one hand, and, on the other hand, those slightly younger than themselves (like Cowley)—and hence, less tied up with the responsibilities of life—whose disenfranchisement is the subject of his essay: "And we who, because of one obligation or another, must for a shorter or longer time stay behind, can not we be permitted to accord to youth as it ventures forth our admiration for its courage and perhaps envy it a little? Can not we do something to make it possible that the answer to the question set forth as the title of this paper must not forever be— Get out!" (*Young Intellectual* 168). Stearns sees "youth" as a vanguard whose impatience and independence enables it to get out, while it is the responsibility of those older and more involved in what American cultural institutions do exist to "do something" to make staying in America a less repellent prospect. In other words, he is not, as is universally held, telling young people to "Get out" as much as he is admonishing his contemporaries to do something to prevent an otherwise inevitable exodus. Although he is pessimistic about the possibility of change, he clearly sees it as a challenge and necessity, and regards getting out as a regrettable last resort.[9]

Although Stearns certainly shared his "young intellectual's" disillusionment with the prospects of change in America, his own motivations for leaving the country were personal and idiosyncratic rather than programmatic. Just a year before the completion of *Civilization in the United States* and *America and the Young Intellectual*, the death in childbirth of Stearns's wife, Alice MacDougal, had launched him into what his neighbor Alfred Kuttner "was pleased to term [his] moral collapse," but what, according to Stearns's own account, was a long period of almost constant drunkenness and despair: "I was as close to impossible as it was for any normal-appearing man to be and yet to escape murder. I was trying to cure the distemper—have not men done it before?—by intoxication through strong drink, even though outwardly, in the ordinary way, I looked conventional and even dull. But the plain truth is I was drunk all the time, terrified only of being caught sober" (*Street* 190). Although Stearns alludes to "the shadows of prohibition and intolerance, all the unlovely aftermath of the great Wilsonian crusade [that] were closing in on me too fast for my comfort," he makes it clear that it was his "old restlessness," the miserable rootlessness and loneliness he felt after Alice's death, that led him to embark on the *Berengaria*: "Europe was calling me again, or—and it came down to the same thing—what I thought was Europe. If Alice had lived, things might have been different; I am sure they would have been different. But as it was, I felt exhausted and tired and a little bitter" (202–3). The "genuine work" demanded by his two book projects kept him "busy and occupied and safe from the one thing of all things I dread and fear the most—being alone" (192). But Stearns makes it clear that the loss of his wife continued to haunt him and that work had merely deferred a breakdown far more elaborate than the drinking binge immediately following her death: "Well, I ran away to France, when I lost her" (176).[10]

If we read Stearns's expatriation as being motivated by personal rather than cultural despair, the example he represents is no longer accounted for in a narrative like Cowley's, where the biographies of even highly neurotic individuals (such as Hart Crane and Harry Crosby) are invoked to confirm through hyperbole a thesis about an entire generation. "The example that [Stearns] sets, and . . . the ideas that he clarifies and sets in motion" (*Young Intellectual* 50) not only represent a powerful *direct* indictment of the intellectual and cultural temper of the United States in the first decades of the century but force us to pay attention to individuals whose lives as lived amount—*indirectly*—to a critique of their culture. The stories of the American male intellectual told by such ex- and repatriation narratives as Cowley's and Stearns's demand that we read them as strategic self-constructions that both canonize a particular intellectual pose and foreground the categories in which the intellectual chooses to be evaluated. While Cowley's portrait of his generation willfully subordinates the private life to what he represents as the life of the mind (and, as if it were the same thing, of a group of male intellectuals), Stearns's portrait of himself (in the context of many of the people and institutions that populate Cowley's text) emphasizes the idiosyncratic over the general, the neurotic over the normative, and insists upon the interpenetration of personal and professional as well as male and female worlds. By disregarding or intentionally breaking down the distinctions—above all, the gender distinctions—that structure Cowley's rendition of the expatriate decade, Stearns's text opens up the possibility of a critical commentary on not only the canonical version of the expatriate experience of the 1920s but also the American cultural coming-of-age that is often taken to be its direct result.

In *The Street I Know*, Stearns presents himself as having inherited but a marginal claim to legitimate membership in society. In a coy play on the beginning of *Tristram Shandy*, by his near-namesake, Laurence Sterne, Stearns entitles the first chapter of his autobiography "Accidentally I Get Born" and proceeds, as does Tristram Shandy, both to give himself a father and to call his patrimony into question. Stearns calls himself "a posthumous child. My father had died three months before I was born," and reports how he was told that his father's "death . . . had so upset [his mother] . . . that she had temporarily lost her mind [and] . . . forfeited all claims to what little property [his father] had intended to leave but didn't (dying intestate)" (*Street* 12–13). Although Stearns accepts his mother's self-characterization as "a penniless widow with two children to support," his biographer, Mark Orwoll, calls him a "bastard," and Stearns, himself, hints at another version of his origins: "My brother, . . . for no good reason I ever was able to discover, gratuitously made my childhood miserable with—whenever I thought of them—dark hints that I did not 'know the whole story' " (13).[11]

Needless to say, the reader never gets to hear the "whole story," although the story that Stearns continues to tell is governed by the trope of fatherlessness and marginal legitimacy together with a remarkably unsentimental and respectful—although not unambivalent—attitude toward women: "In any case, my mother fought a valiant and surprisingly successful battle to keep her children and to keep up a home. Not many women would have had her courage. As a boy, I was supersensitive to her small faults; as a man, I now want to pay tribute to her indomitable spirit" (*Street* 13). Stearns's strategy—at least in his adult life—for navigating between the Scylla of his mother's "small faults" and the Charybdis of her "indomitable spirit" seems to have been to avoid her as much as possible. His almost compulsive failure ever to return to Boston in the thirty years after his graduation from Harvard and the guilt he claims to feel over this failure constitute a leitmotif of *The Street I Know*: "I have planned a real visit to Boston; several times I have started to go. Somehow, I can't seem to make it. I don't exactly know how to express it clearly. . . . Getting up to Boston always presents ridiculous and insuperable problems" (88).

Stearns attributes his sense of being "one of those unfortunate people who really are homeless and spiritual vagabonds" (*Street* 88) to his mother's "restlessness" (59) and to the lack of a "properly corrective home environment . . . the confidence and guidance of a father" (57). Whereas his home situation seems to have freed Stearns from any sentimental nostalgia for "roots" he didn't have, it also condemned him to a perpetual version of the homelessness and uprootedness he experienced as a child, moving from one town to another, often several times a year. His lifelong fear of returning to Boston to discover "that the New Englander in me has died" seems to belong to the same emotional economy that compels Stearns to tiptoe intellectually around both the facts of his patrimony and those of his mother's social situation: "I was to be an alien and an outsider to the special spot of the earth that had given me birth and . . . an education" (88).

It was not until he entered Harvard that he felt that he was a legitimate member of anything resembling the symbolic order; the authorization and legitimacy denied him as an "outsider . . . [with] no father and regular family status in the community" (*Street* 40) was at least provisionally conferred by the *nom propre* of the institution: "It was partly this feeling of inferiority, I think now, which made me decide to go to Harvard, for I knew there was no laughing *that* off" (56). Considering the compensatory importance for Stearns of his Harvard affiliation, it is surprising how little his memoir indulges in social snobbishness. Having witnessed, early in his freshman year, the "class and personal politics . . . pettinesses, absurdities, and loyalties, too" of the senior class and recognizing that "social ambitions have little glamour if you are 'broke' " (72–73), Stearns focused on academic distinction ("If you didn't want to become an educated man, it was nobody's business but your own. The college gave you the chance"; "Incredible as it seems to me now, I had a strong urge for scholarship—or thought I did" [70–71]) and the camaraderie of "men of my own age, and to a greater extent than my youthful pride then permitted me clearly to see, men of approximately the same natural intelligence and ability." And he continues: "Once the class elections were over—and the selections for the more exclusive clubs—there was not much point any longer in being 'up stage.' One began to make friends naturally, and without thinking too much of the possible social consequences to your college career" (75–76). Assuming his place in "a tradition of irreconcilability, as William James has so finely written" (76),

Stearns claims to have maintained a degree of immunity from the coercive—or exclusive—snobbism that colors Cowley's account of his Harvard years and to which his biographer suggests he at least partially succumbed.[12]

In fact, Stearns's experience at Harvard pointed him intellectually in a direction directly opposite to the one that Cowley chose upon arriving in Cambridge. Whereas Cowley pursued literary distinction—and specifically, recognition as a poet—Stearns turned away from the "purely literary view towards life, such as I was then naturally inclined towards" and toward precisely that involvement with the world outside Harvard Yard that Cowley indicts the American university for neglecting fatally. Stearns writes:

> I tried to do some general reading, of course, and I kept up with current news better than the average youngster—chiefly because of my experiences as a reporter, I now believe. . . . Even in my freshman year [a senior, R.S.] Holmes had made me feel that a *purely literary view towards life, such as I was then naturally inclined towards . . . was feminine and inferior and dull. I had partly for that reason turned to philosophy rather than to so-called pure literature*—and I had contracted the habit of watching the newspapers and forming my "own" opinion on politics as well as on other topics. (*Street* 81, emphasis added)

This turn away from "pure literature" and the reasons for it are crucial to an understanding of both Stearns's future career and—as I hope to demonstrate—the careers of Cowley and his "generation." Stearns never says that he, himself, found literature to be "feminine and inferior and dull"; indeed, his passion for Rabelais, his book reviewing, the tenor of his concerns about culture, and the literary pleasure he takes in his own writing suggest that he continued to indulge in this "natural inclination." But, perhaps to a greater extent than his contemporaries whose familial origins and social connectedness grounded them more securely in American institutions and whose family structures reproduced something more generally approximating normative gender arrangements, he seems to have been sensitive to what it took to qualify as a "Harvard *man*" (*Street* 82, emphasis added). The Harvard affiliation served as a supplement to the nomadic, fatherless family unit in which Stearns achieved maturity, and contributed significantly to his ability to recognize and take advantage of what privilege he did enjoy. Stearns undertook, he tells us, to "express [his aristocratic impulse] intellectually rather than socially": "As I was 'free, white, and twenty-one,' a New Englander and a Harvard man to boot, I suffered no early feeling of racial or even family inferiority—sketchy as my actual family life had been" (82). Because of the importance, within the context of Stearns's particular "family romance," of being "a Harvard man," the stigma attached to the literary life— "feminine and inferior and dull"—represented a particular obstacle, and the attempt to avoid this stigmatization was significantly to determine how—and where—he pursued the intellectual life.

IV

> Amidst the racket, Harold Stearns is quiet. He
> In fact is strangely quiet for this Latin,
> Ebullient city, where such piety
> Is rarer than in puritan Manhattan;
> And rather would he brave the fires of Hades
> Than meet the glances of the Paris ladies.
> —MALCOLM COWLEY, "Three Americans in Paris"

The association of the literary with the feminine in American culture was, of course, nothing new. Ann Douglas has claimed that the cultural alliance between the American clergy and "middle-class literary women" had created, by the nineteenth century, a middle-brow popular culture focused on domesticity and sentiment, "that exaltation of the average which is the trademark of mass culture" (*Feminization* 2). In Douglas's account, "feminized" American literary culture propagated "the potentially matriarchal [but, in reality, sentimental or sentimentalized] virtues of nurture, generosity, and acceptance, to create [a] 'culture of the feelings'" and produced the reading consumer, the leisured seeker of entertainment and mild uplift (10). The feminization of which Douglas writes is by no means feminism; rather, she sees the sentimentalism that came to be associated with women as reinscribing them within the limits of the domestic sphere and guaranteeing the continuation of male hegemony in different guises (11).

Yet this hegemony—if hegemony it was—remained precarious. Although recent scholarship has discerned more nuanced, critical negotiations between sentimentality, domesticity, and gender than those described by Douglas,[13] I think it is fair to say that the received idea equating the literary and the feminine was potently behind the admonition that moved Stearns to abandon "pure literature" and turn toward philosophy, psychology, and social criticism. Male intellectuals, especially, have repeatedly felt called upon to describe and delimit those aspects of cultural life that they could not help but concede to the "feminine," and then to defend "manly" scholarship against the threats—imagined or real—of feminization. Part of the task Ralph Waldo Emerson sets himself in "The American Scholar" is to construct the "manlike" scholar. This construction demands that he distinguish between the scholar as an active "delegated intellect . . . *Man Thinking*" and what he calls a "mere thinker . . . the parrot of other men's thinking" (54). Part of this distinction rests in the American scholar's assertion of independence from European thought, "the sere remains of foreign harvests" (53), but the more important characteristic of Emerson's "Man Thinking" lies in his active engagement with the world, with his ability to be inspired, rather than disabled, by books and learning: "They are for nothing but to inspire. I had better never see a book, than to be warped by its attraction clean out of my own orbit, and made a satellite instead of a system" (57). The kind of scholar—one thinks immediately of George Eliot's Casaubon—who escapes the challenges and truths of nature by pursuing its shadows in books does not only deserve the scorn of his contemporaries; he is hardly a man at all:

> There goes in the world a notion, that the scholar should be a
> recluse, a valetudinarian,—as unfit for any handiwork or public
> labor, as a penknife for an axe. The so-called "practical men"
> sneer at speculative men, as if, because they speculate or *see*, they
> could do nothing. I have heard it said that the clergy,—who are
> always, more universally than any other class, the scholars of their
> day,—are addressed as women; that the rough, spontaneous conversation of men they do not hear, but only a mincing and diluted
> speech. They are often virtually disenfranchised; and indeed, there
> are advocates for their celibacy. As far as this is true of the studi-

ous classes, it is not just and wise. Action is with the scholar subordinate, but it is essential. Without it, he is not yet man. (59–60)

In his effort to rehabilitate the scholar from the "sneers" of "practical men," Emerson explicitly attacks those whose misperceptions of the
scholar's activity are responsible for his reputation and, more tacitly,
chides those individual scholars whose example has fostered this faulty
generalization. Lest the scholar be "sneered" at, "addressed as women,"
and "disenfranchised" for his vapid, unmanly performance, Emerson
demands that he partake of the spirit of the pioneer: "Free should the
scholar be,—free and brave" ("American Scholar" 65). His knowledge
must be a source of courage, "for fear is a thing, which a scholar by
his very function puts behind him. Fear always springs from ignorance"
(65). His mandate to pursue the difficult, the dangerous, the provocative
belies his contemplative pose: "It is a shame to him if his tranquillity,
amid dangerous times, arise from the presumption, that, like children
and women, his is a protected class; or if he seek a temporary peace by
the diversion of his thoughts from politics or vexed questions, hiding his
head like an ostrich in the flowering bushes, peeping into microscopes,
and turning rhymes, as a boy whistles to keep his courage up. So is the
danger a danger still; so is the fear worse. Manlike let him turn and
face it" (65). The challenge of and to the scholar—and here we see how
Emerson's exhortation stands behind Stearns's view of the role of the
intellectual—is to take "manlike" risks, to have the "confidence in the
unsearched might of man [that] belongs, by all motives, by all proph-
ecy, by all preparation, to the American Scholar" (70). Like Stearns after
him, Emerson distances himself from "decorous and . . . complaisant"
belletristics, on the one hand, and "the principles on which business is
managed," on the other.

By the end of the essay, Emerson has sublated the opposition between
contemplation and action and projected a portrait of the American
scholar cleansed of the dross of both effete pseudo-cultural complacency
and rank mercantilism: "If the single man plant himself indomitably on
his instincts, and there abide, the huge world will come round to him"
("American Scholar" 70). Yet despite Emerson's blueprint, the association of intellectual activity and the feminine—especially as set against the
equally tenacious coupling of business activity and the masculine—con-

tinued to haunt American cultural life. Pondering the anomaly of American gender relations in *The American Scene*, Henry James recalls observing the comings and goings in Harvard Yard and speculates about the "young men" who populate the university. Although he begins with ethnic speculation, the question he raises, "*whom did they look like the sons of?*" immediately shifts the focus of his interrogation. An issue far more pressing, it would seem, than the ethnic origins of the young men of Harvard is what we might call their gender inheritance. Recalling first that "no impression so promptly assaults the arriving visitor of the United States as that of the overwhelming preponderance, wherever he turns and twists, of the unmitigated 'business man' face" and that, in contrast, "nothing, meanwhile, is more concomitantly striking than the fact that the women, over the land . . . appear to be of a markedly finer texture than the men" (*AS* 64–65), James wonders aloud how and whether education will enable young Harvard men to reconcile "the canvas" supplied by the American man and "the embroidery" that is the province and the achievement of the American woman: "In what proportion of instances would it stick out that the canvas, rather than the embroidery, was what [the Harvard undergraduate] would have to show? In what proportion would he wear the stamp of the unredeemed commercialism that should betray his paternity? In what proportion, in his appearance, would the different social 'value' imputable to his mother have succeeded in interposing?" (66). Having pointed to "the appearance of a queer deep split or chasm between the two stages of personal polish, the two levels of the conversible state, at which the sexes have arrived" (65), James defers drawing conclusions about the effect on American culture of the gross incompatibility of its men and women.

Later in *The American Scene*, however, reflecting that Washington society—significantly, the first he has encountered where business does *not* set the tone for social interactions—is "the only one in the country, in which Men existed" (345), James resumes his meditations on the cultural tasks appointed to men and women in America. When, as James puts it, "the Man, the deep American man, retire[d] into his tent" of business "and let down the flap" (348), the American woman found herself responsible for "the lonely waste, the boundless gaping void of 'society'; which is but a rough name for all the *other* so numerous relations with the world he lives in that are imputable to the civilized being" (345).

While the men who have retreated into the business sphere remain wilfully and blissfully indifferent to what they have surrendered, the women are overburdened with the responsibility for managing social, cultural, and familial relations. Here, James falls short of saying that the ensuing feminization of all walks of life outside the business sphere is necessarily bad; rather, he calls it "unnatural" (348). And while he finds this phenomenon endlessly fascinating—as his fiction attests—he seems to remain unconvinced that it is beneficial to the culture at large.

In "The Speech of American Women" and "The Manners of American Women," two essays he published shortly after his stay in America, James expresses real disapproval of the gender division of cultural labor that he describes less crankily in *The American Scene*, taking American women to task for their unmodulated, unrefined speech and their failure to cultivate and practice the kinds of manners that govern social intercourse in Europe. While these two essays seem directed at American women, the real object of his concern—and to a certain extent, his scorn—turns out to be the American man, whose concession to women of the hegemony over the cultural and social realms that I have described above renders them—the men—responsible for the cultural deficits of their female contemporaries and, by extension, of the society at large: "However it may be with the man, the 'educated' man, of other countries, the American male, in *his* conditions, is incapable of caring for a moment what sounds his women emit: incapable of caring because incapable of knowing—of knowing, that is, what sounds *are*, what they may be, what they should or what they shouldn't be. Of what sounds other than the yell of the stock-exchange or the football-field does he himself . . . give the cheering example?" ("Speech, Two" 1104). Asking "Isn't it everywhere written that the women, in any society, are what the men make them?" James is forced to acknowledge that this is true in America only to the extent that the men's lack of interest in "invent[ing] the standard and set[ting] the tune and . . . constitut[ing], in the whole matter, the authority" has "made" the women take "[the authority] over without blinking, . . . encamped on every inch of the social area that the stock-exchange and the football-field leave free" (1105). Once the men have disenfranchised themselves, the women must be held responsible for a state of affairs that, James suggests, culturally engaged men would not tolerate.

The problem is thus not with the women, but with the men, who have "treacherously abjured the manly part of *real* appreciation—letting, in the guise of generosity, the whole question of responsibility, of manly competence and control, example, expectation, go by the board" ("Manners, Four" 649). Before American women can acquire—or can be made to want to acquire—the competences and graces that would truly distinguish them, before they can channel—and thus, paradoxically, set free—their indisputable energy into culturally appropriate tasks, American men must reassert their concern for and authority over the social and cultural spheres:

"In societies other than ours the male privilege of correction springs, and quite logically, from the social fact that the male is the member of society primarily acting and administering and primarily listened to—whereby his education, his speech, his tone, his standards and connections, his general 'competence' . . . color the whole air, react upon his companion and establish for her the principal relation she recognizes" (650). In the apparent absence in the America he confronts of the kind of men willing or able to exercise this "privilege of correction," James, by writing his critiques of American women's speech and manners, presents his own credentials: the American male writer, the American male intellectual is the missing figure, "primarily acting and administering and primarily listened to," whose "standards and connection" and "general 'competence'" are being made available to American society for its improvement. To the extent that he sees the verbal and social skills he advocates as being necessary to navigating "a world, the very interest of which is exactly that it is complicated" (650), James aligns himself with Emerson's "manly" scholar, whose knowledge enables him to brave those aspects of the social and cultural landscape for which the tools of the traditional man of action are inadequate. Like the male citizen of Washington, whom he describes as "the victim of effacement, the outcast at the door," the returning expatriate, James, has "*talked himself* back" into "some share at least in the interests of civilization, some part of the social property and social office" (AS 350–51).

Yet despite James's insistence that "the [American] woman . . . is never at all thoroughly a well-bred person unless *he* [the American man] has begun by having a sense for it and by showing her the way," the image of the American man as a pioneer of breeding and culture seems to have failed to secure itself in the culture's imaginary. As I hope to have shown in my discussions of Emerson and James, the stigma attached to the male person who is not conspicuously a man of action, combined with the conspicuous sociocultural activity of the female person in America, produces an uneasiness about the gender of intellectual life. That the term *intellectual life* remains vague is, I think, part of the reason that the question of its gender is so volatile; nowhere in Emerson's or James's texts are the boundaries of this intellectual life staked; where, for instance, does James draw the line between the *social*—his generic term for all that has been capitulated to women—and the *intellectual*, which he would seem to regard as a subset of the social (at least, to the extent that it is not within the province of business) but not within the proper domain of women (although he does not expressly claim it for men)? Is, furthermore, the continuum between the social, as practiced in Europe, and the cultural as seamless as James seems to suggest? And, perhaps most important, how does James reconcile his own work with the gender he attributes to it? Or does his expatriation have everything to do with the attempt to locate himself outside of, and thereby to claim exemption from, a gendered division of labor that would place him so clearly in the province of women?

James's and Emerson's defenses of the life of the mind are haunted, first, by the sense that this life threatens to be an irredeemably feminized one, and second, by the attempt to define the manly in terms of a specter of the feminine that ultimately eludes specification. Stearns's otherwise clear-minded excursus on "The Intellectual Life" in *Civilization in the United States* (1922) continues in this tradition, inspired by the work of George Santayana, with whom he had studied, and Randolph Bourne, whom he greatly admired. This essay demonstrates how powerful—and how confused—the association of feminization with the deficiencies of American intellectual life remains. Whereas Stearns recalls being warned in college in general terms that the "purely literary view towards life" was "feminine and inferior and dull," here he diagnoses a specifically American association of the feminine with the intellectual life and proposes a genealogy of this association that recalls both Emerson and James.

Like Emerson, Stearns attributes the "poverty of intellectual things" in America to the tenacity of a "pioneer tradition" understandably hostile to someone who might call into question the validity of its ideology of activity and expansion: "[The thinker] is a reproach and a challenge to the man who must labour by the sweat of his brow—it is as if he said, 'For what end, all this turmoil and effort, merely to live? But do you know if life is worth while on such terms?'" (*Civilization* 135–37). With the closing of the frontier, the pioneer ethos transmuted into that of the businessman: "The facts have changed, but we have not changed, only deflected our interests. Where the pioneer cleared a wilderness, the modern financier subdues a forest of competitors. He puts the same amount of energy and essentially the same quality of thought into his task today" (138). Yet while the pioneer's antagonism to "the distractions of art or the amenities of literature" (137) was justified by the demands of survival, that of his progeny is a sign of the country's philistinism. Having declared his independence not only from the political shackles of the Old World but also from the cultural and social heritage that might give value to something other than the pursuit of lucre that has replaced that of the frontier, the American man has no concept of the "good life," no notion of what to do with his leisure.

While, Stearns continues, the American man continued to make money "because there is nothing else to do," the middle-class American woman had nothing to do but accept her husband's gift of leisure: "But if the successful pioneer did not know what to do with his own leisure, he had naive faith in the capacity of his women to know what to do with theirs. . . . He gave them leisure exactly as the typical business man of today gives them a blank check signed with his name. It disposed of them, kept them out of his world, and salved his conscience—like a check to charity" (*Civilization* 141). Like the women in James's genealogy of America's feminine cultural hegemony, Stearns's women were more than happy to participate in this division of labor, and, like James's women, those Stearns imagines were able to appreciate and capitalize on the gift they had been handed as if by default:

> Unluckily for him, his mother, his wife, his sisters, and his aunts
> were of his own blood and breeding; they were the daughters
> of pioneers like himself, and the daughters of mothers who had
> contributed share and share alike to those foundations which
> had made his success possible. . . . The majority were strangely

discontented (strangely, that is, from his point of view) with the job of mere Victorian ornament. What more natural under the circumstances than that the unimportant things of life—art, music, religion, literature, the intellectual life—should be handed over to them to keep them busy and contented, while he confined himself to the real man's job of making money and getting on in the world? (141)

The effect of this division of labor is that boys and men associate the arts and the life of the mind with effeminacy: "sissies" are interested in poetry; the boy who plays the piano is "queer." The puny salaries of "male teachers, male professors (secretly), male ministers, and male artists" (142) testify to the low esteem in which they are held.

Thus far, Stearns's argument follows—personal idiosyncrasies notwithstanding—the general lines of Emerson's and James's. He continues in their spirit when he complains that women's influence on culture has refined away the "native gaiety . . . sexual curiosity . . . play . . . creative dreaming, or . . . adventure" that are the "more genuine," "manly" intellectual impulses (*Civilization* 142). But then, Stearns parts company with his predecessors: following this sketch of what he calls "the cruder historical forces that have led directly to the present remarkable situation" in which cultural activity is almost exclusively the province of women (143), he dissociates the attributes "feminine" and "masculine" from women and men, thus introducing the distinction between sex and gender that remains unexplored in the discourses of his predecessors. In other words, it might indeed be true that female human beings are in command of the life of the mind in America, but it need not follow that the life of the mind is feminine. In fact, it will turn out that the mind, as Stearns understands it, has two lives: a "feminine," pragmatic one (the life lived by the minds of most men and women in America) and a "masculine," disinterested, abstract one. This distinction enables him to pay tribute to the "genuine intellectual camaraderie" (143) between some men and some women resulting from "suffrage, the new insights into the world of industry which the war gave so many women for the first time, the widening of professional opportunity [and] co-education," while concluding: "Where men and women in America to-day share their intellectual life on terms of equality and perfect understanding, closer examination reveals that the phenomenon is not a sharing but a capitulation. The men have been feminized" (143).

While Stearns's characterizations of the "masculine" and "feminine" approaches to the intellectual life initially strike one as inconsistent with the expectations generated by his genealogy, they are, in fact, its logical consequence.[14] In a culture where women—who are more pragmatic, less philosophical than men—set the agenda for intellectual affairs, intellectual life is going to reflect their biases. And the men whose education and intellectual orientation reflect the values of this culture are going to assume that what Stearns deems a "feminine," "sociological activity" is indeed intellectual activity of the noblest sort. Hence Stearns's disclaimer:

> I have by implication rather than direct statement contrasted
> genuine interest in intellectual things with the kind of intellectual
> life led by women. Let me say now that no intention is less mine
> than to contribute to the old controversy concerning the respective
> intellectual capacities of the two sexes. If I use the adjective "mas-
> culine" to denote a more valid type of intellectual impulse than
> is expressed by the adjective "feminine," it is not to belittle the
> quality of the second impulse; it is a matter of definition. Further,
> the relative degree of "masculine" and "feminine" traits possessed
> by an individual are almost as much the result of acquired train-
> ing as of native inheritance. The young, independent college girl
> of to-day is in fact more likely to possess "masculine" intellectual
> habits than is the average Y.M.C.A. director. I use the adjectives
> to express broad, general characteristics as they are commonly un-
> derstood. (*Civilization* 143–44)

The best minds in America, male and female, find themselves engaged in the application of "knowledge and skill to the formulation of a technique for the better solution of problems *the answers to which are already assumed*" (145, emphasis added). What is missing is the learned and passionate engagement with the problems themselves, as well as the consciousness of the innate value and pleasure of abstract intellectual pursuit: "We are deeply uncomfortable before introspection, contemplation, or scrupulous adherence to logical sequence. Women do not hesitate to call these activities cold, impersonal, indirect. . . . That the life of the mind might have an emotional drive, a sting or vibrancy of its own, constituting as valuable a contribution to human happiness as, say, the satisfied marital felicity of the bacteria-less suburbanite in his concrete villa has been incomprehensible" (145–46).

Stearns's introduction of a constructionist distinction between the "masculine" and "feminine" lives of the mind begins the process of rehabilitating abstract thought as an honorable, manly activity. Disinterested interest in intellectual things needs to be disembarrassed of its feckless, libertine reputation ("wayward and masculine; and, cardinal sin of all, useless" [*Civilization* 144]) and to be pursued with passion and true intellectual purpose. America must become a place where "Man Thinking"—and even man dreaming—can be a real man and a respectable man.

V

And does he then, remembering his article,
Expound to us Three Roads Proposed to Freedom!
And does he paint the town? No, not a particle;
His eyes are innocent as those of Edom.
Less bad than bashful, less in joy than fear,
He hides his glances in a glass of beer.
                    —MALCOLM COWLEY, "Three Americans in Paris"

The way Stearns involves gender in his analysis of the intellectual crisis of early twentieth-century America encourages us to speculate about the role it played in the way he tells the story of his life and especially of his ex- and repatriation. Although in *The Street I Know*, he never thematizes the issue of gender as he did in the essays he wrote prior to his expatriation, the book contains ample evidence that Stearns remained conscious of and preoccupied with the gender trouble associated with the intellectual life; moreover, what he regards as the improvements in the lot and self-presentation of American women occupies the foreground of his tableau of America rediscovered. In his presentation of his own gender relations, Stearns suggests—through omission as well as description— that the ineluctable form of his mother haunted the development of his life and career and that the prospect of understanding the dynamics of his relation to this woman would open up an otherwise foreclosed understanding of why his life took the course that it did. Although Stearns's mother makes but one brief appearance in his narrative of his adult life, she is a presence in his ruminations and particularly in his inventories of his shortcomings. Caught between a fear of presenting himself to his mother as a failure and an equally strong sense of responsibility for her well-being, Stearns never asks her for help and continually postpones visiting her until it is too late: "I felt so helpless and so ashamed of feeling helpless; I should have to wait until I was 'on my feet.' I couldn't bear it, nor did I want her to bear it either—the thought that I was a failure" (404). He makes no connections between her ambivalent role in his early life and his own unconventional relations with women, but the force of his avoidance of her, coupled with the force of his discomfort with his own behavior, suggests that his upbringing has both "prepared" him for the bohemian gender arrangements he will experience, and guaranteed that these arrangements will remain less than satisfactory.

Stearns's representation of the "Mid-Town Bohemia" to which he moved upon completing his Harvard B.A. degree in 1912 foregrounds its truly cosmopolitan sexual, gender, and intellectual arrangements. He records substantial, collegial friendships with "two of the most interesting and brilliant girls I ever knew, lovely Mary Pyne, and the dynamic, talented, curiously handsome Djuna Barnes," as well as more intimate relations with women whose names he does not reveal but whose intelligence and professional savvy dominate his descriptions of them (*Street* 96). He is candid and unapologetic about the comfortable fraternity he enjoyed with men: "'Ike's' [bar] was one of the gathering-places of newspaper men, composers, playwrights, the more literate actors, and book publishers. It was convenient and quiet and purely 'Stag'—and a fondness for the security given men by that is something even my many years in Paris, with its so-to-speak bi-sexual bars, did not completely destroy" (100). The opportunity to enjoy both the friendship of women and the brotherhood of men contributes significantly to the mood of his first year in New York, of "goodnature [sic], a mood of feeling secure, a mood of tolerance towards other countries, other people, and even other people's ideas. . . . A mood (I like to think it is the old and traditional American mood) of willingness . . . to try experiments, even on occasion to welcome them" (101).

If midtown life sustained gender eccentricity, Greenwich Village institutionalized it and set it in opposition to the mainstream "America" to which Stearns has tried to assimilate it. In the teens and 1920s, Greenwich Village was, as Ellen Kay Trimberger puts it, "a code word for cultural and personal revolt against the American middle class" (132). In its atmosphere of dissent in "dialogue with the mass media and those who uphold and shape the dominant morality," many intellectuals and artists of Stearns's generation envisioned what Christine Stansell has termed "a modernism experienced as an artful, carefully crafted everyday life" and sought "to repudiate the cumbersome past and experiment with form, not only in painting and literature . . . but also in politics and love, friendship and sexual passion" (2). Stearns's move to Greenwich Village following a short trip to Europe that coincided with the outbreak of the First World War represents a shift in his relation to the "old and traditional American mood." In the Greenwich Village context, the unconventionality of Stearns's social ties was itself almost conventional; the way he lived, the company he kept, and the opinions he held—and the fact that he did so in Greenwich Village—set him in official opposition to mainstream culture.

Yet even in Greenwich Village's climate of nonconformity, Stearns seems to have remained something of an outsider; although his mores resembled those of his friends and contemporaries, his agenda—conscious or unconscious—was idiosyncratic, and, I surmise, unreliable. Although the publication of *Civilization in the United States* earned him the reputation of being something of an instigator among Greenwich Village intellectuals, his figure is absent from, or earns at best a footnote in, most of the major accounts of the period.[15] He was less than regularly employed and often dependent on the largesse of the women he obviously had no difficulty attracting.[16] He records one relationship in particular with a woman he calls Felicia, a fashion artist who took care of his material needs: "My girl . . . made more than her share of what was needed to keep up the semblance of a ménage, though as a matter of fact she lived out of town and 'commuted,' hence her contribution to the ménage was more in the nature of a manager than a resident. She bought everything; she prepared some of my meals; she paid the bills and saw to it that I had new clothes when my old ones could no longer be repaired—and all this, as if it were the most natural thing in the world" (*Street* 127). He, in turn, taught her "French and history and English literature—so well, in fact, that later on she was able to edit trade magazines successfully and competently at really decent salaries" (127). Later, he and "Felicia" lived in separate apartments in the same building, "so that I had all the advantages, whatever they may be, of 'living with' a girl, and at the same time of being independent and having a place of my own to which I could invite my friends occasionally for dinner" (136).

Stearns's unembarrassed (if perhaps not unambivalent) acceptance of Felicia's financial support documents a willingness to be kept by others—most often, but not exclusively, women—that continues through his expatriation and until the end of his life.[17] That he regards tutoring Felicia as his contribution to their ménage implies that he saw his own intellectual assets as a powerful commodity but one not immediately useful in the battle for survival. Stearns explains but remains unapologetic about his limited ability to convert his interests and skills into the necessities and tangibles of life: "It was the characteristic pot-boiling existence of the time—except that I had few of the proper ingredients to put in the pot, even when I could find it. What I could do best was too special, perhaps too intellectual, for the kind of helter-skelter life of an occasional article here, a little piece or interview for a newspaper there, a book review somewhere else. I never could—and I didn't then—make a go of it" (Street 126). As long as he resists capitulating to the market's demand for what, at the end of the decade, he would call the "feminine approach," which measured "ideas ... for their value by terms outside the ideas themselves" (Civilization 144), he is not compromising himself by assuming the traditionally feminine position of being supported by a more regularly working partner. Rather, he exempts himself from "the characteristic pot-boiling existence of the time" in order to do truly masculine work ("too special, perhaps too intellectual") and enjoy the company of men, leaving the pragmatics of daily survival to a female companion, whose earning power has been augmented by his tutelage.[18]

That Stearns was not overly troubled by the power dynamics and the apparent threat to "masculinity" such a relationship would entail is perhaps further explained by his childhood experience of being supported by a single woman. Yet this dynamics assumes a particular form in the account of his adult life that becomes clearer when we probe in some detail into a short paragraph in which, chronicling a brief sojourn in Chicago in 1916, Stearns alludes to the "indelible impression" made on his mind of an experience that showed him "what sensuality might mean" (*Street* 134). Without vouchsafing any details, Stearns signals that this interlude "with a pretty young woman I had known only by sight before at the old Liberal Club in New York" represented an upheaval of no small proportions. He describes the "purely sensuous impression" left by this encounter as being "almost as vivid as those we read about with startled shame-faced recognition in later adolescent years in the confessions of Rousseau" (135) and suggests that this extramoral experience, rather than any repertoire of responsibilities or relations with "social" implications, effected the profound change that made him, "in the deepest sense, a grown-up man. Intellectual, sensual, emotional naïveté was gone forever" (136).

Before I speculate about the nature of this "sensuality," it is crucial to note Stearns's need to explain this only indirectly specified experience in relation to what he here calls "morality"; "morals," he writes, "are concerned with action in its social significance—they are not, or at least ought not to be, concerned with personal sensations that have no general implications" (*Street* 136). The logic of this passage recalls Stearns's characterization of masculine thought in *Civilization in the United States*. Like the masculine thought that Stearns defined by its independence from criteria of social applicability, this sensuality is a purely personal matter, an action that, having no "social significance," is morally irrelevant. The experience that turned him "in the deepest sense" into "a grown-up man" was thus one that had no place—and, as a truly "sensuous" experience, could have no place—even on the most permissive of Greenwich Village moral maps. Yet, he maintains, it is also a quintessentially, profoundly—and structurally—"masculine" experience, even if, as we shall discover, it seems to be one that scandalizes and profoundly threatens masculinity as it is commonly conceived.

Stearns's allusion to Rousseau and to the "shame-faced recognition" attending the young man's reading of *The Confessions* demands that we recall to just what kind of sensuality the French philosopher was referring. Rousseau's blissfully "shame-faced" confession that to "fall on my knees before a masterful mistress, to obey her commands, to have to beg for her forgiveness, have been to me the most delicate of pleasures" (28) opens up a line of speculation about Stearns that seems to bring into focus both the peculiar shape of his curriculum vitae and the strange repertoire of aversions, sympathies, and ambivalences it inspired. Nothing could be less to my purpose than to explain away the case of Harold Stearns by overreading a passage in which he seems to confess his masochism; yet I do not think we can adequately appreciate the resonances of his figure and its effaced centrality to the Lost Generation's story of its self-discovery unless we examine the figure of the masochist and explore how it troubles and even disrupts the kind of mythography that has installed *Exile's Return* as the definitive narrative of the Lost Generation. It is neither productive nor necessary to attempt an anamnesis of Stearns's sexuality, although the peculiar relation to his mother to which he gives us some limited but symptomatic access in *The Street I Know* and the force he attributes to his fatherlessness and putative illegitimacy suggest a blueprint that might—but certainly need not—tend to favor the development of masochistic tendencies.[19] Rather, I wish to examine how what I take to be Stearns's masochism responds to a dominant cultural discourse that, in the important ways I have discussed above, compensated for his lack of a "properly corrective home environment" and the "confidence and guidance of a father" (*Street* 57) and provided him with the parameters of identity that his particular personal situation denied him ("I knew there was no laughing *that* [Harvard] off" [56]).[20] I want to suggest furthermore, that Stearns's response is but a candid and exacerbated version of, and hence an embarrassingly revealing commentary on, the gender relations to culture informing *Exile's Return* and the mythos of the Lost Generation. If we recall Stearns's—and others'—insistence on the appropriation by women of the intellectual life that he would have define his manhood, we can see how the masochistic position represents a characteristic and even paradigmatic response to the crisis of the male intellectual that I have discussed in detail above.

If the sensuous interlude in Chicago marks the moment when Stearns became "a grown-up man," it is particularly significant that he deems this transformation intellectual and emotional as well as sensual. The trip to the Midwest that included Stearns's sojourn in Chicago appears to have shattered the complacency of his relation to the social order to which Harvard had seemed to admit him. Witnessing at first hand the desolation produced by "industrialism untempered by anything more gracious than a desire for all the profits going" (*Street* 134) and enjoying "enormously" an interview with Bill Haywood, a founder and leader of the Industrial Workers of the World (IWW), Stearns seems to have been shocked into the awareness of the need for and the existence of forms of resistance to the dominant ideology ("I learned . . . what sabotage really meant" [135]), to the possibility of strategies for political action, on the one hand, and pleasure, on the other hand, which, while not socially sanctioned (or, perhaps, because they are not socially sanctioned), address the interests of the subject in question rather than those of the hegemonic discourse ostensibly constituting this subject. Hence, "sabotage" and the sensual experience that Leo Bersani terms a "shattering" of the self (38) participate similarly in different registers—sabotage in political intervention and masochism in the realm of sensuality—as resistances "structured by official power but in deconstructive excess to it" (Siegel 19).

Recent discussions of male masochism tend to see what Freud termed the "most common and most significant of all the perversions" (67), in which pleasure is taken in submission, debasement, and physical pain, as both a response to and an articulation of the ongoing crisis in masculinity that is modernity.[21] In a Freudian reading of masochism, the male's subjecting himself to ritualized abuse at the hands of a dominating female enacts both the wish for the father and the impossibility of representing that desire (Savran 29). The unconscious desire for the father and identification with the mother—a clearly and "unacceptably" "feminine" and "homosexual" desire—is repressed, remodeled, and, most importantly, heterosexualized by endowing the mother with the attributes and characteristics traditionally attributed to the father. Since, for the male subject trapped within the logic of the Oedipus complex, the desire for the father necessarily implies conflict with him, this self-positioning represents a monumental ambivalence, a will to power that can only be articulated as a will to powerlessness: the father is "taken on" through the proxy of the mother in light of the a priori admission that the oedipal conflict can be sustained only if (1) the father does not participate in it, and (2) the pain of the subject's inevitable defeat and submission can be experienced as pleasure. The guilt that suffuses this transaction ensures the bond to the symbolic order that gives it its efficacy. Its ideological yield seems to be the constant calling into question—through feminization—of an instance of domination whose *structural* necessity is just as constantly affirmed. It seems particularly important to an understanding of this "perversion" that we see it as not only masculinizing the (female) woman but also as feminizing the (male) figure of domination. That is to say, if the male subject cannot dispense with domination, he can, by submitting himself to the domination of a woman, recover a—however weakened—hegemonic position within the male-female binary. The presence of the woman, whose gender is nonhegemonic, reinstates the simple, culturally enforced opposition that enables him to align himself (however negatively) with masculinity and power. In this way, too, masochism both declares war on a hegemonic order and reiterates its structural reliance on it.

By analogy, within the cultural realm as Stearns has gendered it, this economy would situate both the male intellectual and the maleness of the intellectual in a masochistic relation to an intellectual realm designated "female." That the "female" intellectual realm is not the real thing (just as the abusive mother is not the father) rescues, according to the binary logic demonstrated in the preceding paragraph, the masculinity of the authentic male intellectual from the specter of feminization. At the same time, however, it reinforces the (authentic) need for an inauthentic, "feminized" intellectual realm in relation to which the true intellectual realm can be delineated and also demeaned. Since this realm, while gendered female, is inhabited by both men and women and is only considered inauthentic by the self-declared "authentic" intellectuals it deems "feminized," it is capable of wielding the hegemonic and abusive power that the "authentic" intellectual requires to authenticate himself. Authenticity is thus defined in abused opposition to the dominant intellectual culture as that which cannot be recognized or appreciated by it.

Stearns never again alludes to the kind of experience he had in Chicago; in fact, the phrase, "the indelible impression . . . of what sensuality *might mean*" (*Street* 134, emphasis added) suggests that it is not a form of experience he pursued further. Instead, he seems to have sublimated the structure of masochism and experienced its yield in other domains. His account of his relationship with and brief marriage to Alice MacDougal recalls the dynamics of domination I have just described, although emotional and social, rather than sexual, domination characterized the relationship—at least as he describes it.[22] In fact, although we assume that his wife's pregnancy was a result of their partnership, Stearns seems relatively uninterested in sex, to the point where, in a 1928 letter to F. Scott Fitzgerald, later published in *Scribner's Magazine* as "Apologia of an Expatriate," Stearns confesses that "sex does not bother me; I seldom think much one way or the other about it," and he characterizes himself further as someone who "happens . . . not to have much to do with sex" (341). While Stearns claims not to have been interested in sex, he does seem to have liked and appreciated women; his ability to indulge his masochistic tendencies in nonsexual, or only incidentally sexual, relations of domination or abuse seems to have freed him from regarding women as sexual objects and enabled him to enjoy real friendships with them. As it is recorded in *The Street I Know*, his relationship with Alice MacDougal seems to have been the healthiest of these deployments of the masochistic structure I describe above, engaging it emotionally, intellectually, politically, socially, and perhaps even sexually.

Stearns's positioning of his account of this relationship within the narrative explicitly aligns it with those other domains of concern that were of such importance to him. Stearns mentions his proposal of marriage to Alice—who has not appeared in the narrative prior to this moment—as his response to the end of the war that he had defied public opinion by opposing. His account of his opposition to the First World War suggests that he saw it as threatening the "disinterested," masculine cast of mind that he championed: to fall for the government's "preparation, consolidation of public opinion . . . and training for slaughter" (*Street* 144) was to become "hysterical"; to indulge one's own rage at this same spectacle was to succumb to the same "feminine" agitation. Only the men who had yielded to conscription were immune from the hysteria of the times: "I know that many times I wished [that the mechanism of the draft might reach out to me]. Anything seemed better than this indecision and waiting and impotence; I began to understand why the boys looked really cheerful, almost gay, when I saw them marching clumsily through the streets to the railroad stations to entrain for the draft camps—things had been settled for them; there was no longer any need to feel responsible" (145). While the rest of the country—and indeed, an entire younger generation of intellectuals that would volunteer for duty out of curiosity and return from Europe to declare itself "lost"—succumbed to "war hysteria" (141), Stearns endured the "indecision, waiting and impotence" that were the only responses reconcilable with his political stance: "The only way . . . in which I could 'carry on' . . . without becoming hysterical" was to live a "curious, unreal, monastic life" reviewing books and writing articles that "had no immediate, contemporary implications" (144). In a situation where any critical engagement with the issue drew him into the "hysteria" he associated with the war, "disinterested" masculinity was to be had only by fighting the war or pretending that it wasn't taking place.

The draft exemption he was able to garner during his 1917 stint in Chicago as editor of the *Dial*—the first regular, salaried job he'd held since 1914—represents an ironic twist to the gender trouble surrounding Stearns's opposition to the war. He obtained his exemption by sending a portion of his salary to his mother; thus, while maintaining his unconventional and unpopular stance in resistance to the war, Stearns, for the first and perhaps only time in his life, assumed the conventionally male and popularly sanctioned role of provider. Yet the transaction that enabled Stearns to respond to the dictates of his conscience was at variance with the "disinterested," masculine intellectual stance that was so important to him and, through his mother's dependence upon him, reinscribed him in the dependent relation to her that he seemed so determined to avoid. His relief at the end of the war must have been compounded by the cessation of this pact both with the governmental powers that be and with maternal power. Until this contract was dissolved, he was quite literally not man enough to enter into a contractual emotional and sexual relation with anyone else.[23]

The fact that in *The Street I Know*, Stearns uses his proposal to Alice MacDougal as the literary device through which he celebrates the end of all the obscenities and distortions the war has represented to him seems at first glance mere convention: "That was the night I asked Alice if she would be my wife—for though I think she knew perfectly well that I intended to ask her anyway, I was determined not to do it until peace formally arrived" (171). He explains his reluctance to propose during the war with his fears of induction should it continue and his unwillingness to "exploit any feeling of sympathy" that Alice might not have for him "in normal times." This understandable desire "to act as people do in ordinary peace-time days, not depending on the mere emotional upsets and illusions of abnormal excitement" does not, however, explain why Alice, who has clearly been a presence in his life in the war years ("She said . . . that she had known all along how I felt about it" [172]), has not been mentioned up to this point in his narrative. Alice seems to have represented to him a positive embodiment of culture and the intellectual life *as feminine*; in her thrall, and buoyed by her financial independence, he was both free and compelled to deliver on the intellectual scruples that had always kept him from frequenting Grub Street. He clearly promised himself from marriage to this brilliant and well-born woman access to a realm of hitherto unavailable normality on terms that were not irreconcilable with his intellectual self-fashioning. Yet in the atmosphere of war hysteria, where masculinity as Stearns conceived it for himself had no place, the official, legal consolidation of this relationship could only be postponed.

There is no doubt about his respect for Alice—even allowing for some elegiac exaggeration, it is clear that he deemed her his intellectual equal and emotional and social superior: "She knew [her fondness for me] was absurd; she even, on a few occasions, said so. But it didn't seem to make any difference. She realized that everybody has to have some weakness—and I was hers" (*Street* 175–76).[24] Alice comes across as the better disciplined of the two, the instigator as well as enforcer of his intellectual ambitions. During their post-wedding trip, she admonishes him:

> "You must work, when we get back to New York. You know you want to do that book on liberalism, and that somebody ought to do it. It may not be so good as you hope it will be, but you must do it just the same. You must do something to distinguish yourself; I want you to."
>
> "But I married you," I replied. "Isn't that distinction enough?"
>
> "No," she came back quickly. "It certainly isn't. I admit that matrimony is the only definite traditional thing some men seem able to achieve. But if I had thought your marrying me was the most important thing you had to do—well, I never should have married you at all."
>
> "That's it. That's modern 'love' for you. Something else always than what it is in its essence." I was almost angry.
>
> "No," said Alice, "that's just common sense." . . .
>
> She had the final word: "And don't think common sense is incompatible with a love much deeper than the romantic novelists ever dreamed of." (180)

I have quoted from this passage at length because I think it summarizes a—in this case potentially productive—power dynamics structurally similar to the dynamics of masochism I described above. The authority Stearns represents his wife as wielding in this passage is remarkable, even for a New Woman. The total reversal of roles manifested in his "I married you . . . Isn't that distinction enough" and her "No . . . I admit that matrimony is the only definite traditional thing some men seem able to achieve" suggests that Stearns's submission to Alice, his devoted enjoyment of her practical, "feminine" dominion and authority ("that's just common sense"), was crucial to his renewed critical engagement with the structures and institutions that had silenced dissent during the war; she forced him to observe the "regular work habits" without which he considered himself "miserable and unhappy" (*Street* 126) and enabled him to envision a productive, bourgeois life. Stearns articulates this vision following his account of Alice's departure for her parents' home in California, where she awaited the term of what threatened to be a risky pregnancy:

> I remember I thought with a touch of bitterness of my traditional use of the word "home." For I had never really had a home, as it is ordinarily defined, either when I was a boy—or now, when I was grown up and a married man. A married man and a prospective father, too. Yet there I was, as always and forever except for brief happy interludes, alone again. Alice at least had her own family to which she was going—and somehow, strangely, that reflection comforted me. It was bad enough for one of us to be a spiritual orphan; thank God, both of us weren't. Well, I said finally to myself in that inner discussion, a few more months, just a few more months of patience and work and waiting and loneliness—*then, once and forever, the life of an ordinary member of the community. A taxpayer, a citizen, a voter, a father. Vagabondia was over with; I could—and would—do what every man in his heart at some time or other believes he wants to do, that is, settle down.* By the time I reached my room I had become, if not cheerful, at all events more composed. I had begun to think again of my work. (182–83, emphasis added)

Stearns would never achieve the fusion of his critical faculties and his bourgeois dreams. The irony of Alice's injunction that he complete *Liberalism in America* during her pregnancy—that he and she should, as it were, give birth at approximately the same time—is, sadly and appropriately, that while her discipline saw him through, there was nothing he could do for her. After Alice's death, Stearns found himself indifferent to the fate of his book; the "disinterested" attitude that he considered so important in the conduct of intellectual affairs extended to all domains of his life. He took on odd jobs, collected the essays that would comprise *America and the Young Intellectual*, edited, in one final burst of engagement, *Civilization in the United States*, and then took indefinite leave of the world on whose threshold his brilliance and his marriage had placed him.

It is worth noting that the chapter in *The Street I Know* recounting Alice's death is entitled "What Can a Young Man Do?" This question is, of course, also the title of the final chapter of *America and the Young Intellectual*, whose final words, "Get out!" have been so widely misinterpreted as Stearns's announcement of the reasons for his own departure. The citation from his earlier work makes it clear that the conundrum *for him* was raised by personal loss, which, as I have tried to demonstrate, shattered the perversely and precariously structured critical working relation to the dominant culture that his unconventional relation with Alice had initiated. Had she stayed alive, he would, I suspect, have made his way as a resident renegade. She would have forced him to work, to be worthy of her, to be a good father, to live a relatively healthy life, and to go to the dentist regularly. And he would have taken pleasure in her dominion. Without Alice's entrepreneurial manipulation of his masochism, he disengaged himself from the America in perverse opposition to which his capacities best engaged themselves to pursue and achieve more direct abjection in France.

VI

Picture instead a little sidewalk table
In Montparnasse, or rather, at the Dôme;
Picture the drinkers (if you are still able);
They called each other Tom and Dick at home;

Picture the action: our Manhattan notables
Are busily imbibing potables.

—MALCOLM COWLEY, "Three Americans in Paris"

Although Stearns continued to write in Paris, his work was generally of the Grub Street variety for which he'd considered himself temperamentally and intellectually unsuited. In fact, Stearns seems to have opted out of the debate in which he was such a prominent participant and suspended his intellectual scruples and ambitions for the duration of his sojourn in Paris, living in what was at best a "rêve à Paris" (*Street* 209) and more often a nightmare. In his account of his one trip back to the United States, five years into his eleven-year expatriation, Stearns reflects on this apathy; he realizes how much, in Paris, he "had wanted the realities of life," but he continues: "Now that the dearest of [these realities, Alice, whose memory was so bitterly revived during his visit with his son, Philip] was gone, I could find no genuine impulse of ambition or desire; slowly the conviction in me grew that I had to get back to Paris once more—to a slight, a derivative, a fundamentally unsatisfactory reality, but still, the only one I knew" (247). Stearns is quite candid about the self-destructive disposition that led him to leave America, squander his brilliance, and court catastrophe; he presents his account of his expatriate "reality" first and foremost as an individual case study, but he also suggests that it represents a psychogram of a certain kind of American man abroad who exchanges a conflicted and sexually troubled native landscape for a reality that, however "slight, derivative [and] fundamentally unsatisfactory," enables him to opt out of or defer confronting what most troubles but would also most satisfy him. In Stearns's mythology as in Henry James's before him,[25] "in Paris . . . the American will (at least the American will-to-work) is enfeebled, and many a man, who, had he remained at home and worked hard with what special capacity he had, would have made a modest second-rate success, suffered just a sufficient sea-change to let the will, competent in the home environment to generate some activity, relapse into mere wishing and dreaming" (298).

Here we find the logical consequence of the critique launched in *America and the Young Intellectual*; the "sturdy individualism . . . which still constitutes the real American national genius" has not adapted itself to the demands of a culture that has long left the frontier behind and become a culture of "belligerent individualism" (18). Whereas his pioneer forefather went west, "strik[ing] out for himself [to] lead the kind of life he chose" when the pressure of conformity became too great, the American of Stearns's generation has been forced to go east to Europe. Yet those modern-day seekers of freedom, returning to a continent whose social constraints were the reason for the exodus to America in the first place, are not equipped to deal with Europe, where a whole nexus of custom, religion, history, and tradition engender in the individual an "inner restraint," a kind of submission that can, in Americans, only be enforced through what Stearns calls "outward compulsion" (20). In Europe, the "belligerent individualist" finds, instead of the belligerent resistance that would curb or discipline his compulsions from without, the utter indifference of a society that subtly regulates such excesses from within. The paralysis of the American will that James, Stearns, and others associate with Paris derives from the absence, in the French cultural landscape, of the conspicuous instances of discipline (the "blunderbuss well polished and hung in a conspicuous place on the wall" [18–19]) that keep Americans in line and out of trouble. Americans, Stearns suggests even before he could demonstrate the process in his own person, are culturally unprepared to decipher, master, and deploy to their own benefit the kinds of codes structuring European society.

The bitter irony of Stearns's situation is that, although he craved the French indifference that he called "freedom" and continued to expound its virtues even after his repatriation, he was more dependent than most—for both productivity *and* pleasure—on what he calls "outward compulsion," that same domination from without—be it sexual, emotional, or cultural—that he criticizes American culture for providing in overabundance. Hence, without being able to reconcile for himself the conflict between the desire for "freedom" and the need for "constraint," he is more attuned than other chroniclers of Paris in the 1920s to the way that lack of discipline, self-delusion, and the "arrogance of being an American" (*Street* 298) compound the oft-documented brilliance, creativity, and Bohemian rebellion to produce the phenomenon that has come to be known as the Lost Generation.

Moreover, Stearns suggests, as his contemporaries do not, that this issue is one of gender. Being American in Paris is indeed all about being American, but in the cases of Stearns, Cowley, and the Lost Generation, it is also about being a man. Stearns, who boasts that "masculinity" was not something of which he often felt compelled to "boast" (*Street* 218), is less afraid than his contemporaries to name and anatomize the lost American man, whom he considers essentially "childish";[26] as interested in women as he may consider himself to be, he is happiest in such "world[s] untroubled by politics and sexual disappointments and money worries" as the race track, the late-night newsroom ("the Never-Never-Land of male irresponsibility, absurdity, and entertainment, of which all men in their hearts forever dream—and so seldom ever reach" [335]), and the stag dinner "of which every true American male has, at some time or other, dreamed . . . where those dreams came true—all except any sexual side to them, I hasten to add, for they were strictly, entirely, and whole-heartedly alcoholic" (296).[27]

If the "rêve à Paris" to which Stearns compares the unproductive passing of expatriate time is disciplined at all, it is disciplined not by French culture but by the same imported American institutions that foster the dream: until he was overwhelmed by the illness that made him incapable of functioning at all, his job as racing correspondent for an American newspaper and the camaraderie it enabled structured the permanent, one-man stag party that his life threatened to become.[28] Thus, however sordid his personal circumstances, "my life . . . is regular and takes me every day to the different French race-tracks around Paris. It keeps me in the open half the day, rain or shine; it gives me a routine and stabilizes my life; it tires me in a healthy way; and it gives a genuine external objective interest. . . . My mornings are free for reading or work or, if I stay up too late, for sleep. Sex does not bother me; I seldom think much one way or the other about it" ("Apologia" 340–41). It took the utter breakdown of this routine and the body it just managed to discipline—the mysterious illness and ensuing loss of his job and teeth—to send Stearns back to America. Without the external constraints of routine, Stearns was like a child without a mother to rescue him; it is utterly fitting that the American Aid Society, do-goodish, pragmatic ambassadors of the country he had fled because of its do-goodish, pragmatic, meddling, feminine cast of mind, secured him a passport and a berth on a steamer headed west.

VII

The young man cannot grow who lives in fetters,
'Tis only by experience he learns;
So go abroad if you love Art and Letters.
        —MALCOLM COWLEY, "Three Americans in Paris"

Stearns returned home to a country in which, as his friends told him, "things were very bad, but . . . there seemed a faint chance of their getting better, simply because the bottom had been reached" (*Street* 377). His friends' description of the state of the country could fairly be applied to Stearns's own condition when he disembarked; he had reached a stage of abjection that matched that of America in the depths of the Depression. At this historical moment, when misfortune crossed class, race, and gender lines, Stearns, for all the "loneliness" of which he continues to complain, was not alone in having "nothing of my own, no dignity, no security, no convictions, no happiness" (404). In essence, he faced the same task of total self-restoration as the country, and he was able to borrow for personal purposes on a national rhetoric of and project for rehabilitation as well as on the "latent fund of good-will and neighborliness and decency" (379) that he discovered the Depression to have called forth in the general public.

Summing up his repatriation in the penultimate chapter of *The Street I Know*, Stearns claims to have fitted back "into the pattern of my old American life and ambitions" so well that "sometimes, it is not easy for me to realize I have ever been away at all" (400). Yet the passage from the "slight, derivative, . . . fundamentally insubstantial reality" of Paris life to "my real, my American life" (400) is far more complex and ambivalent than such formulations let on; the changes both in Stearns and in the country that play such a substantial role in his narrative also play a substantial role in this mutual accommodation. Stearns does not return to America with his young avatar's "confidence in oneself, belief in one's attractiveness, certainty of one's talent and of one's ability to get on in the world" (404). The humiliation, shame, anxious insecurity, and homelessness that are his only baggage on his homeward passage seem to articulate, perhaps even to perform, some essential aspect of himself that was hidden from view—even from his own view—by his earlier persona.

Although the Stearns legend thrives on the spectacle of what William Shirer terms "the slow degeneration of one once so splendidly endowed and so promising" (220), *The Street I Know* suggests a continuity between the "Young Intellectual" of 1921 whose departure from America became legendary and the man whom misfortune has instructed to "'go home, that is the place for you. Go home to America'" (370). If the "pattern of [his] old American life and ambitions" seems replicated by what amounts to an entirely new one, it is because the young Stearns was pursuing masochistically what the older Stearns has achieved through abjection. At least as he tells it in *The Street I Know*, Stearns's successful repatriation involves assuming a new, chastened persona with the dignity that his old persona needed to squander in order to constitute itself.

"Everything seemed at once something I had always known and been an unconscionably long time away from" (*Street* 373): Stearns's feelings upon return anticipate the uncanny "shocks of recognition and nonrecognition" that Gertrude Stein was experiencing while he was writing his autobiography and about which she would write a few years later. Stearns's desire "to see [the skyline of Manhattan] as if I had never seen it before" is baffled by a "lack of any feeling of strangeness, a kind of vague wonder and doubt as to whether or not you really have ever been away at all." The complexity of this experience is reducible to "the simplest thing in the world . . . *I was coming home*" (373, emphasis added). Whatever "home" means to Stearns, it imbues him with a sense of purpose, what he elsewhere calls "a renewal of that buoyancy and enthusiasm, our American sense of still infinite possibility" (*Rediscovering America* 14). Although Stearns worries early and often about his ability to remake himself in America and goes so far as to compare himself to an immigrant ("even some immigrants . . . have come to America as late in life as I am doing, and sometimes with but the feeblest command of English. If they can do it, why cannot I?" [*Street* 374]), he takes comfort in the familiarity of his Greenwich Village terrain and the welcome of his friends: "On the docks in Jersey, I had felt, for a few moments, almost like an immigrant—and it wasn't true! There were still quite a few who remembered me; perhaps . . . they would even be glad to see me 'home' again" (376). With a return of the initiative of which his Paris sojourn seemed to have sapped him, he quickly manages to interest *Scribner's* in commissioning an article on his repatriation ("A Prodigal Returns"), with whose advance he rents a typewriter and takes a room in a hotel.

Fits of purposeful activity and almost patriotic euphoria alternate, during Stearns's first year of repatriation, with bleak moments of feeling "disinherited." When the proximity and generosity of his old friends does not help him to feel at least allied with, if not a member of, the privileged few whose skills, education, and connections allow them to survive the Depression with dignity, he is assailed by the reality of being homeless, "of being without a job, of not belonging" (*Street* 385). Living by his wits, he can feel like part of his old world when he has secured the occasional commission to write an article or review, but he just as often finds himself identifying with the immigrants and beggars whose fortunes are indeed closer to his own. After the death of his mother, whom he, characteristically, has not been able to bring himself to visit, this feeling is exacerbated; not only is he "really . . . alone in the world," but he has missed the chance to bring any resolution to a relationship that he could never pursue but also never abandon.

As always, Stearns bounces back when he can work, and America, unlike Paris, inspires him to do so. During the difficult first two years of repatriation, his ability to pay for and keep his typewriter becomes a "curious symbol of success or failure—but a real symbol to me. If I lost that, I lost my reason for living at all" (*Street* 392). It is, thus, as a writer, as someone whose proficiency in the English language distinguishes him from the immigrants with whom he identifies in so many other ways, that Stearns begins the work of reconstituting himself as a resident of his native country. Work—writing—keeps the demons of self-loathing, on the one hand, and his too-acute perception of his surroundings, on the other hand, at bay.

In fact, Stearns discovers that his needs and motivations for work are, perforce, very American ones. His response to the "appalling dreariness of semi-industrial American suburbia" during a brief residence in Newark echoes his observation in *Civilization in the United States* that American men don't "make money because they love to do so, but because there is nothing else to do" (140): "It seemed hardly credible to me . . . that men could have struggled and worked, dreamed dreams, had wars and revolutions for centuries just to produce this. Bad as it was, I was glad to get back to our little flat, where I could . . . work. Work, blessed and healing work, which took my mind off my surroundings." He continues: "For if you did not work, you might look around and reflect; and the results of that might be just too awful. In the kind of America which Newark represented . . . your one salvation was activity" (*Street* 389–90).

Work, Stearns realizes, is a kind of intoxicant; like alcohol, it enables one to get through the day without having to confront the full shock of one's surroundings. The yield of the kind of "looking around and reflecting" that is the métier and the authority of even the most abject Parisian flâneur is bearable in America only if it is counterbalanced by and processed through the activity of writing. If, in the highly regulated French social landscape, "there is something to amuse you when you loaf" (*Street* 390), in America, leisure is terrifying. In this context, Stearns claims finally to understand that "the whole psychological intensity back of our early wall-motto incitements of young men to industrious habits" (389–90) derives from the American fear of and, hence, antipathy toward the kind of unproductive reflection that, in his earlier essays, he designated "masculine." Americans need to get and keep working, and they need habits, compulsions, and external incentive to get to work. The compulsive nature of the American work ethic became painfully apparent to Stearns through the experience of a foreign culture in which he was increasingly cut off from the nexus of motivations and imperatives that forced him to work and in which he could no longer persuade himself that what he was doing when he wasn't working was "masculine." Thus, without making an explicit connection between his newfound ambition and his earlier criticism of American men who lose their will to work in Paris, he suggests why, during his years of expatriation, he had allowed himself to go "to hell" and why repatriation has reversed this process. Stearns discovers that he is a truly American writer because only in America is he compelled to write. And it is as a writer—although no longer as a spokesman or even a member of the cultural and intellectual elite—that Stearns manages to negotiate the vagaries of fortune of his first years of repatriation and ultimately to capitalize on them.

In *Rediscovering America*, Stearns writes: "If affairs go badly with you in a foreign country, I believe the normal thing is to come back home. If they go badly at home, there is only one thing to do—to hang on, to fight, to work as intelligently and diligently as one can until they go better" (40). There was much about America that Stearns still did not like, and, as James W. Lane's review of *The Street I Know* suggests, the nostalgia for the French way of life that accompanies his rediscovery of America did not necessary please his American public (110). Paris, Stearns maintains, remains the most congenial venue for "a lonely man, who happens also to be a foreigner," and he clearly misses "the kind of *café, bistrodial,* surface existence of casual acquaintance and fleeting intimacy" (*Rediscovering America* 30–31). But Stearns also recognizes that this kind of comfort is not good for him; indeed, as he documented in a 1929 article written from Paris, this kind of comfort had ceased to be comfortable. The "bitterness of being an expatriate" involves

> physical discomfort, the humiliation of friends avoiding you
> because your condition distresses them, the silent pity of those
> whom ordinarily you would like to ignore, the necessity of asso-
> ciating with second-rate people and bores until you could scream
> with impatience, the chilling of vitality which comes from cheap
> food and sometimes none at all, the weariness of spirit that results
> from working hard and well and being paid hardly enough to
> cover your hotel bill, the sense of isolation and at the same time
> knowing that all sorts of fantastic yarns are being composed about
> you. ("Apologia" 338)

What Stearns did experience in Paris—and seems to have experienced as hospitable—was the absence of the superstructure of compulsion that he required in order to work.[29] Yet without this superstructure, Stearns was compelled into abjection, which Julia Kristeva describes as "experienced at the peak of its strength when [the] subject, weary of fruitless attempts to identify with something on the outside, finds the impossible within; when it finds that the impossible constitutes its very *being*, that it *is* none other than abject" (5). And whereas this Parisian indifference might have counterbalanced the discomforts of expatriate life as long as Stearns was more or less afloat, it offered no anchor whatsoever—no resistance, no compulsion to improve, not even the recognition afforded through punishment—as soon as he was adrift: "Abjection is elaborated through a failure to recognize its kin; nothing is familiar, not even the shadow of a memory" (5).[30] In order to reassemble the pieces of his life, "to hang on, to fight, to work as intelligently and diligently as one can," he had to "come back to more deeply familiar things" (*Rediscovering America* 40). Returning to America, Stearns is down-and-out, but no longer abject, reentering into the neurotic and productive relation with his surroundings that he calls "the pattern of my old American life and ambitions." As soon as he resituates himself in an American symbolic order whose efficacy and necessity for him he has come to acknowledge even as he continues to detest it, he begins to write again. He reentitles himself to his old opinions at the same time as he opens up the possibility of writing his way toward new ones.

In a predictably unsympathetic review of *The Street I Know* in the *New Republic*, Louis Kronenberger reproves Stearns for not having "toughened intellectually" during his idle Paris years, for not "during a convulsed era, moved ahead with life" (319). Much as Kronenberger errs egregiously in calling the 1920s in Paris a "Venusberg"—neither Stearns's memoir nor Cowley's presents the expatriate adventure as a particularly erotic one—he also misreads the genre of Stearns's text and the focus of his interest. The writing with which Stearns restores his respectability as well as his self-respect differs significantly from the writing that made him famous in the teens and early 1920s. Stearns's early work takes on grand themes—"Liberalism in America," "America and the Young Intellectual," "Civilization in the United States"—in an impersonal, confident, even magisterial voice. His late work is self-consciously, even self-effacingly, autobiographical. While it manifests Stearns's continuing critical interest in the culture and politics of his native country, it addresses cultural, political, and social issues in a discourse that is both personal and local; Stearns is careful always to situate himself in relation to the phenomena he is recording and to emphasize the particularity of his subject position: "I am not going to try to generalize about experiences I haven't gone through—besides, I don't know how" (*Rediscovering America* 41–42). Moreover, Stearns shies away from grand cultural pronouncements, examining instead local phenomena he considers representative of American society and attitudes. This attention to representative detail is borne out in the list of Stearns's own "special interests" in the "Who's Who of the Contributors" to *America Now*, the symposium he convened to update the portrait of America presented in *Civilization in the United States*: " . . . outside regular work of writing, editing, and reporting . . . trotting racing, gardening, the poetry of Walt

Whitman . . . statistical studies in gambling (particularly on horse-races), television, French politics and literature . . . and American history. Has a morbid interest in baseball and murder trials. Present interest: Preparing a book on American foibles—from trick gadgets and zippers to self-help and religious revivals" (*America Now* 591). This list certainly reflects the freedom to occupy himself with whatever he wishes that Stearns enjoyed after his marriage to a wealthy woman, but it also reflects the absorption with and appreciation of the texture of everyday life that he brought back with him from France. His comparative leisure allowed him to contemplate what people do with the "infinite possibility" that, for better as well as for worse, American society offers them and what their leisure activities reveal about American culture.

Stearns's relation to the phenomena of everyday life is generous but not uncritical; he recognizes the extent to which the practices of individuals as well as entire social classes articulate relations to social and cultural phenomena to which the ordinary individual can have no direct access. Moreover, he recognizes that since every American is nothing more—or less—than an ordinary individual, the practices of self-appointed elites are subject to the same kinds of critical scrutiny as those of the generally less enfranchised members of society that elites tend to scorn, patronize, sponsor, or champion. Americans, he suggests, need to be held more responsible for their cruelty or pretentiousness, for their racism, intolerance, and covetousness, than for their unconscious or semiconscious vulgarity. The project of improving America, then, lies in accepting the implications of democracy and making not simply the best of it, but, rather, the very best: "What *is* important is what we make of our own life, and what is important about American life is not how many elements of it were taken from European, but what—in the American scene and with the American social experience—we do with those elements" (*Rediscovering America* 221).

Stearns regards the improved situation of American women as the most dramatic example of what can be done with the elements of American democracy. In "A Prodigal American Returns," the first essay he wrote after his return, he rejoices in the self-confidence and stylishness of American women—"the difference in these United States of the whole stage setting of sex"—and declares "the era of political disability for women [to be] already as remote in feeling as in fact" (*Rediscovering*

America 21–22).[31] In the third chapter of *Rediscovering America*, unfortunately entitled "The Girls," Stearns examines how the availability of birth control, suffrage, equality before the law, what he calls "full opportunities, on the same economic level . . . as men in the professions, the arts, and many aspects of business" (56), the abolition of prostitution, and "practically the same educational opportunities as young men and certainly the same adventurous ones" (56) have brought about a revolution in the status of women that is, simultaneously, a challenge to and a potential boon for men. Although there is much in Stearns's discussion that is naive and even occasionally retrograde, in his two major arguments—that self-sufficiency and economic independence are the prerequisites to a good partnership and that "motherhood . . . to keep even its traditional dignity, to say nothing of its intrinsic satisfactions, must be purposeful, something intended intelligently and planned intelligently, instead of something just accidental and haphazard" (47)—he is intent on demonstrating what is required in order to maintain a society in which the promises of democracy are truly available to women and what is to be gained—for everyone in the society—from such democratization. Despite the lapses in his argument (he claims that "the old fashioned feminist would have to admit, in modern America women have obtained about everything," and he alludes to "a virulent and restless group of women, sexually embittered, socially jealous, economically ambitious, resentful of men's control, and pulchritudinously below the mark of the dumbest 'one-arm' lunch-room waitress" who would seem to dispute his claims [58, 64]), Stearns recognizes the need for legislation that ensures women's rights and champions the friendship, partnership, and collegiality of equally endowed male and female human beings that such legislation makes possible.

No longer under the thrall of his own distinction between an authentic "male" intellectual life and its all-too-prevalent "feminine" counterpart, Stearns approves of the "practical sex'[s]" acceptance of the ways in which, through the vicissitudes of the Depression, men have been transformed, perforce, from "vain and boastful 'provider[s]'" into "considerate and loving husband[s]" (*Rediscovering America* 61). In his account of his own life, the new self-confidence he ascribes to American women assumes a bittersweet cast: the "fair Dora" to whom he alludes briefly has proved to be wary of his penury and unwilling to "gamble":

"I had forgotten that American young women—especially if they are in-dependent and have a good job of their own—resent a man's economic insecurity much more than the old-fashioned 'sheltered' girl of a genera-tion ago, chiefly because they have no romantic notions about 'earning one's living'" (*Street* 401). There is regret in this passage, but no resent-ment; the reader has the sense that the masochistic structures that deter-mined Stearns's earlier relations to women and to society have collapsed, leaving in their place an acceptance of the challenge of what he calls "the continuity of life" and a certain confidence of his ability to meet it (401).

It is certainly not accidental that Stearns opens the first chapter of *Re-discovering America* with the following epigraph from Benedetto Croce: "What we do not understand we do not dominate; on the contrary, it dominates us" (25). Stearns's return to America and the self-understand-ing that has come from writing about it seem to have invalidated the structures of domination that had determined both his earlier pursuit of success at home and his pursuit of abjection abroad. As I have argued, in Stearns's earlier gendering of the American cultural realm, the authentic, masculine intellectual constitutes himself in abused relation to an inau-thentic and feminized dominant intellectual culture, which confirms his authenticity by refusing to recognize or appreciate him. Stearns's experi-ence of true abjection in an indisputably hegemonic European culture, which—to his American eyes at least—is plagued by no such problems of gender and authenticity and to which he has and makes no claims seems to have released him from the dominion of this essentially masochistic economy.

Stearns returns from France having conceded defeat in his war against civilization in America and retains, for all his renewed hopes, on the one hand, and exasperation with American racism and commercialism, on the other hand, a freedom from the structures and traditions of the in-stitutions against which he formerly waged his battles. He becomes able, as I have shown, to recognize himself as subject to the same pathology regarding work and leisure that in 1921 he regarded as the province of the American philistine. Indirectly, at least, he assumes personal respon-sibility for the estrangement from his mother as well as for the failures of friendships that, in the course of the book, he has represented as having mysteriously dissolved. In short, he represents himself as having gotten over or given up on the hierarchical structurings of culture, society, and personal relations that were the subject of his early work and the nexus that generated his early successes and subsequent failures. Masochism affirms the structural necessity of hierarchies at the same time that it declares them invalid. In *America*, Stearns's relation to high culture required the ongoing deconstruction of the hierarchies it sought to maintain. During his sojourn in France, Stearns turned into his own abject, the embodiment of every American intellectual's nightmare autobiography.

At the end of *The Street I Know*, Stearns recalls the nadir of his French sojourn, when with "nothing of my own, no dignity, no convictions, no happiness" he wonders, "what had availed the fact that I had at least tried to make my thought honest?" (404). *The Street I Know* attempts to answer this question. "Keeping [his] thought honest," Stearns reconsiders the achievements and motivations of his early career, mourns the losses to which he had clung but had not accepted, and accepts for better as well as for worse the spectacle of abjection that has made him "legendary." When he returns to America in the middle of the Depression "with no teeth, few friends, no job and no money" (370), he is forced—and able—to identify with "the beggars who made the walk of a few blocks a lesson in how to stifle one's generous impulses" and to recognize that his own penury preempts generous impulses before he can stifle them. However, he must reconcile the sense of privilege and entitlement that reminds him of his difference from these beggars with the memories of a not-so-distant past when the figure he cut would have been indistinguishable from theirs. What he has come to understand is the simultaneously liberating and troubling possibility, within democracy, of negotiating with, and hence exposing, the contingency of its constitutive intellectual, cultural, and gender hierarchies. This means that the individual is both more and less important than his or her European counterpart. America lacks the amenities of Paris; its "*petites choses*" do not add up to a consoling notion of a "home" that comfortingly determines—but also limits—the individual and his or her possibilities. Its opportunities are vaster, and because there are limits set neither on self-realization nor on self-destruction, much of the advantage that has been taken of them is vulgar and misguided. Yet, as he realizes when, wearing a borrowed shirt, he walks into Scribner's and sells "A Prodigal Returns," "one couldn't do that in France, if you were God Almighty" (378). Stearns's reward for "keeping his thought honest" is his return to America with an understanding that has disengaged itself from the structures of dominance in such a manner that his life and writing represent a challenge to those who would maintain them.

CHAPTER THREE

Wo Mama war, soll Dada werden

Malcolm Cowley's Odyssey of Legitimation

S HORTLY AFTER THE PUBLICATION OF *The Street I Know*, Malcolm Cowley completed *Exile's Return*, an account of the expatriate decade that has become the official narrative of the Lost Generation. This book, which Cowley substantially revised and reissued in 1951, tells the story of a group of young men, largely from the Midwest, who attended college in the East, went to Europe during the First World War, and returned home from the war divested of their illusions. In the course of the 1920s, they went back to Europe in search of culture only to return once more to their homeland, where they became the literary and intellectual elite of the United States in the mid-twentieth century. The "intellectual odyssey" that took the best and the brightest from their rural homes into a world of high culture satisfied their ambitions but alienated them permanently from what Cowley calls their "roots." *Exile's Return* tells the story of how this generation survived its uprooting by creating for itself a new home in the world of American letters. Unlike Stearns, who, unable to get himself to go to Boston to see his mother, sits in a borrowed New York apartment watching the evening boat to Boston make its way up the East River as he talks to her for the last time on the telephone, the Cowley of *Exile's Return* seems to have made peace with his abandonment of the dramatis personae of his youth, even if—or perhaps, to the extent that—he evinces nostalgia for its landscapes. Yet, in a poem he wrote at the age of seventy-seven, Cowley makes an explicit and belated connection between the people—or more precisely, his mother—and the land that clarifies the relation between the ambitions and the gender ideology of his Lost Generation and thus helps to explain his antipathy to Stearns and his particular "rediscovery" of America.

Cowley's mother died in 1937. Forty years later, in the poem entitled "Prayer on All Saints' Day," he imagines himself kneeling at the graveside he has never visited, "offer[ing his] testimony" to what he has made of her "gift" of life:

> Your hope, all that was left, you placed in me:
> I should outshine the neighbors' children,
> grow up to be admired,
> have worldly possessions too.
> Those were modest aims you gave me, Mother.
> I have achieved them all. (*Blue Juniata* 151)

After "boasting" of the accomplishments that satisfied the "modest" agenda in which his mother invested what was left of her life's portion of hope, Cowley strikes a more rueful note, "detail[ing]," as he puts it in a prose tribute to her published in 1983, "some of my lapses in sympathy, for herself and others" ("Mother and Son" 35), and associating these lapses with the anything but modest agenda that he set for himself:

> There was a time
> I called myself a bad son, but a poet.
> "My world has deeper colors than yours,"
> I boasted, "and the words will come
> to match the colors."
> Words were like horses loose in the back pasture;
> I bridled and saddled them,
> rode off with a tight rein at a steady trot,
> came back and paid my debts one day,
> survived. . . . (152)

Cowley makes it very clear that there is a serious conflict between being a good son and being a poet and that this eulogy represents his attempt to "pay his debts," in his own currency, to the figure whom he saw as standing in the way of this calling: through poetry, that mistress in pursuit of whom he once left home, the "bad son" can make up for all the years of being "imperceptive and short of funds and busy with [his] own affairs" ("Mother and Son" 34), memorializing both his mother and his good intentions. If "words" were the means of escape from his mother's thrall, to be harnessed, made to bear the weight of his ambition, and managed "with a tight rein," they are also the medium through which he affects his belated journey home. Despite its transparent patina of remorse, then, the poem confidently sets out to justify Cowley's pursuit of what he elsewhere calls "the writer's trade."

"Prayer on All Saints' Day" does not yield a particularly attractive picture of its author-speaker. Yet it is important to distinguish between what is intentionally unattractive and what the poem unwittingly reveals about its persona. This is not "Sailing to Byzantium": the aging, feeble, deaf poet seems heedless of the sensuality of anything but his own decrepitude: he "fart[s] and fiddl[es] among papers," describes how he has outlived all his "great coevals" ("now I write epitaphs for the dead lions"), and wonders pathetically, "Does that make me a jackal?" Yet it turns out that he has been feasting on carrion for years, albeit of a far less illustrious pedigree. He admits that his conscience is burdened by his lack of generosity to a former servant who once appealed to him for money to save her farm; although he wrote to her "warmly and at length" to justify his inability to help her, he now seems to suspect that his otherwise so efficacious words might not have settled his moral accounts with the woman "who served our family for how many years / and was paid three dollars a week and saved all three": "She didn't answer my letter. / I don't know when Ora died." Along similar lines, Cowley reviews his failure to visit a helpful associate dying of cancer "forty miles away," and wonders, "Is there a circle of thorns around the dying? / a circle of ice around the aged, / ice at the center too?"

Cowley attempts to raise the temperature of the "ice at the center" by cataloging the kindnesses of "easier moments," recalling "the unpaid days, the uncredited work / for the craft, for brilliant youngsters, for the town, / or the yearlong struggle to make the words come right." But the distinction he draws between his public and professional engagement, on the one hand, and his personal aloofness, on the other hand, suggests that the "circle of thorns around the dying" and the "circle of ice around the aged" are emanations of his own prickliness and coldness and that the survival he speaks of earlier in the poem is a product of having maintained this distinction. It is thus difficult not to include Cowley's mother in the company of those whose too-personal (read: nonliterary) claims on him nag at his complacency without altering his behavior, whose demands crystallize the "ice at the center":

> Trust me to be here, not complaining,
> not making excuses, not letting my envy speak,
> not ever slipping a knife in the back.
> In other things don't trust me too far.   (*Blue Juniata* 153)

"Here," at the scene of writing, Cowley is capable of a sort of limited and negative virtue ("not . . . not . . . not . . ."); elsewhere, "in other things," he is a cantankerous old man who, however much he might regret his "lapses in sympathy" and "absences," is entirely unwilling to relinquish the strategies for "survival" to which these shortcomings were crucial.

Cowley concludes this "prayer" of homecoming with the following apostrophe:

> There in the last grave
> in that unvisited family plot,
> smile up at me through the earth, Mother,
> be jubilant for what you achieved in me.
> Forgive my absences.
>   (*Blue Juniata* 153; "Mother and Son" 565)

In this grotesque parody of prosopopoeia, Cowley restores enough bodily integrity to the remains of his long-dead mother to solicit from her both a celebration of what he has admitted to have achieved at her expense and forgiveness for the negligences that were the prerequisites for these achievements. The "circle of ice around" this "aged" man allows him to solicit absolution for his lifelong disengagement from his sentimental roots and thus tap and appropriate their pathos for his own situation:

> Now I am older than you were ever to be,
> deaf as a gravestone,
> incipient cataracts in both eyes . . .   (*Blue Juniata* 153)

Likening himself to a "gravestone," the poet proposes his words as a more efficacious memorial than the "family plot" that he has never visited. Staring death—in the person of his smiling mother—in the face, Cowley borrows the pathos of those he has neglected and exploits the sources he claims to have had to freeze off in order to be a poet. In the course of the poem, he makes the journey home that would have cost him so much at the time and does so at the expense of the dead mother he claims to be honoring.

I

In no country as in the United States have the tragic consequences of the lack of any common concept of the good life been so strikingly exemplified, and in no country has the break with those common concepts been so sharp. After all, when other colonies have been founded, when other peoples have roved from the homeland and settled in distant parts, they have carried with them more than mere scraps of tradition. Oftenest they have carried the most precious human asset of all, a heritage of common feeling, which enabled them to cling to the substance of the old forms even while they adapted them to the new conditions of life.

—HAROLD STEARNS, "The Intellectual Life"

This reading of "A Prayer on All Saints' Day" would seem to be entirely inconsistent with much of what we know about Cowley. Even the most cursory consideration of his life's work reveals a constant preoccupation with what I have called his sentimental roots.[1] Indeed, "A Prayer on All Saints' Day" would not, perhaps, be quite so troubling had Cowley not made nostalgia for the landscape of his childhood such a powerful trope throughout his writing career. But this poem and what it tells us about Cowley's flight from a scenario for which he claims lifelong nostalgia offer us access to a reading of *Exile's Return* that might help to reconcile the story it does tell to others that it suggests—either through exaggeration or omission—but avoids or suppresses. These stories are crucial to our understanding both of the expatriate decade Cowley chronicles and of the decade during which Cowley wrote *Exile's Return* and to whose cultural politics the book is, at least in part, a response.

Exile's Return begins with an evocation of a kind of universal, rural "boyhood . . . country" that is more real and familiar than any encountered in adulthood: "The country of our childhood survives, if only in our minds, and retains our loyalty even when casting us into exile; we carry its image from city to city as our most essential baggage" (15).[2] Cowley sees himself and his contemporaries as exiles from this landscape of the past, striving to achieve through poetry the homecoming denied them in life. Such nostalgia is the subject of "The Urn," the poem with which he closes the invocation of a boyhood landscape that begins *Exile's Return* and introduces the saga of the Lost Generation:

> Wanderers outside the gates, in hollow
> landscapes without memory, we carry
> each of us an urn of native soil,
> of not impalpable dust a double handful
>
> anciently gathered—was it garden mold
> or wood soil fresh with hemlock needles, pine,
> and princess pine, this little earth we bore
> in silence, blindly over the frontier?
>
> —a parcel of the soil not wide enough
> or firm enough to build a dwelling on,
> or deep enough to dig a grave, but cool
> and sweet enough to sink the nostrils in
> and find the smell of home, or in the ears,
> rumors of home, like oceans in a shell.   (15–16)

The handful or two of native earth, smuggled out of childhood into the "hollow landscape" of maturity, is a poetic nosegay, a fetish of perennial adolescent nostalgia. The only edifice for which it is a substantial enough foundation ("not wide enough or firm enough to build a dwelling on / or deep enough to dig a grave") is that of poetry; upon its scent or echoes of home are constructed poems such as "The Urn," chronicles such as *Exile's Return*, and careers such as Cowley's. Cowley is too clever not to question whether the home so achingly recalled "exist[s] outside your memory" (15), but he nevertheless bestows upon this chimera the power to determine the trajectory of a life.

It is important to remember, however, that Cowley first presents this landscape as one of some ambivalence; he writes that it "retains our loyalty even when casting us into exile." This particular sentimental attachment—intense perhaps precisely in proportion to its ambivalence—bears a structural homology to the sentimental attachment to his mother that

Cowley tries to recover in "Prayer on All Saints' Day" and that he describes in some detail in "Mother and Son." In this essay, which began as a brief segment about his mother's death in a book about the late 1930s but "got way out of proportion to what I could use in the book" (35), Cowley explicitly attributes the deterioration of his relation to his mother to his literary bent. When he was a baby, Josephine Cowley was "radiantly proud of her only child" and made him feel that he "was different from ordinary children, a center of the whole mysterious world" (30). Then, he writes: "Things changed for me in boyhood, and I have often wondered why. Perhaps it was because I required and rewarded less of Mother's attention. I must have become a difficult boy, and she hated to be rebuffed. *'You learned to read,' she told me years later, 'and you weren't my boy any more. You lay on the floor reading a book, and I couldn't get a word out of you.' Mother had no interest in books, and I had entered a new world in which she played no part*" (30, emphasis added).

Although Cowley seems to agree with his mother's diagnosis that their special closeness terminated with his entrance into the world of letters, he shows their estrangement to have had a life and dynamics of its own. If Cowley describes himself as having been "difficult" and "unrewarding," he characterizes his mother as negligent. He recalls that she once left the eleven-year-old Malcolm alone in the country for a month, at the end of which he showed signs of severe malnutrition; he also tells of her letting him "walk a mile to school without an overcoat or even a muffler" (32) during three Pittsburgh winters. However, in the space between her loneliness ("Mother must have been starved for affection" ["Mother and Son" 33]) and his ("I had the good fortune to be a neglected child"; "Mother had little time for me" [31, 32]), a compelling relation seems to have subsisted, one whose intensity Cowley strains to recapture: "She wasn't consistently indifferent to what I did. . . . That there was still a bond between us was revealed even when we quarreled, more bitterly as time went on. We always quarreled as equals, almost as a married pair. . . . In spite of our failures to understand each other, we were closer in many ways than I had recognized. She had passed on to me much of herself. . . . For years I found it hard to write anything that might have wounded her deeply if she had been there to read it" (32, 35).

Although Cowley speculates about the oedipal nature of his relation with his mother ("Were there other symptoms of the too-famous Oedipal complex?" ["Mother and Son" 32]), his presentation of it suggests a dynamics of troubled mutual identification rather than desire.[3] He clearly needed the frictions of his relation with his mother in order to define himself as the intellectual she so clearly wasn't. Although toward the end of the essay he claims to wish he had inherited her "nervous energy" and "instinctive kindness to waifs and strangers," he has already discredited these qualities, shown them to be the effects of what, taken together, amounts to her gender: "a tragedy of frustrated hopes and misdirected vitality, but also of uncalculating affection . . . a large human potential on which she was unable to draw because of circumstances" (35). Cowley's descriptions of his mother's zany, intermittent projects (she raised canaries, made quilts, and bred chickens; she alternately paid "little attention to cooking meals" and was then "seized with a rage for baking" [31]) constitute a portrait of someone who never fully mastered the cultural lesson of sublimation. She was unable to conceive of her ambitions for her son in terms other than those that dictated her own life; hence, according to Cowley's account, it is not until he divorced his first wife, "a Greenwich Village type, irreligious and a bad housekeeper" and married a "beautiful and orderly" woman that Josephine Cowley found something to identify with and celebrate in her son: "Mother . . . was entranced by my new and final wife; here was someone beautiful and orderly in whom she could confide. When we gave her a grandson she was in raptures" (33).

Cowley's first marriage, to the bohemian divorcée Peggy Baird, had enacted and enforced his break with his childhood landscape. Yet, as I explore in detail later, Peggy Baird Cowley represented a disorder, a version of femininity even more untenable than the maternal one, and she had, of course, in her turn to be sacrificed to Cowley's methodical, journeyman-like practice of "the writer's trade." After he achieved "a fairly steady income and a place in the literary world" (ER 9), he was able to cast off the wife who represented its superficial, bohemian allure and marry the kind of woman ("my new and final wife") of whom his mother would approve. Having secured himself a place in a Lost Generation that had fled its native landscape and disavowed its mothers, Cowley could assuage the "guilty sense of malfeasance" he felt toward Josephine

Cowley by giving her a grandson, by participating in the production of generations as she understood it.

II

In my own day at Harvard the Westerners in my class looked with considerable suspicion upon those who specialized in literature, the classics, or philosophy. . . . Only "sissies," I was informed, took courses in poetry out in that virile West.
　　　　　　　　　—HAROLD STEARNS, "The Intellectual Life"

The process through which Cowley achieved independence from his identification with his mother is also the process, chronicled in *Exile's Return*, through which Cowley achieved respectability as an intellectual. Indeed, I claim that achieving respectability as an intellectual—as an American, male intellectual—is what *Exile's Return* is about. As my preliminary discussion of Cowley's relation to his mother suggests, the ambivalent process that he repeatedly called "exile" is, first and foremost, a self-distancing from femininity as represented by a maternal instance whose attraction and curse is its independence from the symbolic order. Cowley constitutes himself as an intellectual not through any oedipal identification with or rebellion against the intellectual legacy of his bookish, Swedenborgian father, but rather by distinguishing himself from the mother who had been taught "to write a fine, legible hand but not how to punctuate" ("Mother and Son" 29). The movement into the world of letters and the commitment to the symbolic realm it celebrates takes place in relation to and at the expense of the questionably literate mother who, because she cannot follow where she cannot tread, can be seen as sharing the responsibility—or blame—for the estrangement. Like the boyhood landscape of *Exile's Return*, which "refuses to take [one] back, to reincorporate [one] into its common life," either because it has disappeared or because one is oneself "so changed or uprooted," Cowley's mother, in this representation, remains complicit in the mutual estrangement upon which his career is founded, "retain[ing] our loyalty even when casting us into exile" (*ER* 15).

Cowley's writings about his mother suggest that Ann Douglas's notion of a "matricidal" agenda among American male intellectuals in the second and third decades of the twentieth century does not get at either the subtleties of the relation between these men and their mothers or the creative power generated by this relation. Rebelling against their overbearingly and energetically moral mothers, Douglas argues, these men

> discovered that they could enjoy what purported to be a moral crusade without believing in it, and get something, even possibly great art, out of destruction and chaos without idealizing them. They could take the adrenaline rush that fills the days and rides the nights, and leave the Victorian content and bogus rhetoric behind. The writers who fought in the war threw off, in its name, all efforts to check their development or define their aims; open disillusion was the sharpest weapon they had in waging the real war, the war against Mother. (*Terrible Honesty* 220)

Even in the examples Douglas proposes, it is what she herself terms "ambivalence," the ongoing dialogue with and rejection of what the mother represents, rather than any desire to silence her once and for all that characterizes the "revolt against the matriarch" (224).[4] The mothers Douglas introduces incur their sons' exasperation and anger for their attempts to follow their sons into adulthood, for their irritating ineptitude in bridging the gap between the feminized world they inhabit and the masculine world to which their sons aspire. Cowley and his contemporaries need their mothers, but they need to have left them behind in a never-never land of childhood that remains accessible when the strains of adult life grow overwhelming. Thus, in a 1929 letter to his oldest friend, Kenneth Burke, Cowley urges a summer expedition to the rural haunt of his childhood, Belsano: "It's an opportunity for a flight backwards into adolescence, into a life with only the future shadow of women (walks along dusty roads, Chopin at twilight on an out-of-tune piano, books, possibilities, Mother in the kitchen)" (cited in Jay 439). Cowley's nostalgia for a lost, and thereby fetishizable, pre-oedipal connectedness with the abjected maternal landscape provides him with the trope that will determine the shape of his individual works and his entire career.

The fact that the "brief segment about his mother's death" that he planned to write for a book on the late 1930s "got way out of proportion to what [he] could use in the book" conforms entirely to the storytelling logic governing his career in general; the truly personal—as opposed to the representatively personal—has no place in the public mythography of this man of letters. Yet Cowley's description of the process in which the "brief segment" about his mother threatened the economy of the volume ("And then I began to think and feel about her life . . . [and t]he piece got way out of proportion") suggests the power of the material that, in his dotage, he finally isolated and published elsewhere. Unlike Stearns, the text of whose life is haunted—and perhaps determined—by his failures and near failures to accommodate the specter of his mother, Cowley shapes a career that reads like an extended and successful detour away from the Mother in order then, when he is "older than [she was] ever to be," to acknowledge that she has been a motive force all along. If Stearns can be regarded as having carried his mother around with him in a self-destructive, imperfectly sublimated form, Cowley, through his notion of exile, effectively relegated his mother to a pre- and extratextual realm whose energies he appropriated as he repeatedly declared its concerns to be irrelevant to the construction of the American male intellectual of the twentieth century.

The "urn of native soil" of which Cowley writes in the poem discussed above is sublimation's gender-neutral, poetically viable version of "Mother in the kitchen." With this substitution of a general, ungendered "homesickness for childhood" for the nostalgia for "Mother in the kitchen," Cowley sets up a rhetorical and ideological system that enables him to suppress and ignore the issues of gender that troubled the self-styling of so many American male intellectuals. There is no place for "Mother" and very little for women at all in the portrait of a generation that Cowley substitutes for the portrait of himself—or rather, in which Cowley sublimates his self-portrait. As I hope to demonstrate in the discussion that follows, it is only once he has written women out of the saga of early twentieth-century American literary production that Cowley can construct for himself the persona of the intellectual picaro, "one representative of a new generation in American letters, one person among many, and otherwise as a young man without special qualities" ("Looking" 582). In the chronicle whose singular title (*Exile's Return*) claims to represent a collective experience, a group of postadolescent males of above-average intelligence and literary ambition becomes a "generation"; the lonely, insignificant "I" becomes the collective, signifying "they." The adventure of one of these young men becomes a composite history, "the story of a whole social class, how it became aware of itself and how it went marching toward the end of an era" (13).

The true exile's return would entail Cowley's return to his mother's unvisited grave in order to restore to its source the fetishized "handful of native earth" that has accompanied him throughout his lifelong "literary odyssey." Every "return" he chronicles and celebrates prior to this octogenarian poetic moment can be seen as both a displacement and a rehearsal of the trajectory suggested in the juxtaposition of "The Urn" and "Prayer on All Saints' Day." I would like now to examine how Cowley constructed the "return" he chronicles in *Exile's Return*, how his tale of the Lost Generation borrows the energies of, transposes, works variations on, and displaces the "return" that it denies and for which it is standing in. If the personal narrative is indeed to become a "narrative of ideas" or "a literary odyssey," as the subtitle of the 1951 reissue claims, what transformations are performed upon the intellectual or literary baggage with which he begins he journey? And if Cowley's journey (*Exile's Return*) is to become a paradigm for the career of a generation whose individual narratives, one takes it, would only repeat with minor, idiosyncratic differences the story Cowley has already told, what kind of self-presentation, which omissions and embellishments, which contextualizations, and which rhetorical strategies best serve the interests of this group portrait? How do the "ideas" that Cowley chooses to narrate—or, regarded from a slightly different angle, the kind of literary odyssey he constructs—contribute to a particular portrait of the American intellectual in 1934? And finally, how does the trope of return organize a narrative so that it serves particular interests and begs particular questions that would be crucial to a critical evaluation of the portrait of a generation that Cowley proposes?[5]

III

Free . . . of any common heritage or tradition which might question his values, free, also, of the troublesome idealism of the older revolutionary mood, the ordinary man could go forth into the wil-

derness with singleness of purpose. He could be, as he still is to-day,
the pioneer *toujours*.

—HAROLD STEARNS, "The Intellectual Life"

"So it was to be the Lost Generation. . . ." The first sentence of *Exile's
Return* introduces a note of inevitability to the construction of the group
portrait of "probably the first real [generation] in the history of American letters" (7).[6] The social forces at work around the turn of the century were such, Cowley claims, that young people coming of age in the
mid-1910s should experience a commonality of experience, vision, temperament, and ambition yet unprecedented in American history. These
sons of middle-class midwestern families attended public high schools
and then ventured East to go to college, where "they were divested of
their local peculiarities, taught the standardized American idiom and introduced to the boundaryless world of international learning. Soon they
would be leaving for the army in France, where they would experience
the same boredom, fear, excitement, pride, aloofness, curiosity" (8–9).

Common sense tells us that a "literary generation" is never composed
of more than a handful of people. With every comma in his list of common traits and experiences, Cowley whittles his "generation" down to
just such a handful at the same time as he strives for a certain universalizing pathos.[7] Without ever really exaggerating, Cowley makes it seem as
though *his* (literary) generation is representative of *its* generation:

> The Lost Generation . . . was lost, first of all, because it was up-
> rooted, schooled away, almost wrenched away, from its attach-
> ment to any region or tradition. It was lost because its training
> had prepared it for another world than existed after the War (and
> the War prepared it for nothing). It was lost because it chose to
> live in exile. It was lost because it had no trustworthy guides, and
> had formed for itself only the vaguest picture of society and the
> writer's place in it. The generation belonged to a period of con-
> fused transition from values already fixed to values that had to be
> created. (*ER* 11)

And finally, "the story of the Lost Generation and its return from exile is
something else besides: it is partly the story of a whole social class, how
it became aware of itself and how it went marching toward the end of

an era" (13). Like most elites, this particular group *can* be representative only because it *is* not. Not only do Cowley and his cohort enjoy the education, intelligence, and relative prosperity that enable them to reflect productively on an experience that undid many of their less fortunate contemporaries, but they are also in the position to determine who belongs in the group that is to represent its generation.

While Cowley is candid about the socioeconomic, geographical, and educational commonalities of his "generation," he is less so about its gender. After one early reference to "young men and women," it becomes clear that Cowley is interested only in the men. Indeed, the criteria he gradually sets out explicitly exclude any woman with the intelligence and self-consciousness necessary to have qualified for the "generation" in the first place (at one point he writes that the "members of [the postwar New York intellectual set] had about the same experiences . . . the year in the army if they were men, the unhappy love affair that took its place if they were women" [*ER* 216]). Readers who are attentive to both what they are and are not being told as they attend to Cowley's narration could easily become uncomfortable with the vehemence with which the experiences of this select handful of overeducated young men is projected as characteristic of "a whole social class" or even "an era." "All of them" to whom he attributes the same postwar "emotional collapse" and who followed, until the end of their and the century's third decade, a common "geographical pattern of life, one that can be expressed briefly by the names of two cities and a state: New York, Paris, Connecticut," are in reality a small cohort of men who have achieved by 1929, "a fairly steady income and a place in the literary world" (9).

Once this group has been made to stand for its "generation," Cowley's story can be told as its representative narrative. From the vantage point of the "place in the literary world" they have come to occupy, Cowley can cast their story as a narrative of exile and return: "I want to set down the story of this Lost Generation while its adventures are fresh in my mind. I want to tell how it earned its name (and tried to live up to it) and then how it ceased to be lost, how, in a sense, it found itself" (*ER* 12). Prior to the "return" celebrated by his book's title, Cowley and the other members of his generation passed through a series of forms of exile—the original, existential exile that makes the sons of the fin de siècle feel that they had to leave the "country of their childhood" (52), the East Coast urban college life that "uprooted [them] in spirit" (90), and military or ambulance duty in Europe during the First World War, which "physically uprooted . . . hundreds of us, millions, plucked from our own soil as if by a clamshell bucket and dumped, scattered among strange people. All our roots were dead now" (55). With the end of the war, the young men returned to a United States whose Prohibition Amendment "publish[ed] a bill of separation between itself and ourselves; it wasn't our country any longer." They settled in New York, "the homeland of the uprooted, where everyone you met came from another town and tried to forget it" (56). Soon, this exile from exile demanded an exile of its own: Cowley's generation emigrated to Paris en masse, where it sought a world in which it really belonged and declared itself to be officially "Lost." Their (usually brief) sojourns ended, the members of the Lost Generation returned to the United States and undertook to transform the lessons of their exile into an American cultural mainstream.

Cowley was not alone in his attempts to will into being a "literary generation" with whose countenance and concerns he could identify. The latent association of intellectual activity with femininity that I discussed in the previous chapter, as well as the conspicuous literary achievements of women and African Americans during the period with which Cowley is concerned in *Exile's Return*, provoked numerous attempts to paint a portrait of literary America that would resemble the face that Cowley saw when he looked in the mirror. In his 1983 essay, "Race and Gender in the Shaping of the American Literary Canon: A Case Study from the Twenties," Paul Lauter examines the cultural processes that culminated, by the end of the 1920s, in the virtual elimination of black, white female, and working-class writers from the American literary canon (435). Lauter attributes the deliberate establishment of a canon of American letters to what he terms "a significant shift in cultural authority from female-defined to male-defined institutions," from a genteel tradition regarded as dilettantish and feminine to a more self-consciously theoretical, professionalized institutionalization of the study of literature that is also self-consciously and aggressively "male." By canonizing texts that represent grand cultural labors and demand intricate interpretational work, the men of letters of the early twentieth century rescued their profession from the specters of feminization, sentimentalism, frivolity, and even gentility that haunted it. Lauter quotes Cowley's friend, Allen Tate:

[The] critical responsibility [of the man of letters in the modern world] is thus . . . the recreation and the application of literary standards. . . . His task is to preserve the integrity, the purity, and the reality of language wherever and for whatever purpose it may be used. . . . The true province of the man of letters is nothing less (as it is nothing more) than culture itself. . . . It is the duty of the man of letters to supervise the culture of language, to which the rest of culture is subordinate, and to warn us when our language is ceasing to forward the ends proper to man. (450)

This kind of program salvages the moral authority that the "American Scholar may have lost with the decline of the ability of the educated classes to establish standards of conduct"; colleges, universities, and professional associations such as the Modern Language Association serve as fora for this mission of cultural improvement and masculine self-legitimation.

Unlike those of his contemporaries whose cultural projects Lauter examines, Cowley professed independence of and often contempt for the universities, the professors, and the canon makers. Yet as Cowley's response to the culture wars of his time, *Exile's Return* performs many of the same functions as the debates at the universities and professional associations, grounding a particular conviction about and program for American literature in a universalizing context and narrowing down the roster of its practitioners to the familiar canon of white men. While his academic contemporaries decree which texts best represent a "useful," aesthetically viable version of American culture, Cowley shows how a particular set of cultural tenets and literary standards develops as the educated, sensitive, and worldly young man's response to the cultural, political, and economic exigencies of American society. The freelance writers, poets, editors, and journalists who were Cowley's intellectual cohorts regarded themselves as more in touch with real life and contemporary literature, closer to "the writer's trade," and worldlier than the professors and thus uniquely qualified to assess which kinds of literature most adequately responded to the world as they saw it. Moreover, they claimed for themselves the authority to judge America through the lens of Europe at the same time as they now judged Europe through the lens of knowledge and experience rather than that of cultural inferiority and romantic desire. In retrospect, their literary biases look very much like the ones we associate with the academic canon; at the time, however, their stated goals were less to determine the course of the study of American letters than to create an intellectual atmosphere congenial to the production of a literature and a cultural discourse that accurately represented what they took—or willed—America—and, by extension, themselves as Americans—to be.[8]

Cowley presents his own experience as representative of what Marc Dolan terms "a shared and presumed generational identity" (88), and he constructs a narrative in which a certain notion of what literature should be is the inevitable result of the "exile" and "return" that were the hallmarks of this generation's experience. In order to be able to ground a cultural program in a personal narrative, however representative it may be, this narrative must be shown to transcend its own contingency. Dolan argues that Cowley draws on the conventions of myth in order to "structur[e] his generational narrative around an ideal sequence of life experiences": "Cowley's text is a myth of the *intellectual* as hero, in which the tests are aesthetic philosophies; the helpers, the 'good writers' of canonical modernism; the dark world, the world of European art circles and the false religion of art; the ordeal, the moment of avant-garde experimentation; and the return, the act of reintegration into American culture and society" (101). Dolan takes his cue from Cowley's own invocation of the traditional quest narrative in the epilogue he wrote for the 1951 reissue of *Exile's Return*:

> The story . . . seems to follow the old pattern of alienation and reintegration, or departure and return, that is repeated in scores of European myths and continually re-embodied in life. A generation of American writers went out into the world like the children in Grimm's fairy tales who ran away from a cruel stepmother. They wandered for years in search of treasure and then came back like the grown children to dig for it at home. But the story in life was not so simple and lacked the happy ending of fairy tales. Perhaps there was really a treasure and perhaps it had been buried all the time in their father's garden, but the exiles did not find it there. They found only what others were finding: work to do as best they could and families to support and educate. The adventure

had ended and once more they were part of the common life.
(289)

Cowley's presentation of *Exile's Return* as a fairy tale manqué is based, of course, on a particular allegorization that needs to be examined: the "cruel stepmother" is urban American society, epitomized in Cowley's text by New York City, and particularly by Greenwich Village. This "homeland of the uprooted" (*ER* 56) is also, as Cowley himself points out, the "homeland" of Stearns's critique of "feminized" American intellectual life (85–90). Although Cowley cites Stearns in order to point out the limitations of *Civilization in the United States*, he does not actively refute its claims, and nothing in his own analysis challenges Stearns's excoriation of an America that refuses to nurture the young people placed in its care and forces its "youngest generation" into exile to seek the treasures of their birthright in the Old World. Unlike Stearns, however, who sees the promise of America in the revolt of young urban intellectuals, Cowley is wary of cities and insists upon the ties that bind his generation to the landscapes of their past. While Stearns's generation "had revolted and tried to break new trails [and] never got letters from home," Cowley and his contemporaries "had never broken with [their] parents, never walked stormily out of church, never been expelled from school for writing essays on anarchism" (81–82). Cowley attributes this difference to his generation's disabused acceptance of the realities that made cynics of Stearns's. But there is an additional difference: Cowley's generation may not have been "so close to their fathers and mothers that . . . they had been forced to quarrel with and reject them," but, having been "placed at a greater distance from [their] elders" (82) they also developed a nostalgia for the landscape of their childhood that made them loathe to abandon it completely. (Stearns, as we remember, writes of his fond memories of his childhood landscape, but expresses no nostalgia; in fact, he regards his own failure ever to return to the Boston area and visit his mother as almost pathological.) Thus, to return to the language of Cowley's fairy tale, behind the specter of the (urban) stepmother there lurks, of course, the ghost of an idealized real mother—one is tempted to call her Mother Nature—whose inheritance remains to be realized and who, the fantasy insists, would have nurtured differently: "Somewhere behind them was another country, a real country of barns, cornfields, hemlock woods and brooks tumbling across birch logs into pools where the big trout lay. Somewhere, at an incredible distance, was the country of their childhood, where they had once been part of the landscape and the life" (52).

As I pointed out above, Cowley is aware that this scenario is an idealization. Unlike the "grown children" in the fairy tale, Cowley's "generation" do not possess the magic necessary to bridge this "incredible distance"; they are adults and not "grown children." Moreover, these young men are aware that what Cowley calls their "survival" depends on maintaining the distance that is the governing trope of their creativity. Finally, in Cowley's mythology, fathers don't have gardens. In fact, fathers—to the extent that Cowley's text mentions them at all—are distinctly urban creatures; their gardens are those offices, factories, and, at best, publishing houses and editorial offices where fantasy and desire come up against the reality principle. When Cowley describes the "landscape and the life" of his rural childhood summers, he introduces his father—and specifically, his father as professional person and breadwinner—as the figure who interferes with the childhood idyll, dragging him back from the birthplace that he "thought of as [his] home" to the "bigtown" where the process of deracination begins: "I was born in a farmhouse near Belsano, in Cambria County, Pennsylvania. . . . All my summers were spent there, and sometimes the long autumns too—fishing, shooting cottontails and pine squirrels, or simply wandering through the woods by myself; I thought of Belsano as my home. *But my father was a doctor in Pittsburgh and I attended a big-town high school*" (ER 16, emphasis added). The business of being an adult man who has to "educate and support a family" seems to be incompatible with country life, and especially with what it means for Cowley. We can read Cowley's career as an attempt to reconcile his nostalgia for the country with the realities of adult male life, to return on his own terms and in full manhood to the land from which he feels exiled. *Exile's Return* establishes those terms and charts the development of an intellectual who refuses to sacrifice his ties to the land and whose work will enable him to buy back his birthright in the form of a small farm in Connecticut.

Of course, no farm in Connecticut can replace the lost world of childhood; we recall that the pursuit of the "writer's trade" requires the flight from this maternal landscape. As Cowley acknowledges: "Of course they couldn't go back: their own countrysides or Middle Western towns would offer no scope to their talents, no opportunity for earning the sort of living to which they had grown accustomed" (*ER* 218). The fruits of working as steadily at the "writer's trade" as the paternal generation did at their professions enable Cowley to complete the "European" mythic pattern in a particularly American way: he buys land and plants his own garden instead of digging for hidden treasure in his father's plot.[9] In the master-narrative that Cowley derives from its European avatars, he purchases through hard American work a landscape reminiscent of but at a sufficient distance from his that of childhood: "Perhaps they could make a compromise, could enjoy the advantages of two worlds by purchasing a farm somewhere within a hundred miles of Manhattan and spending their summers in the country without separating themselves from their urban sources of income" (218).

This "compromise" makes it possible for Cowley to circumnavigate the demands of both the rural mother and the urban stepmother; to the extent that it secures this compromise, *Exile's Return* is not simply the fairy tale manqué in which the young exiles return to collide with a reality principle that denies them the treasure they have sought. If the "story in life . . . lack[s] the happy ending of fairy tales" (*ER* [1951] 289), it does not lack another genre of "happy ending." With its allusion to the exiles' discovery of "what others were finding: work to do as best they could and families to support and educate," *Exile's Return* inscribes itself within the conventions of the nineteenth-century narrative of renunciation and then announces its triumph over the genre. Return is not simply a sobering reencounter with the philistine world to which the high culture of Europe seemed the only antidote; it is, rather, constructed to be a gesture of self-affirmation in which a repertoire of real cultural possibilities set into motion by the complex experience of exile is made available to the trajectory of desire. Although the narrative of this experience must acknowledge the difficulties that life still places in the path of the returned exiles, its accounts of the stultifying office work required to pay the bills and the returnees' buffo attempts to transplant Dada to the shores of the Hudson, even its rendition of the murder-suicide with which Harry Crosby marked the "end of an era" serve to highlight the particular accomplishments of those who "survived."[10] If the exiles returned "with a set of values that bore no relation to American life, with convictions that could not fail to be misunderstood in a country where Dada was hardly a name, and moral judgments on literary matters were thought to be in questionable taste" (180), they soon gave up their "efforts to apply in one country the standards [they] had brought from another" (205) and began the process of creating and arbitrating what has come to be regarded as American high culture. Even as Cowley milks the pathos of his generation's uprootedness, his text is already carving out a space that resituates him outside the terms in which he construes exile. Locating himself halfway between the city and the country of his childhood, Cowley creates a space in which he can work unbothered by the gendered phantoms that render these two places uninhabitable in his cultural and emotional economy.

IV

We know exactly how Mr. Jiggs feels when Mrs. Jiggs drags him
away to a concert and makes him dress for a stiff, formal dinner,
when all his heart desires is to smoke his pipe and play poker with
Dinty and the boys.
                —HAROLD STEARNS, "The Intellectual Life"

According to Cowley, the narrative of *Exile's Return* is only superficially the tale of how he and his contemporaries survived the perils of ex- and repatriation and established themselves in a life in which the ideas gestated in the country were negotiated and sold in the intellectual marketplace of the city. *Exile's Return* is, he maintains, "not so much a record of events as a narrative of ideas." He goes on to qualify what he means by "ideas": they "will be of a certain type: they are not the ones people thought they believed and consciously expressed in books and book reviews. The ideas that concern me here are the ones that half-unconsciously guided people's actions, the ones they lived and wrote by" (12). Cowley's sense of the critic's mandate to question and reevaluate writers' "consciously expressed" positions and self-presentations legitimizes a reassessment of both his narrative and his ideas, an examination of what might have "half-unconsciously guided" the actions that Cowley himself "lived and wrote by."

I have already foregrounded the importance for the curriculum vitae recounted in *Exile's Return* of the critical relation between Cowley's nostalgia for the countryside of his childhood and his ambivalent flight from a precultural, pre-oedipal scenario I have figured as "Mother in the kitchen," as well as of the equally vexed relation to an urban cultural landscape that figures as the "cruel stepmother" in the fairy-tale summary he presents in the 1951 revision of the book. The "compromise" between these two unlivable worlds, the rural-suburban world outside exile toward which *Exile's Return* points, is a world that is purged of the threat of the feminine—and by extension, of any critical engagement of the issue of gender. Women figure, if at all, almost exclusively negatively in Cowley's narrative of his entrance into a world of letters that he presents as, simultaneously, the world of mature sexuality. Yet the issue of gender that he barely addresses—and the fact that he barely addresses it—"half-consciously guid[e]" what he presents as an intellectual journey. If, at the "end of [the] era" of exile, Cowley's generation has "found itself," this self-discovery is not simply a matter of having discovered that America is just as good as Europe and that literature exists not in and as a purely aesthetic realm with its own laws, but rather in dialogue with the set of social realities it represents. It is also—and significantly— the discovery that there is a way of living as an intellectual in America as a man among men, untroubled both by whatever gender struggles might accompany everyday life and by the crisis of masculinity that has often been the corollary of American intellectual life.

The odyssey that Cowley traces in *Exile's Return* is an odyssey away from women and from a cultural landscape where the specter of the feminine haunted the prospect of the intellectual life. Unlike Stearns's narrative, it nowhere mentions the crisis of intellectual masculinity that figures so prominently both in the discourse of the time and in the commentaries on it.[11] Rather than taking on the issue, it ignores it. As Cowley writes in a slightly different context, comparing his generation to that of Stearns, "'They' had revolted and tried to break new trails. . . . We had avoided issues and got what we wanted in a quiet way, simply by taking it" (81– 82). It is precisely by avoiding this issue so central to the concerns of his near-contemporaries that *Exile's Return* tells the story of how, by the time Cowley and his friends returned from Europe, they had written this specter out of their cultural text and created for themselves what Christine Stansell has described as "a decidedly masculine world . . . where young men bellowed at each other about fine points in Gourmont and young women cleaned up" ("Hermit" 29).

Instead of *recording* the "determined, if unconscious, effort to reinscribe 'the artist' within a proper fraternity" ("Hermit" 29), Cowley's account of his intellectual odyssey *performs* it, replacing the image of "Mother in the kitchen" with the tableau of "two or three young men [content to sit in the kitchen] with our feet on the bare table, discussing the problem of abstract beauty while we rolled Bull Durham into cigarettes and let the flakes sift down into our laps" (*ER* 82). The very marginal presence of women in the text is strategic, if not, perhaps, intentionally so; in the course of Cowley's saga of ex- and repatriation, women are represented first as objects of postadolescent sexual desire, then as a (marital) burden to be borne, and later as the violators of at least the male partner's understanding of the marital pact, and hence, an encumbrance of which the serious artist must divest himself. By the time Cowley writes *The Dream of the Golden Mountains*, the chronicle of the period during which *Exile's Return* was written, women have become the literary device through which he represents the boundary between culture and its Other. Before examining how *Exile's Return* sends not only women but also the issue of gender into exile as it instates Cowley's generation at the center of American creative and intellectual life, I would like to use the more flagrant example of his memoir of the 1930s, *The Dream of the Golden Mountains*, in order to demonstrate the purposiveness of Cowley's cultural misogyny.

Cowley begins *The Dream of the Golden Mountains* with a description of the brownstone in Chelsea that housed the offices of the *New Republic*, whose literary editor he became in 1929. Within the genteelly shabby building, "the atmosphere was of a home where one family had been living for a long time. . . . The moral atmosphere, too, was that of a family rather than of a business office. There were family jokes and mild family quarrels and the sound of laughter in the hallways, sometimes mingled with the smell of cooking" (2). Cowley's extended description suggests that, except for the secretaries, who "had cubbyholes that used to be hall bedrooms" and "Lucie the cook, who was actually North Italian [and] lived in the basement with her husband, Etienne the butler," the *New Republic* "family" was a household of fathers and well-appreciated, well-behaved sons: "Everyone felt sure of his job and hardly anyone was angling for a better one" (2–3). A good deal of "family life" centered on the dining room table, where, Cowley boasts, the lofty conversation could be rather daunting. Instead of giving his reader an example of the discourse at a *New Republic* luncheon, he illustrates the atmosphere in the following manner: "Strangers were likely to be intimidated. A painter's wife, invited for the first time, was so nervous that she kept rubbing her hands on her skirt; then she looked down and discovered that her thighs were bare. That day she didn't enjoy the good French cooking" (2). In this cruelly gratuitous passage, Cowley makes it clear the offending woman has penetrated the inner sanctum as a "painter's wife" and not as anyone in her own right. The painter remains unnamed, perhaps so that he be spared the embarrassment of this unseemly female behavior in a document addressed to posterity. And the nervous offender is triply punished: first, she disgraces herself in "intimidating" company; second, she is denied enjoyment of the "good French cooking" that is a perquisite of the initiated; and third, her faux pas becomes part of the lore of intellectual life in the 1930s.

If this were the only anecdote of its kind, it could, perhaps, be overlooked as a harmless, albeit tasteless, attempt to inject local color into the description of the editorial offices of a highbrow periodical. But it is followed, a scant three pages later, by another passage in which, again, a woman is made the object of ridicule for her inability to deal with the high seriousness of the *New Republic* family: "More and more people were coming to see us. . . . I seem to remember dozens of correspondents back from Russia, either inspired by the Five Year Plan or else disturbed by the omnipresence of the political police and the signs of hunger. 'In the provinces people are dying by thousands,' one of them said. His wife took another helping of Lucie's *boeuf bourguignon*. 'Yes, and in Moscow,' she added, 'They gave us nothing but just chicken, chicken, chicken'" (*Dream* 5). Either women commit faux pas that make it impossible to enjoy the food or their enjoyment of it becomes a faux pas in and of itself. Were Cowley prone to peppering his narrative with such anecdotes, touching on the foibles of men and women alike, such material could, conceivably, be accommodated by a general tableau of human pretense and frailty. But such passages are the exception rather than the rule, and only women are subjected to such representation. Cowley's catalogue of the "cranks and crazy people" who beleaguered the *New Re-*

public offices with their mania, their phobias, and their "cure[s] for the depression" begins as a list of "types" ("Some of the worst. . . . Others") and ends with the detailed description of one, by now predictably female individual: "One woman carried a big sealed envelope in which she said was a series of articles that would shake the nation. She wouldn't let us open the envelope unless we accepted and paid for its entire contents in advance. 'I know you editors,' she said, 'You'd steal my ideas and print them under a different name. You'd steal the pennies from a dead man's eyes'" (6). Overlooking, for a moment, the fact that the woman's assessment of journalists is neither unprecedented nor unwarranted and that Cowley, at less prosperous moments of his own career, was capable of waxing cynical about the probity of his colleagues, we can interpret the woman's unopened and unremunerated envelope as representing a boundary between serious writing and its debased Other. Cowley never entertains the possibility that the envelope's contents might be, if not "nation-shaking," valuable, and he uses the example of this woman to secure the uncontaminated seriousness of his publication and its world.

Cowley uses the story of the breakup of his first marriage and Hart Crane's suicide to distinguish the intellectual, political, and emotional climate of the period during which *Exile's Return* was written from the atmosphere of the decade it chronicles. These "two events in my nonpolitical life that had helped to prepare me for new convictions" (*Dream* 51) occasion both a critical summary of what Cowley retrospectively regards as the revels of the 1920s and his participation in them and his renunciation of their ethos of pleasure and excess. Both Peggy Cowley's flamboyance and promiscuity and Crane's alcoholism and homosexuality threaten the discreet, conventional gender normativity that underwrites the self-construction toward which he is striving. Cowley describes the situation that led him to seek a divorce as follows: "Peggy and I had tortured each other in many heedless fashions. As time went on she had casual affairs, and I had less casual ones. She was a heavy drinker, though not an alcoholic like Hart Crane. I felt responsible for Peggy, but after I went to work for *The New Republic*, I could no longer lead the old bohemian life. Often when I came home from the office I found the apartment full of her boon companions; bottles galore, but nothing to eat" (52).

It is hardly necessary to elaborate on this characterization of Peggy

Baird Cowley; it remains to examine what is at stake in this representation of her decadence. Her "casual affairs" are set in contrast to her husband's "less casual ones"; her "bohemian" mores clash with Cowley's work ethic; her drinking companions are "boon companions," while his are fellow writers or the "family" at the *New Republic*. As Cowley tells the story, his wife's way of life sends him into exile again, causing him to lie "in bed staring at the shadows on the ceiling" and then "to roam the streets or stand alone at a crowded bar" (52). After a frightening encounter with "an extra-large man with a blackjack" in a disreputable late-night speakeasy, Cowley is comforted by a policeman: "The policeman put a fatherly hand on my shoulder. 'Son,' he said, 'you shouldn't go *in* to places like that'" (52). This exchange provokes the meditation that leads to Cowley's divorce: "I went home sober and lay awake until it was time to get dressed for the office. *There was, I had learned, a special world in New York for men who couldn't sleep*; it consisted of speakeasies, all-night lunchrooms, and the waiting room of Grand Central Station, where one sat on snowy nights and read the bulldog edition of the morning papers; but it wasn't a world designed for permanent habitation" (52, emphasis added).

The discovery of a special urban nightmare world reserved "*for men*" is what precipitates Cowley's divorce; in other words, it is not his wife's actions per se, but the fact that they make him an exile from the world "for men" to which he aspires—a world of work, letters, routine, balanced meals, and clean clothes—that motivates an action that Cowley was reluctant to take. The man who "survived" Harvard, the trenches of the First World War, "exile" in Europe, and the penurious years in Greenwich Village in the company of his "generation" comes up against the limits of his sanity and his capacity to endure when confronted with the discomforts of his wife's household ("nothing to eat"), on the one hand, and the "special world in New York for men who couldn't sleep," on the other: "I began to feel that my only choice was between getting a divorce . . . and going off to a sanitarium" (*Dream* 52).

For Cowley, the divorce marks more than the end of a marriage; his account of it in *The Dream of the Golden Mountain* functions as a ritual sacrifice in which he "writes off" Peggy Baird and Hart Crane, two close companions of the 1920s who, between them, assembled the vices that threatened the persona Cowley was in the process of constructing. He

then rededicates his energies to a life privately more respectable and politically nobler than the one that has him at the threshold of skid row.
When Peggy Baird Cowley went to Mexico to seek a divorce, she began
an affair with Hart Crane. Although Cowley claims to be "delighted for
both of them," the relationship could not have been entirely untroubling.
On the one hand, as Hans Bak stresses in his biography, Cowley was
professionally indebted to both Peggy Baird and Crane; she secured him
many valuable connections at the outset of his New York career, while
Crane was responsible for the publication of Cowley's volume of poems,
Blue Juniata (127ff.). On the other hand, however, they represented a way
of life that was becoming increasingly distasteful to Cowley: to Peggy's
drinking, carousing, and infidelity, Crane added serious alcoholism, pug-
nacity, poetic genius, and a homosexuality that Cowley tried to overlook
or tolerate ("I regarded it as an item of personal gossip, as if I had been
told that he had a birthmark on his back or suffered—as he did—from
constipation. He did not look or talk like a homosexual. . . . Instead of
being delicate, his poems were solidly built and clumped on heavy feet,
like Hart himself" [*Second Flowering* 196]) but that he always invoked
as the sign of the loss of control, which was what irritated him most
about Crane ("he was obeying the iron laws of another country than
ours. . . . He had entered the last phase of his party—a familiar phase . . .
when he cruised the waterfront looking for sailors and sometimes ended
by being beaten or jailed" [215]).

The proximity of vice and virtue in these two figures, combined with
the obvious attraction they exerted on him, made for an ambivalence
that might have threatened Cowley had he not figured out how to enlist
it in service of his "survival." In a book whose purpose was to record a
time in history when, by "surrendering their middle-class identities [and]
joining the workers in an idealized army" (*Dream* xii) intellectuals might
devote themselves to a political goal that transcended their individual
concerns, the introduction of intimate material seems rather odd. Yet
Cowley has no qualms about quoting at length from Peggy's private letters to him and exposing the indignities of his good friend's final months.
The details of the affair between Crane and Peggy Cowley are mildly
lurid but not particularly interesting; that it inspires Crane to write one
final, good poem might be slightly more so. Most revealing, however, is
the rendition of this literary event by Cowley the critic. He quotes from

the letter in which Crane sent him a copy of "The Broken Tower": "I'm wondering whether or not you'll like the above poem—about the 1st I've written in two years . . . I'm getting too damned self-critical to write at all any more. More than ever, however, I do implore your honest appraisal of this verse, prose or nonsense—whatever it may seem. Please let me know" (78, ellipsis in original). Cowley never responds to Crane's request: "I thought the poem was splendid, but I was so taken up with *The New Republic* and my after-hours work for the NCDPP that I put off writing Hart from day to day" (80). A month later, Crane was dead and Peggy, who was on board the ship from which he jumped and who blamed herself for not having stopped him, was back in New York: "I helped Peggy through customs with her collection of Mexican baskets and serapes. She was staying with friends whom I didn't want to see at the time, so I put her into a taxi and kissed her goodbye" (81).

Too busy fighting the cause of Appalachian miners to answer his friend's letter and disinclined to reenter the distraught Peggy's bohemian world, Cowley sacrifices his companions of the 1920s to the concerns of the 1930s. With the kiss that sends Peggy and her baubles back to Bohemia, Cowley takes leave of the last remnants of the era he celebrated in *Exile's Return*: "Having mourned for Hart a year before he died, I now felt that his suicide and Peggy's decree of divorce were echoes of an era that had ended. It had been a good era in its fashion, full of high spirits and grand parties, but also, it seemed to me now, inexcusably wasteful of time and emotions. We had lived on the reckless margins of society and had spent our energies on our private lives, which had gone to pieces" (*Dream* 81–82). He continues, articulating the monogamized, professionalized, compartmentalized, politicized modus vivendi that is the antithesis of everything that Peggy Baird Cowley, Hart Crane, and also, to some extent, the Malcolm Cowley of the 1920s had stood for: "Now I wanted to get married again and stay married, I knew to whom. I wanted to live as simply as possible and turn my energies toward the world outside. I wanted to write honestly, I wanted to do my share in building a just society" (82).

Drawing a line of decorum between the public and private worlds whose interpenetration is one of the hallmarks of the 1920s as he has represented them, Cowley enters into the bourgeois personal arrangement with the woman he will later call "my new and final wife" at the same time as he dedicates himself to radical politics. Although from a later perspective he will suggest that "writing honestly" and "building a just society" might "come into conflict," there seems no doubt that the respectable, discreet marriage to a woman of whom his mother will approve serves to underwrite rather than threaten these ambitions.

V

Hardly any intelligent foreigner has failed to observe and comment upon the extraordinary feminization of American social life, and oftenest he has coupled this observation with a few biting remarks concerning the intellectual anaemia or torpor that seems to accompany it.

— HAROLD STEARNS, "The Intellectual Life"

The gender politics established in the section of *The Dream of the Golden Mountain* devoted to Cowley's divorce form the context in which *Exile's Return* was written. The marriage with Muriel Maurer as it is represented here—a conventional marriage, which, like that of his parents, would produce one son—needs to be read as one of the "returns" that I described earlier in this chapter and indeed as the one that most closely rehearses the return to his mother's grave imagined in "Prayer on All Saints' Eve." As I have suggested, however, *Exile's Return* itself orchestrates a very different relation between the private and the professional worlds in that it does not radically separate them and then distinguish them by gender. Whereas, by the end of *The Dream of the Golden Mountain*, "Mother" has been quite literally returned to the "kitchen," and the domestic and procreational world has been sealed off from the world in which men work and create culture, *Exile's Return* has the more difficult task of portraying an era in which "generation" is a cultural category and is carried out, to return to Cowley's own formulation, by "two or three young men [content to sit in the kitchen] with our feet on the bare table, discussing the problem of abstract beauty while we rolled Bull Durham into cigarettes and let the flakes sift down into our laps" (*ER* 82).

We can begin to discern the very different—and more subtle—way the Malcolm Cowley of *Exile's Return* manages the incursions of feminine

unrule if we examine a passage that is remarkably similar to the one leading up to his decision to divorce in *The Dream of the Golden Mountain*.
In the section of *Exile's Return* entitled "The City of Anger," Cowley
describes his return to New York after two years in France and his and
his fellow "exiles'" attempts to "readjust . . . [themselves] to this once
familiar environment" (182). After a few references to the conjugal "we"
that disembarks and to the attempt "with my wife" to "redecorate our
flat in Dominck Street," Cowley's narrative abandons Peggy Cowley to
focus on his attempts "with [Matthew] Josephson, [Ramon] Guthrie and
a few others [to reproduce] in New York the conditions that had seemed
so congenial to us abroad, and [to continue] to appreciate and praise the
picturesque American qualities of the Machine Age and the New Economic Era while living under their shadow" (183–84). Their amateur,
futile attempts to sustain the journal *Broom* and the tempest in a teapot
surrounding Ernest Boyd's caricature, "Esthete: Model 1924," in the first
issue of the *American Mercury* combine with intragenerational quibbling
and general poverty to leave Cowley "dispirited, exhausted, licked." In
defeat, he retreats to a friend's unheated shack in Woodstock, New York,
where they spend a long weekend freezing, drinking, and courting the
muse. Upon his return to New York, he finds himself locked out of his
apartment. After breaking down the door, he discovers two men who
have been sitting there in the dark and drinking for about as long as
he has been away. To his question "Where's Peggy?" they answer, "She
went out. Frances insulted Peggy and went out too. She went out last
Monday." Giving up on receiving any coherent information about his
wife's whereabouts, Cowley goes upstairs to his room:

> The room was cold, not like Bill's shack in the country, but like a
> sealed tomb. . . . I found my notebook, filled a fountain pen, and
> began to write a letter: "My dear Malcolm . . . it would be wise
> to admit that you . . . cannot, while working for Sweet's Cata-
> logue Service, Inc., be editor, free lance, boon companion, literary
> polemist. Instead you must confine yourself to essentials: think-
> ing, reading, conversation, writing, livelihood, in about the order
> named. At this moment you must strip yourself of everything
> inessential to these aims; and especially of the functions of editor,
> free lance, drinking companion, and literary polemist. You must

arrange your life against interruptions; you must sleep, exercise, earn your living and pass the other moments beneath a lamp or talking. Too many excitements: at this moment you are tired and discouraged. . . . You have left the stage and you did not even bow . . ." (209–10)

In *The Dream of the Golden Mountains*, Cowley surveys the disorder of his surroundings and decides to change them; here, he resolves to change himself. Certainly, eight additional years of living in the midst of his wife's version of a movable feast must have strained a tolerance that, in 1924, retained some resiliency. But the difference between the two *texts* has also to do with the different ways they stage women. In *The Dream of the Golden Mountain*, women are introduced in order to designate the other side of the boundary inscribing the public realm of normative bourgeois masculinity and the work performed under its aegis; the women who are made visible in the text make it clear why this boundary is necessary, while the women whose existence is indicated but who do not achieve representation—Muriel Maurer Cowley is the prime example of such a woman—testify to its efficacy once it is in place. In *Exile's Return*, women share and participate in the world in which men work. While they cannot be expected to self-efface like midwestern housewives, they must be marked as "inessential" so that the men can confine themselves "to essentials: thinking, reading, conversation, writing, livelihood"; the man who finds his house a mess must be able to put domestic matters behind him and rededicate himself to the pursuit of what matters even if he cannot rely upon his wife to clean up.[12]

Exile's Return strives to represent the world of culture as an all-male world. The irrelevance of women to this world is best documented, of course, by marking their omnipresence as essentially negative and in opposition to the pursuit of culture. Thus, for instance, Cowley signals the end of the self-indulgent and debauched "long furlough" following his return from service in the First World War in the following manner:

It couldn't go on for ever. Some drizzly morning late in April *you woke up to find yourself married (and your wife, perhaps, suffering from a dry cough that threatened consumption)*. If there had been checks from home, there would be no more of them. Or else it happened after a siege of influenza, which that year had curious effects: it left you weak in body, clear in mind, revolted by humanity and yourself. . . . There was no army now to clothe and feed you like a kind-hateful parent. No matter where the next meal came from, you would pay for it yourself. (59–60, emphasis added)

This is Cowley's first reference to his first wife; marriage is represented here not as an act of desire or of the will, but as something that happens when one is not in full possession of one's faculties and whose consequences—physical weakness, moral revulsion, and time wasted—like those of the flu, need to be minimized.[13] Marriage is but one more element of the crisis faced by every young man after the war when he realizes that the fun is over. Its antidote is a high-minded rededication to the role of breadwinner, the pursuit of high culture, and the society of men devoted to it.

Cowley's marriage to the woman whose "dry cough that threatened consumption" recalled him from his postwar flirtation with irresponsibility brought him closer to the women's movement than he acknowledges anywhere. Hans Bak writes that Peggy Baird "sided with many of the causes championed by the New Women," was imprisoned and brutalized along with other representatives of the National Women's Party for picketing the White House in 1917, and was one of the first Village women to bob her hair. Although not a radical feminist, she "mocked conventional notions of femininity [and] insisted on a woman's right to economic independence" (126).[14] Cowley never mentions his wife's feminism; nor does he ever really take a stand for or against the emancipation of women, that part of the prewar bohemian agenda that he describes as "women [claiming to be] the moral and economic equals of men. They should have the same pay, the same working conditions, the same opportunities for drinking, smoking, taking or dismissing lovers" (ER 70). But his examples of the kinds of equality the women's movement demanded, as well as the images he uses to describe the popularization and commercialization of Greenwich Village values and mores, suggest that he considered the growing social and political equality of women to be one of the obstacles to real cultural development in the United States in the period after the war and prior to his expatriation in the early twenties. If cultural work is what men do (and if smoking, drinking, and taking and dismissing lovers are the perquisites of men's work) and women seem to be doing everything that men do, then the existence of a world of unadulteratedly male cultural work seems seriously threatened. This, of course, is a version of Stearns's argument, but it is a superficial version that foregrounds the personal fears of the young aspirants to culture rather than the kind of critical—and self-critical—awareness of the long and troubled intellectual tradition we see in Stearns.

Cowley criticizes the superficiality of "Bohemia's" commitment to culture ("Bohemia is Grub Street romanticized, doctrinalized and rendered self-conscious; it is Grub Street on parade" [ER 65]) and traces the loosening of morals during and after the First World War and the trickling down of Greenwich Village bohemian mores into the *Saturday Evening Post*-reading strata of the American population: "[Greenwich Village] was dying of success. . . . It was dying because women smoked cigarettes on the streets of the Bronx, drank gin cocktails in Omaha and had perfectly swell parties in Seattle and Middletown" (76). Although Cowley will go on to conclude that "American business and the whole of middle-class America had been going Greenwich Village," the examples he uses above represent "going Greenwich Village" as essentially a mode of degeneration and feminization, a kind of carnevalization of an originally serious cultural critique that has given midwestern and suburban women—people like "Mother"—license to indulge in the dissipations he and his cohorts considered characteristic of male intellectual life in New York.

While the world from which he came was indulging in sins made in Bohemia, the Greenwich Village to which Cowley and his generation returned after the war was in crisis. We recall Stearns's account of the traumatic experience of remaining a civilian during the First World War in *The Street I Know*. Cowley, too, sees the war as representing a watershed for Stearns's generation of Greenwich Village radicals. Whereas, in the early 1910s, social and political rebellion (what he calls "bohemianism") and the revolt against capitalism ("radicalism") went hand in hand, fought the same causes, and wore the same uniforms, the war forced people "to decide what kind of rebels they were." While bohemianism and the trappings of its way of life had survived the war, "almost all of the radicals of 1917 were defeated by events" that left "the Village . . . full of former people" (ER 77): "To stay in New York during the

War was a greater moral strain than to enter the army: there were more decisions to be made and uneasily justified; also there were defeats to be concealed" (81). This passage would suggest some kind of sympathy for such figures as Stearns, who also represents the decision to oppose the war and steer clear of the army as an excruciating one. But, instead of sympathizing with them, Cowley emasculates them. He concludes that postwar Greenwich Village was "empty of young men." In other words, all the men left in the Village were old men, if, indeed, they were still men at all: "Nobody seemed to be doing anything, now, except lamenting the time's decay" (78).

Having killed off the fathers, even those a scant seven years his senior, Cowley and his generation still faced—and at least Cowley himself married into—a generation of Greenwich Village women whose battles were not "former battles" and who were not as easily written off as Stearns and his coterie of "former" men. While a younger generation of women—represented in Cowley's narrative by an unnamed Radcliffe graduate who bites people in the arm and breaks a great Chinese vase at the Liberal Club dance of 1917 before going on to seek an abortionist, marry, and have a baby—appear in the Village, make a scene, and disappear back to domesticity in the suburbs and the Midwest, the older women seem to have survived both the war and the influx of frivolity. They terrify Cowley: "The women had evolved a regional costume . . . hair cut in a Dutch bob, hat carried at the side, a smock of some bright fabric, . . . a skirt rather shorter than the fashion of the day, gray cotton stockings and sandals. With heels set firmly on the ground and abdomens a little protruding—since they wore no corsets and dieting hadn't become popular—they had a look of unexampled solidity; it was terrifying to be advanced upon by six of them in close formation" (ER 80). Those who don't wear the uniform sport either "tight-fitting tailored suits with Buster Brown collars," a five-gallon hat, or riding boots and a crop (80). In other words, the women are all feminists or dykes or both. The comparison Cowley uses to sum up the prewar generation's rebellion—"they had slammed doors like Nora in A Doll's House" (81–82)—suggests that its spirit of engaged dissent is a feminine, even feminist, one—one, in fact, that will leave husband and children behind to pursue its ends.

Here, Cowley unwittingly joins Stearns's critique of American intellectual life as engaged and, hence, feminized, although while Stearns is criticizing the quality and limits of intellectual discourse, Cowley directs his scorn at those who practice what the intellectuals preach. Each, although for entirely different reasons, regards a position of "disengagement" to be superior to what both regard as the feminized scramble for reform. Whereas Stearns points to the limits of a pragmatic "feminized" American intellectual life—as opposed to reformist activities themselves—in order to champion the intellectual ideals of "introspection, contemplation, or scrupulous adherence to logical sequence [that w]omen do not hesitate to call . . . cold, impersonal, indirect" (*Civilization* 145), Cowley represents himself as wary of the reformist activities themselves: "We couldn't see much use in crusading against Puritanism: it had ceased to interfere with our personal lives and, though it seemed to be triumphant, it had suffered a moral defeat and would slowly disappear. Female equality was a good idea, perhaps, but the feminists we knew wore spectacles and flat-heeled shoes" (*ER* 83–84). The intellectual case against Puritanism might be no more than the unnecessary flogging of an old, if not dead, horse, but the spectacle of women in "spectacles and flat-heeled shoes" assumes an "unexampled solidity" of its own and seems to represent a source of considerable discomfort to the "disinterested" persona that Cowley is in the process of constructing. Cowley does not seem to think that the "terrifying" Village women will follow the example of Puritanism's moral defeat and eventual disappearance; the language and affect with which he describes them suggests that he regards them as an impediment to the pursuit of unexceptional normality, which he projects as his generation's answer to the old Villagers' rebellions.

It is important to remember that, prior to his expatriation, Cowley lived in the same world as Stearns. For all his equivocation about the boundaries between one "generation" and the other, the "old Villagers" worked for the same journals and publishers and frequented the same establishments as the new. In Cowley's case, the "generations" intermarried. Indeed, Peggy Baird Cowley, under her first married name, Peggy Johns, is listed as a member of Stearns's clique in his rehearsal of his "typical Bohemian existence" (*Street* 126). Furthermore, it was Peggy's close friendship with Clarence Britten, whom Stearns appointed as his assistant during his stint as editor of the *Dial*, that secured Cowley his first paid writing assignments. The distinctions Cowley draws between the Greenwich Village generations thus often seem to be distinctions without a difference, unless, of course, the creation of the difference is the point of making the distinction. What is at stake for "the young men" in whose name he speaks is the relegation of the "old"—along with that of the decadent—to the realm of the feminine. Long before they achieve distinction, the "new," cynical, disabused, "young men" distinguish themselves through their disengagement from the social and political passions of their "elders" and the single-minded pursuit of literary distinction that exile in Europe will authorize.

VI

Never in any national sense having had leisure, as individuals we
do not know what to do with it when good fortune gives it to us.
Unlike a real game, we must go on playing *our* game even after we
have won.

—HAROLD STEARNS, "The Intellectual Life"

If *The Street I Know* represents a New York life devoted to intellectual matters and an "exile" in Paris during which these matters are neglected, if not forgotten, *Exile's Return* represents something of the opposite trajectory. Prior to the sections that deal with Cowley's sojourn in France and his return to Greenwich Village, *Exile's Return* focuses on the experiences and general socio-intellectual passions of the Lost Generation as well as the ambient atmosphere of ideas in which it developed. Although Cowley's letters and the two biographical studies devoted to his early life document significant writerly production and intellectual development during the years that led up to his "exile," *Exile's Return* gives the impression of a young man trying out personae, hustling for work, and looking for a set of circumstances in which to begin work that other evidence tells us had clearly already begun.[15] Such a presentation heightens the reader's impression that the real life of Cowley's mind began when he and his generation returned to Europe "to recover the good life and the traditions of art, to free themselves from organized stupidity, to win their deserved place in the hierarchy of the intellect" (91). *Exile's Return* would fall short of its mission, of course, if it represented the "exiles" as having found what they sought in Europe. Cowley's near pun, "Having come in search of values, they found valuta," (91) is, however, a cheap and inadequate introduction to the process through which the young intellectuals discovered, from the perspective of Europe and armed with some of the intellectual practices of the Old World, an America worthy of their talents, ambitions, and pretensions and gained the conviction that they were "men of letters" worth of its advocacy.

In taking up the issues of poetic form, of the relation of the artist to society, and of art's dual responsibility to the world and to itself—all issues that had occupied Cowley since his Harvard years—only after the Lost Generation had taken up exile in Europe, *Exile's Return* enacts in its structure, if not in its substance, the received ideas about America's inability to nurture native talent and Europe's hospitality to serious thought and art. Since in its substance, it traces the process through which, between 1920 and 1930—the expatriate decade—America came to be regarded as a land capable of high culture, it enforces Cowley's claim that the exiles of the 1920s "played their part" in this change. As he tells it, Europe gives the exiles exactly what they needed: "They had merely to travel, compare, evaluate and honestly record what they saw. In the midst of this process the burden of inferiority somehow disappeared—it was not so much dropped as it leaked away like sand from a bag carried on the shoulder—suddenly it was gone and nobody noticed the difference" (*ER* 106). This process, as seemingly passive as marriage in Cowley's representation ("you wake up to find yourself married"), is, in fact, its obverse and antidote. Instead of culminating in a pathology requiring therapy, it reveals to the young Americans that they are not, after all, inferior, or even all that different: "They decided that all nations were fairly equal . . . [the Americans] were simply a nation among the other capitalist West European nations. Having registered this impression, the exiles were ready to find that their own nation had every attribute they had been taught to admire in those of Europe" (106).

The "voyage of discovery" on which the "exiles were preparing to embark" was thus less the *tour d'Europe* than a preparation for their *re-tour*, in which, "standing as it were on the Tour Eiffel, they looked southwestward across the wheatfields of Beauce and the rain-drenched little hills of Brittany, until somewhere in the mist they saw the country of their childhood, which should henceforth be the country of their art" (*ER* 107). At this distance, the "landscape of their childhood" is a vista rather than an appeal. The emotional material that makes for the ambivalence of this landscape has no place among the "ideas which the exiles . . . carried duty-free across the Atlantic" (108). Without the specters of "Mother" and feminization that constitute the tax that talent has to pay to dignity in America, "American themes . . . had exactly the dignity that talent could lend them" (107). In what they were able to perceive as the all-male world of European letters, the exiles set out to construct the intellectual personae whose dignity was commensurate with their sense of their own talent.

This dignity, rather than any particular intellectual or cultural content, is what the Lost Generation found—or rather, constructed for itself—in Europe. Fleeing a country where the association of intellectual activity with feminization was a commonplace and where women's ubiquity in the intellectual and political worlds he inhabited threatened the persona he was in the process of constructing, Cowley interpolates himself and his ideas into what he represents as a monolithically male European intellectual landscape in which a crisis of gender, however present, was not present to him.[16] The first thing Cowley represents himself as doing after his arrival in Europe is composing an essay entitled "This Youngest Generation." Written for an American audience, the essay declares the exiles' allegiance to the tenets of literary modernism ("form, simplification, strangeness, respect for literature as an art with traditions, abstractness") that Cowley sees as having derived from the French intellectual and literary tradition: "Certainly the French influence is acting on us today; there remains to be seen just what effect it will bring forth" (ER 111). Once he immerses himself in his host country's culture, the process of intellectual repatriation begins in earnest. Not only does the French admiration for an America whose "picturesque, surprising, dramatic, swift, exuberant, vigorous, 'original'" qualities fulfill their "esthetic standards of judgment" (115, 114) cause him to begin reevaluating his critique of his native country; the exiles' experience of the realities of Europe teach them that "America is just as God-damned good as Europe—worse in some ways, better in others" (119).

It is, however, not simply the lesson of cultural relativity that sends Cowley and his cohorts back to America with an enhanced sense of American culture as a viable and livable reality. The experience of Dada, of artists and intellectuals boldly and legitimately acting like a boisterous group of fun- and mischief-loving boys without doubting for a moment their status as men, gives Cowley and his contemporaries the confidence to return to America and arbitrate its cultural future. In the survey of potential literary role models that occupies the central section of his account of his European sojourn, Cowley assesses the achievements and limitations of the great modernist writers of the preceding generation. He rejects the aestheticism and contempt for the "real world" and correspondingly effete personae of T. S. Eliot ("We should continue to honor Eliot's poems, and the integrity, and clearness of his prose, but . . . we didn't agree with the idea that . . . the present is inferior to the past" [*ER* 128, 125]); James Joyce ("He had achieved genius . . . but there was something about that genius as inhuman and cold as the touch at parting of his long, cold, wet-marble fingers" [132]); Marcel Proust ("We had neither the wish nor the financial resources nor yet the intellectual resources to shut ourselves in cork-lined chambers and examine our memories" [133–34]); and Paul Valéry ("the thinking man . . . does nothing, desires nothing, occupies no position, is almost completely cut off from society" [139]). Cowley then turns his attention to his French contemporaries, the practitioners of Dada, whose vitality, love of literature, and fascination with things American struck him as the "very essence of Paris . . . young and adventurous, and human" (145).

Cowley's infatuation with Dada accommodates his ambivalence toward what he calls the "religion of art," which he traces from Gautier and Flaubert, through the "Parnassians, the Decadents, the Symbolists" to "the Post-Impressionists, the Cubists, . . . the Neo-Classicists, the Fantaisists" (*ER* 148–49), since Dada, by carrying the tendencies inherent in this tradition "to an extreme," also constitutes a critical commentary on them. As the summary last hiccough of nineteenth-century aestheticisms, Dada tried to uphold the artist's "feeling of liberty . . . from the old artistic mediums" at a time when "everything was said, everything written . . . all the great subjects of poetry and fiction had been seized upon by others, exploited and rendered unusable" (160–61). Cowley concludes that for all its energy and ambition, Dada was dying even as it came into life. Thus introduced, Dada represents an exuberant preparation for whatever artistic, moral, or political commitments its practitioners might adopt in something more closely resembling their adulthood. Its combustibility allows a basically conservative sensibility such as his own to flirt with "adventure" without having to take serious literary responsibility for it. Engagement with Dada promised the thrill of high seriousness, a kind of "duty-free" immersion in the very foreign cultural element Cowley had set out to find in Europe, and, most importantly, the experience of a male artistic persona and a mode of male artistic camaraderie that was contemptuously innocent of the associations of the intellectual life with femininity that overshadowed the American cultural scene.[17]

The Dadaists' mode of existing as artists in the world endears them to Cowley. Although he claims that "Dada, in art and life was the extreme of individualism" (*ER* 158), his representation of Dada "in life" foregrounds its importance to him as a group: he is inspired by its rivalries, energies, manifestoes, spectacles, and "indifference" to the criticism it provokes and spellbound by its ability to absorb and accommodate the intoxications of a group of American literati in search of legitimation. There is a strong element of identification in this description of "a group of young men probably the most talented in Europe: there was not one of them who lacked the ability to become a good writer or, if he so decided, a very popular writer" (162). Unlike their Ivy League counterparts, whom Cowley has described in much the same manner, these "poor young men of middle-class families with their way to make" (164–65) suffer from an embarrassment of cultural riches: "They had behind them the long traditions of French literature (and knew them perfectly); they had the examples of living masters (and had pondered them); they had a burning love of their art and a fury to excel" (162). Cowley's description of his French contemporaries foregrounds his sense of their sense of their integration in their society. If they are rebels, they rebel against a social and cultural fabric that recognizes the meaningfulness of their gestures even if it dismisses or despises their meanings. Their choice to remain at the margins of their society's cultural elite depends upon the existence of a cultural elite worth opposing and implies the central role that would be available to them were they less unwilling to compromise their ideals.

Furthermore, the "young men" of Dada appear untroubled by any questions regarding the gender of their pursuit. They are not a group of "young people" who just happen to be "young men"; there is no room for women as cultural agents in Cowley's portrait of Dada and no question of this situation representing a problem for anyone. Over and over again, the artistic, cultural, and social attitudes of the Dadaists are epitomized by their treatment of "their" women. Cowley introduces André Breton's élan and his Dada entourage in the following manner: "Breton, their present *chef d'école* had discovered a play of which he approved. At least he was not half-hearted in his approval, and he brought along his twenty friends with their wives and mistresses" (*ER* 144). The "twenty friends" are unmistakably male; their "wives and mistresses" are mentioned to underscore and decorate this fact.[18] Among the Dadaists, women don't have to be written out of the scenario, because, at least in Cowley's view of things, they have and make no claims to be written in. Note, for example, Cowley's account of weekend visits from the Dadaists: "Tzara came to visit us with a pretty American girl who smoked sixty cigarettes a day to the great profit of the French government tobacco monopoly, while Tzara made puns, invented games and innocently changed the rules for fear of losing. And sometimes . . . all of André Breton's friends arrived on Sundays, a whole performing troupe of Dadaists with their mistresses or wives. They were very serious, angry young men, on principle, but they laughed a great deal" (168).

The reader must assume that the "us" at the beginning of this passage refers to Cowley and his wife, although, with the exception of a few references to "we," she has disappeared from the narrative since disembarkation. Cowley has no such need to efface his French friends' female companions; a chain-smoking American girl might need to be put in her place, but, as in the passage above, the "wives and mistresses" of Breton's friends seem part of a set piece in which they know their place and do not challenge it. The moral economy to which this gender economy gives rise becomes clear in Cowley's description of the "moral . . . fashion" he acquired from his Dada friends: "A writer *could steal, murder, drink or be sober, lie to his friends or with their wives* . . . but my tolerance did not extend to his writing, from which I demanded high courage, absolute integrity, and a sort of intelligence that was in itself a moral quality" (*ER* 170, emphasis added). The cute turn of phrase notwithstanding, it articulates more than simply a man's unswerving allegiance to the integrity of his art that tolerates all but aesthetic crimes; it inscribes the writer's "friends" as invariably male (otherwise he could not refer to their "wives" so unreservedly) and enforces a double standard in which men are the instance in relation to which morality is measured: if lying to one's friends endangers the bond of friendship, lying "with their wives" is equally a matter between men, at least to the extent that it represents a moral issue.

The same untroubled division of the aesthetic and moral worlds along gender lines appears in Cowley's characterization of his "master," Aragon, in a letter to Kenneth Burke that he cites in *Exile's Return*: "He proclaims himself a romantic. In practice this means that his attitude toward women is abominable: he is either reciting poetry, which soon ceases to interest them, or trying to sleep with them, which they say becomes equally monotonous. He is always seriously in love; he never philanders. . . . He is an egoist and vain, but faithful to his friends" (172). Although Cowley's letters and poetry of the period document Aragon's influence on his writing, what he emphasizes here is the Frenchman's influence on his pose and attitude. This man, who, for all his interest in women, doesn't deign to interest them, indulges his heterosexuality as part of the spectacle that is himself. Cowley's distinction, "but faithful to his friends," tells us, of course, more about the characterizer than the characterized: as in the passages above, Cowley sees a man's "friends" as occupying a different moral universe than his "women."

Cowley's composite portrait of the Dadaists and their importance to him can be summarized in the following sentence, in which he describes Aragon's contemptuous behavior toward the French cultural establishment: "He retains all that hatred of compromise which is the attribute of youth—and of a type of youth we never wholly possessed" (*ER* 172). The rose-colored glasses through which Cowley regards Aragon allow him to see his "master" as uncompromised by the tribute the American exiles have had to pay to youth. Rooted in a French culture he is free to accept or not at will, Aragon inhabits a cultural present that does not exist for Americans, who are caught between their nostalgia for a past they consider unusable and their responsibility for a future that, at the beginning of the American Century, is being attributed to them proleptically. It is in the context of such considerations that the "significant gesture" with which Cowley takes leave of France needs to be read: on Bastille Day, 1923, he was arrested for punching the proprietor of the Café de la Rotonde, a suspected "stool-pigeon," in the jaw and was bailed out by influential French (male) friends accompanied by "nine young [American] ladies in evening gowns [who had not] been present at the scene in the Rotonde the night before" (178). This event represents his—unwittingly but supremely "American"—application of the "youth" he borrows from his French mentors and the yield of their sexual politics.

The Cowley who writes *Exile's Return* in 1934 is aware of the incommensurability of the gesture with which his younger avatar brazens his way into the lore of Montparnasse and the cultural baggage it was meant to carry at the time, but he remains sympathetic to the exile's desire to put compromise behind, to perform at least one manly gesture in the name of culture, and to become, with this "unusual" and typically American act ("French writers rarely came to blows . . . they placed a high value on my unusual action") something of a local hero.[19] Although he is sophisticated enough to suggest some kind of retrospective distance between himself and the "young man" who slugged the proprietor, he cannot entirely play down either the prominence he enjoyed or his enjoyment of it: "Years later . . . I realized that . . . I had performed an act to which all [the Dadaists'] favorite catchwords could be applied. First of all, I had acted for reasons of public morality; bearing no private grudge against my victim, I had been *disinterested*. I had committed an *indiscretion*, acted with *violence* and *disdain* for the law, performed an *arbitrary* and *significant gesture*, uttered a *manifesto*; in their opinion I had shown *courage*. . . . For the first time in my life, I became a public character" (*ER* 179). Cowley's act of insolence represents what he describes as his entrée into cultural Europe: he is interviewed, his articles are solicited by Dada publications throughout Europe, his stories translated into Hungarian and German, and his poems published in Soviet magazines.

This same gesture, however, initiates Cowley's return to America in August 1923. The subject matter of the poems he publishes in Moscow is one "that had been arousing the enthusiasm of Soviet" and other European writers: "They were poems about America, poems that spoke of movies and skyscrapers and machines, dwelling upon them with all the nostalgia derived from two long years of exile. I, too, was enthusiastic over America; I had learned from a distance to admire its picturesque qualities" (*ER* 179). Cowley's integration into the European cultural scene to which he has been aspiring and his affectation of European high culture's fascination with the American popular culture he had always scorned effect his transition back to the United States. The passage continues: "And I was returning to New York with a set of values that bore no relation to American life, with convictions that could not fail to be misunderstood in a country where Dada was hardly a name, and moral judgments on literary matters were thought to be in questionable taste" (179–80).

Here, Cowley sounds uncannily like the Harold Stearns of 1921, extolling America's energy and potential while excoriating its cultural reality. The difference, of course, is that he has borrowed his perspective and his sense of entitlement from his European friends. His account of his return will have to demonstrate how, by mobilizing this sense of entitlement as he abandons his European perspective for a genuinely American one (and, I might add, replaces the European fascination with American popular culture with his earlier contempt for it), Cowley positions himself to write *Exile's Return*.[20]

VII

Or if we are so fortunate as to be "regular" Americans instead of
unhappy intellectuals educated beyond our environment, we go
gratefully back to our work at the office.
        —HAROLD STEARNS, "The Intellectual Life"

I have already traced the process of return through which Cowley repositions himself in an American cultural landscape halfway between the city—which remains the locus of cultural production and where, as Stearns's texts make clear, women are as active as ever in worlds abutting Cowley's—and the mythic rural landscape that continues to inspire him ideologically and rhetorically.[21] It remains to take stock of how Stearns and his text of return intervene critically in Cowley's reading of himself and his times. Although it is clear that, in some ways, Stearns represents Cowley's quintessential expatriate "crack up," his example is not one that supports the story that Cowley has set out to tell: it is Harry Crosby whose life maps out this trajectory in *Exile's Return*. Clearly, Cowley needed to summarize the ultimately self-destructive energies of the 1920s with a figure that ratified his own experience of the First World War and whose drive toward extinction consummated itself with the decade. Stearns's tortured opposition to American involvement in the war disqualifies him from membership in Cowley's generation; indeed, it casts

Cowley's courtship of its sensations in a critical light that history has, perhaps, harshened. While Stearns's Parisian abjection—his drunkenness, his filthiness, his money-making ruses, and his abandonment of high culture for the racetrack—functions in Cowley's construction as the other side of the boundary that constitutes his Lost Generation, his self-resurrection threatens to deconstruct the system that enforced that boundary. It thus serves far less readily than Crosby's demise the purpose of dramatizing the forces particular to the twenties, Cowley's mastery of them, and their inviability beyond the decade. Indeed, Stearns's autobiography and its emphasis on the individual rather than the representative in a human life might even suggest that Crosby's story is just one of many, idiosyncratic, more-or-less-spectacular personal dramas that Cowley has borrowed and rendered exemplary for the purposes of his "narrative of ideas."[22] Certainly, Crosby's adulterous *Liebestod* is a more fitting obituary to Cowley's saga of the 1920s than is Stearns's paean to the American working woman. Moreover, Stearns's American application of the lessons he learned while watching the French be French and his eagerness to take on, however critically, the spectacle and implications of democratic mass culture retain, in the imaginary of Cowley's American cultural elite, a taint of the "feminine" incompatible with the high seriousness of the latter's literary and political commitments.[23] Most of all, however, it is Stearns's brand of critical self-knowledge, his exposure of the personal motives within and behind the grand narratives of cultural history, and the "liberal" suspicion with which he regards left- as well as right-wing radicalism that deconstruct the kind of master narrative that Cowley needs *Exile's Return* to be.

When Stearns's expatriate fellow-drinkers snickered, "There goes American civilization" when they encountered him "hanging on the bar like a crook handled cane" (Ford 112), they were, through denial, speaking for themselves.[24] What Stearns represents in and for the history of the American male intellectual in the first thirty years of the twentieth century explains why Cowley must take such pains to discredit him. In her discussion of abjection, Judith Butler stresses how the repudiation of the "'unlivable' and 'uninhabitable' zones of social life" designated as abject serves to "circumscribe the domain of the subject" and constitutes "the defining limit of the subject's domain." Such scapegoating is not accomplished in one act; it must be performed repeatedly in order that the border between the willed self-constitution and its designated Other be maintained, that the abject be kept in its place: "This disavowed abjection will threaten to expose the self-grounding presumptions of the . . . subject, grounded as that subject is in a repudiation whose consequences it cannot fully control" (3). The power of Stearns's figure—and its power to disrupt the hegemony of Cowley's narrative—are affirmed by Cowley's repeated repudiation of it; "Young Mr. Elkins" and the portrait of Stearns in "Three Americans in Paris" are no more able fully to discredit Stearns's centrality to the intellectual history Cowley is telling than was Stearns himself, whose decade-long attempt to abject himself can be read as an attempt to ratify, through self-exclusion, the American culture he excoriated. Stearns came to realize that he was, for better or for worse, inextricable from that culture and that his survival depended upon his acknowledgment of his relation to it, however deadly or merely disappointing that relation might be. Similarly, his figure and what it reveals—through both its self-knowledge and its blindness—about American culture is inextricable from the self-conscious intellectual "generation" that would found itself upon a repudiation of him.[25]

When Cowley returned to New York from France in 1923, he was repelled by the skyscrapers that had fascinated him at a distance. The accommodation to the reality of America that is *Exile's Return* involves the construction of a persona and a geography within America that is never quite *of* what he too clearly perceives the country to be. By the time Stearns returned in the midst of the Depression, Cowley was ensconced in the editorial offices of the *New Republic*, whence, according to Alfred Kazin, "not knowing what to do for the hungry faces waiting to see him, [he] would sell the books there was no space to review and dole out the proceeds among the more desperate cases haunting him for review assignments" (15–16). Kazin's portrait of Cowley coincides exactly with Cowley's own self-portrait, and it reveals either how completely he had, by 1934, succeeded in occupying the persona he was in the process of canonizing in *Exile's Return* or how totally *Exile's Return* colors the memories of those who knew Cowley in the 1930s:

> This kindliness was also a conscious symbol of the times. Cowley
> had been at Harvard in the time of Dos Passos, he had left Har-
> vard in 1917 for service in an American ambulance unit in the

time of E.E. Cummings, he had drunk in Paris with Hemingway, had ought the *flics* with Aragon, had walked the Village with Hart Crane. Just as he now lived in Connecticut (and *Exile's Return* noted when writers began moving from Greenwich Village to Connecticut), so he was unable to lift his pipe to his mouth, or to make a crack, without making one feel that he recognized the literary situation involved. He seemed always to have moved in the company of writers, literary movements, *cénacles*, to see history in terms of what writers had thought and how they had lived. When in his book he recounted his memories of the Dôme and the Select, hinting at the real names of the characters in *The Sun Also Rises*, I had an image of Malcolm Cowley as a passenger in the great polished coach that was forever taking young Harvard poets to war, to the Left Bank, to the Village, to Connecticut. Wherever Cowley moved or ate, wherever he lived, he heard the bell of literary history sounding the moment and his own voice calling possibly another change in the literary weather. (16)

If Cowley set out to construct the exemplary literary life, Kazin ratifies the edifice, alluding to the "real names of the characters in *The Sun Also Rises*" without uttering them, homogenizing the "company of writers, literary movements, *cénacles*" and celebrating the "great polished coach" that transported potential makers of culture through the hardships of their *Lehrjahre* to an aerie whence, between their sallies into the world of radical politics, they "radiated ease and sophistication" (17).

Unlike Cowley, Stearns was thrilled with the skyscrapers, technical innovations, and urban scenario that greeted him upon his return. Indeed, his documents of exile and return embody and invoke everything that gets left out of the "great polished coach" shuttling back and forth between the townhouse just north of Greenwich Village that housed the offices of the *New Republic* and the farmhouse in Connecticut where Cowley ensconced his "new and final wife" and their son. If the words that the young Cowley "bridled and saddled" enabled him to escape the confines of his mother's world of muted colors and thwarted ambition, "[riding] off with a tight rein at a steady trot," these words now pull the "great polished coach" of institutionalized progressive high culture in America. The vehicle in which he "came back and paid [his] debts one day" is, thus, powered by the medium of his escape and survival. But, as I hope the reading of "A Prayer on All Saints' Eve" with which I began this chapter has shown, he returns too late for any yield other than the satisfaction of having memorialized his mother in a poem about his own decrepitude. This is, of course, a version of the abjection that so revolted him in Stearns and that his "intellectual odyssey" so deftly circumnavigates. But, like the inland territory to whose baffled inhabitants Odysseus must present "a winnowing oar" before he can return home to await a gentle death, such abjection has always been a feature on Cowley's map, albeit one from which he has turned away in a disgust masquerading as moral disapproval, cultural sanction, or incomprehension. It turns out, however, to be a destination he must reach before what he returns to can really be called "home." As Cowley already knew when he wrote "The Urn," an exile's return can never be anything but a figure for a return that has been rendered impossible and unaffordable by the terms and the price of the ticket.

In *The Street I Know*, Harold Stearns tells the story of how, shortly after his return from Europe, Evan Shipman's mother, "a landscape architect of considerable distinction," offered him the use of the office facilities in her home in Beekman Place, where, "when her own work was finished," he could write undisturbed. "She also said that dinner would be served me there, too, so that the rather peculiar hours ought to prove no barrier—a graceful way of doing something nice for somebody without 'rubbing in' . . . their temporary hard luck" (378). He describes an evening when, unable to write, he watched the "evening boat to Boston [pass] by up towards Hell Gate and the Sound" (381) while he spoke to his mother on the telephone for what would turn out to be the last time. This passage invokes irreversible loss and real homelessness and disjunction at the same time as it commemorates the "good-will and neighborliness and decency" among generations and genders that fan the flame of his will to "survive." Like the text of which it is part, it represents the American intellectual as determined by and torn between the seemingly irreconcilable personal and professional demands to which his writing must answer. It is this kind of resolutely personal history, this kind of quintessentially American narrative that Malcolm Cowley needed to write out of his account of an exile's return in order to canonize his generation and steer the course of its "intellectual odyssey."

CHAPTER FOUR

Everybody's Autobiography

The Remaking of an American

> It is queer the use of that word, native always means people who belong somewhere else, because they had once belonged somewhere.
>
> —*Everybody's Autobiography*

*E*VERYBODY'S AUTOBIOGRAPHY (1937) celebrates two homecomings, one to America and a subsequent one to France. In 1934, in the wake of the success of *The Autobiography of Alice B. Toklas* and after an absence of thirty years, Gertrude Stein embarked on an extensive lecture tour of the United States. Stein's return to America is the central event in *Everybody's Autobiography*, and the text's record of her visit to her "native land" does, like *The American Scene*, explore the shocks—what she calls the "shocks of recognition and nonrecognition" (*EA* 180)—experienced by the native confronted by a society and a landscape rendered strange through distance and time. In her "Meditations on being about to visit my native land," written just before her departure in 1934, Stein articulates concerns that recall the agenda that James set for himself prior to his 1904 repatriation:

> I cannot believe that America has changed, many things have come and gone but not really come and not really gone but they are there and that perhaps does make the America that I left and the America I am to find different but not really different, it would be impossible for it to be really different or for me to find that it was really different.
>
> I wonder and ask everybody who has been in America or who comes from America what they eat and the answers make it sound a little different but not really very different. It will be nice so very nice if it is not really different. . . .

Twenty-five years roll around so quickly even when they do not seem to be rolling around at all.

And now I am going back to visit my native land. It may not mean so much to anybody but it does mean a lot to me and I feel gradually a pleasant pleasure both near and far away. ("Meditations" 1)

Stein, like James, anticipates a highly significant encounter with a "native land" whose changes both tantalize and give rise to apprehension. Yet the titles of the texts that document the two authors' reencounters with the United States, *The American Scene*, on the one hand, and *Everybody's Autobiography*, on the other hand, signal the ways in which they differ. Where James set out to render America, and in so doing wrote a text that we now read as autobiography, Stein's text, announcing itself as autobiography, uses the occasion of a tour of America as the occasion for its ruminations on Gertrude Stein, Americans, and "everybody." In the "Meditations," Stein stresses her anticipation not only of the spectacle of America but also of her interaction with Americans: "I am being so very busy in being about to visit my native land that I have not been meditating not meditating very much but if I were not so busy and were to meditate I would meditate a great deal and I would and in a way do meditate upon *what they are to say to me and what I am to say to them those who make in my native land my native land. What will they say to me and what will I say to them*" ("Meditations" 1–2, emphasis added). If James's goal in returning to and writing about America was to ratify the title of "Master" through subjecting his native land to the discipline of his representational strategies, Stein was far more concerned with the dialogue with America and Americans and with the light the American response to her and her works shed on the "identity" of someone who had always claimed to "write for myself and strangers."

The relatively little critical attention that *Everybody's Autobiography* has received is remarkable in its reluctance to take up the subject of Stein's trip to America as in any way related to what the text is about or is doing.[1] *Everybody's Autobiography* might be one of the most consistently cited texts in Stein's oeuvre, satisfying both the biographer's need for anecdote and the critic's interest in the philosophical speculation that characterized Stein's later works, but the question of what is actually going on in the text's 340 pages has rarely been addressed.[2] That it is very centrally about homecoming seems clear. But beyond the simple dynamics of homecoming, the text makes one homecoming (the return to America) the prerequisite for another (the return to France). Or, more precisely, by doing the work of homecoming in her reencounter with America, Stein makes it possible to return to a France that had ceased to serve the function as home on which her being able to work depended.

This chapter explores the way in which Stein narrates her return to America as a self-described "celebrity" such that the "singular," "queer" American becomes the representative American. The representation of Gertrude Stein in America regrounds the representation of Gertrude Stein as American so that she can return to Paris to be the American writer whose mythology of the creative process requires a disjunction between "the country that made me" and the country in which "I made what I made." In this way, Stein completes the trajectory anticipated in the letters James wrote both before and after his American sojourn but not realized in *The American Scene*; although *The American Scene* is clearly written from the perspective of the return to Lamb House, its final sentence, "That was to be in fact my very next 'big' impression," makes it clear that *The American Scene* does not chronicle the round-trip journey that is its occasion. To the extent that Stein completes a task that James left unfinished, she stakes yet another claim to be her "forerunner's" worthy successor as a writer and as an American—which is to say, as an expatriate (*ABT* 86). If James was "the only nineteenth century writer who being an american *felt* the method of the twentieth century" (86, emphasis added), in *Everybody's Autobiography* Stein claims to be *realizing* this equation of the "american" and the "method of the twentieth century" and exploring its implications both for the American writer and for twentieth-century American writing.

I

Poodles are circus dogs they have no sense of home and no sense of being a dog, they do not realize danger nor ordinary life because in the circus there is no such thing.

—*Everybody's Autobiography*

Everybody's Autobiography needs, of course, to be considered in terms of the expatriation that occasioned it. Stein left the United States for Paris in 1903 and, except for a short stay a year later, did not return to her native country until 1934. Her expatriation is variously attributed to her discontent with American higher education, her disinclination to practice medicine, her adulation of her brother, Leo, with whom she joined forces upon her arrival in Paris, and most often, to the fallout from a failed passion for a female fellow student.[3] Yet in the course of the autobiographical project that occupied her in the late 1920s and throughout the 1930s, Stein herself refused to acknowledge any motivation for her expatriation other than a creative one.[4] In *Paris, France* (1939), written after her return from her American tour, Stein explained the artistic need to live in a country other than her native one: "After all everybody, that is everybody who writes is interested in living inside themselves to tell what is inside themselves. That is why writers have to have two countries, the one where they belong and the one in which they live really. The second one is romantic, it is separate from themselves it is not real but it is really there" (2). She expanded on this distinction in a lecture delivered at Cambridge University in 1936, entitled "An American and France": "And so I am an American and I have lived half my life in Paris, not the half that made me but the half in which I made what I made" (1). In these two texts written after *Everybody's Autobiography*, she calls America the country where she "belongs" as well as the country that "made" her. The country in which she "live[s] really" (which I take to mean both "actually resides" and "is truly alive") is the country where she can be artistically productive (where "I made what I made"). True to the notion of the "continuous present" toward which Stein strives in her writing, here she seems to be saying that "inside" herself she still "belongs" in (or to) an America that continues to make her what she is even as this "inside" needs to—can only—"really live" in the France where she makes of it what she makes.

Stein views the artistic function of expatriation far more pragmatically than does the romantic individual who assumes the persona of the exile in order to (self-)dramatize the persona of the artist. Stein sees nothing "romantic" about the person of the artist herself. What is—and must be—"romantic" for Stein is the world in which she lives her "daily life." In order for her to give expression to what is "inside" herself, the world the artist lives in must be "romantic" to the extent that it makes no claims on her and affords her the freedom to focus on the realization—in the literal sense of the word—of her personal (and hence, American) idiom:

> It is very natural that every one who makes anything inside themselves that is makes it entirely out of what is in them does naturally have to have two civilizations. They have to have the civilization that makes them and the civilization that has nothing to do with them. What is adventure and what is romance. Adventure is making the distance approach nearer but romance is having what is where it is which is not where you are stay where it is. So those who create things do not need adventure but they do need romance they need that something that is not for them stays where it is and that they can know that it is there where it is. . . . There is no possibility of mixing up the other civilization with yourself you are you and if you are you in your own civilization you are apt to mix yourself too much with your civilization but when it is another civilization a complete other a romantic other another that stays there where it is you in it have a freedom inside yourself. ("American and France" 1)

Whereas for the romantic "exile," the contingencies of identity are resolved—or at least suspended—by putting distance between oneself and home, for Stein, it is less the distance from home than that from the host civilization, which, by freeing her from worrying about "identity," guarantees the integrity of what, inside herself, seeks articulation specifically through language. In her notion of the "romantic," the foreign (or even the exotic) serves not as a particular attraction or even as a particular obstacle but as the outside of a boundary inside of which there is work to be done that is best performed in sociable cultural isolation. This pragmatics of expatriation leaves no room for speculation about personal motives: "*To be friendly and to let you alone, to be there and to be not needed by it*, that was France in the nineteenth century and so everybody was there and everybody and anybody did what they did in it not being of it because one could not be of it since it was there. . . . *It is not what France gave you but what it did not take away from you that was important*" (7, emphasis added).

Throughout her writings, Stein stresses the structural importance for literary production of this homeostasis—or one could call it a truce—between the demands of the "inside" and the "outside." It is not simply French manners and the notorious French indifference to foreigners that provide Stein with an "outside" to her American "inside." "Being surrounded by people who knew no english," she wrote, "has left me more intensely alone with my eyes and my english" (*ABT* 78). Stein further distinguishes between French as a spoken language and English as a written one, and attributes the freedom she enjoys putting "words next to each other in a different way . . . shoving the language around until at last now the job is done" (Harrison 96) to the absence in France of the competing demands of both spoken English and written French.[5] But her writings also show this truce to be a precarious one, vulnerable to destabilization from within as well as from without. Although Stein prided herself on "talk[ing] French badly and writ[ing] it worse" (*EA* 14), "badly" and "worse" are relative matters, and her translations in and out of French suggest that her claims to limited fluency are best read as a fiction devised to enforce the boundary between "her" English and "their" French, between "her" writing and "their" talking. Indeed, as she demonstrates in "What Is English Literature," a lecture she wrote during the period being chronicled in *Everybody's Autobiography*, conditions of the "outside" can cause severe disjunctions within the "inside": "because of the outside coming to penetrate inside and then having become inside became inside, or because the inside caused confusion in the inside or because the decision of inside made all the inside as settled as if there never had been an outside" ("English Literature" 41–42).

Everybody's Autobiography chronicles the consequences of the destabilization of Stein's working relation between herself and her world following the publication and success of *The Autobiography of Alice B. Toklas*. As Stein's writing (that account of what is "inside [her]self") entered and became part of the public domain, it escaped her control:

> Well anyway my success did begin.
> And so Mr. Bradley telephoned every morning and they gradually decided about everything and slowly everything changed inside me. Yes of course it did because suddenly it was all different,

what I did had a value that made people ready to pay, up to that time everything I did had a value because nobody was ready to pay. (*EA* 45–46)

In "What Is English Literature," Stein articulates a theoretical/literary historical version of this autobiographical predicament. The following passage makes clear that when Stein writes of people's willingness—or not—to "pay," she is addressing the entire issue of reception and the influence upon one's writing of the fact—and demands—of a readership:

When I say god and mammon concerning the writer writing, I mean that any one can use words to say something. And in using these words to say what he has to say he may use those words directly or indirectly. If he uses these words indirectly he says what he intends to have heard by somebody who is to hear and in so doing inevitably he has to serve mammon. Mammon may be a success, mammon may be an effort he is to produce, mammon may be a pleasure he has from hearing what he himself has done, mammon may be his way of explaining, mammon may be a laziness that needs nothing but going on, in short mammon may be anything that is done indirectly. Now serving god for a writer who is writing is writing anything directly, it makes no difference what it is but it must be direct, the relation between the thing done and the doer must be direct. In this way there is completion and the essence of the completed thing is completion. ("English Literature" 39)

The publication and commercial success of *The Autobiography of Alice B. Toklas* transformed a work written to serve god into a work serving mammon—or revealed that it had been serving mammon all along. In the final paragraphs of the *Autobiography*, as Stein prepares to reveal her authorship of Alice's voice, "Alice" writes:

For some time now many people, and publishers, have been asking Gertrude Stein to write her autobiography and she had always replied, not possibly.

She began to tease me and say that I should write my autobiography. Just think, she would say, what a lot of money you would make. She then began to invent titles for my autobiography. (271)

Stein not only anticipated but also solicited the publicity and the infringement upon her private sphere (the demands of "many people, publishers," but also the "money" [271]) that an autobiography would occasion. If Stein even suspected that the smoke-screen of the *Autobiography*'s conceit—Alice's putative authorship—would mitigate this publicity or shield her "inside" from the assault of the "outside," she failed to recognize that the simple facts of public reception and financial gain would change her relation to her work.[6] "The [direct] relation between the thing done and the doer" that distinguishes a work that serves god is rendered "indirect" by its enthusiastic reception and market value.

The author of the *Autobiography* has thus subjected herself to a crisis of identity, despite all her efforts to protect her work (and herself) against it. This change in the relation between inside and outside troubles her productive relation with France and sets in motion a set of circumstances and reflections that lead to the decision to travel to America:

> It is funny about money. And it is funny about identity. You are
> you because your little dog knows you, but when your public
> knows you and does not want to pay for you and when your
> public knows you and does want to pay for you, you are not the
> same you. *Anyway life in Paris began but it was less Paris than it
> had been and so it was natural that sooner or later I should go to
> America again.*
>   *It was less Paris than it had been.* (EA 46, emphasis added)

Success compromises Stein's ability to "be [in Paris] and to be not needed by it" ("An American in France" 7);[7] Paris is hence "less Paris than it had been," or rather, "it was not very exciting, as Paris, but it was very exciting as myself selling The Autobiography of Alice B. Toklas" (*EA* 47). Instead of writing, Stein is living in a world her writing has produced. The articulation of "what is inside" is stymied by the negotiations between "inside" and "outside" that Stein calls "worrying about identity" and that living in the old, indifferent Paris had rendered unnecessary:

> All this time I did no writing. I had written and was writing noth-
> ing. Nothing inside me needed to be written. Nothing needed any
> word and there was no word inside me that could not be spoken
> and so there was no word inside me. And I was not writing. I

began to worry about identity. I had always been I because I had words that had to be written inside me and now any word I had inside could be spoken it did not need to be written. I am I because my little dog knows me. But was I I when I had no written word inside me. It was very bothersome. (*EA* 66)

Stein makes clear here that it is not simply a matter of the outside's having permeated the wall that she had built around her inside; her "inside" has been teased out of itself into the "outside," "romantic," spoken idiom of the France whose difference from her English had made her able to be in touch with and write the writing that was inside her. "Romance" has become "adventure":

The thing is like this, it is all the question of identity. It is all a question of the outside being outside and the inside being inside. As long as the outside does not put a value on you it remains outside but when it does put a value on you then it gets inside or rather if the outside puts a value on you then all your inside gets to be outside. I used to tell all the men who were being successful young how bad this was for them and then I who was no longer young was having it happen.

But there was spending of money and there is no doubt about it there is no pleasure like it, the sudden splendid spending of money and we spent it. (*EA* 48)

II

Now, as they talked on, a dog that lay there
lifted up his muzzle, pricked his ears . . .
It was Argos, long-enduring Odysseus's dog
he trained as a puppy once, but little joy he got
since all too soon he shipped to sacred Troy.
. . . .
Infested with ticks, half-dead from neglect,
here lay the hound, old Argos.
But the moment he sensed Odysseus standing by
he thumped his tail, nuzzling low, and his ears dropped,

though he had no strength to drag himself an inch
toward his master.   — *The Odyssey*

Stein finds self-alienation to be the result of success: "I had always been I because I had words that had to be written inside me and now any word I had inside could be spoken it did not need to be written. I am I because my little dog knows me. But was I I when I had no written word inside me." In the wake of this experience—at least according to the chronology she establishes in *Everybody's Autobiography*—Stein began to meditate on the relation between immediate and mediated experience, which she called "human mind" and "human nature."[8] Following William James's distinction between "functional" and "substantial identity," Stein saw "human mind" as "entity . . . a thing in itself and not in relation," whereas "human nature" is involved with "identity," the self in the context of relations of knowledge and recognition of it.[9] Although, as Shirley C. Neuman points out, "human mind" has no identity of its own, it can meditate on identity (37). The meditations on "I am I because my little dog knows me" that punctuate *Everybody's Autobiography* as well as *The Geographical History of America*, *Four in America*, and "Identity a Poem" are generally taken to recreate such a meditation on identity.[10] The "little dog" represents the audience that, in the wake of the *Autobiography*'s success, had to be dealt with as an independent and potent reality rather than a chimera whose absence was the precondition of her writing ("In writing the Making of Americans I said I write for myself and strangers") at the same time as its potential presence was, paradoxically, its goal ("and then later now I know these strangers, are they still strangers" [*EA* 104]).

In this connection, the nursery rhyme "Lawkamercyme," from which "I am I because my little dog knows me" is derived, enriches our notion of the crisis of identity that sent Stein back to America and that is worked through narratively in *Everybody's Autobiography*. I am conscious of working against the grain both of Stein's own literary project and of some Stein scholarship, first, in claiming to read out of *The Autobiography of Alice B. Toklas* and *Everybody's Autobiography* a crisis of "identity" in the life of Gertrude Stein and second, in claiming that *Everybody's Autobiography* does narrative "work."[11] Yet Stein presents ample evidence in *Everybody's Autobiography* of a crisis in writing that, because it involves the (entirely ambivalent) presence of an audience, can indeed be regarded as a crisis in identity according to her definition of the term. Furthermore, since this crisis precipitates Stein the writer into the quagmire of "human nature," it demands to be worked through "narratively" in terms of the categories of "time," "memory," and "history" that she was working so hard to eliminate from her writing. The project of narrative reworking is presented in the text that is its product; in other words, while *Everybody's Autobiography* may not *be* the working through of Stein's crisis, it is certainly the record of that process. In fact, if *Everybody's Autobiography* can strive to be "a simple narrative of what is happening not as if it had happened not as if it is happening but as if it is existing simply that thing" (*EA* 312), it is because within the frame of this account of "existing," Stein deals with such issues of time, memory, and history, transforming them from process to presence in the course of the text's construction.

Like *Everybody's Autobiography*, "Lawkamercyme" is a homecoming narrative. It relates what seems at first glance a nightmare version of Stein's experience of "serving mammon":

There was an old woman as I've heard tell,
She went to market her eggs for to sell;
She went to market, all on a market-day,
And she fell asleep on the king's highway.

There came by a pedlar, whose name was Stout,
He cut her petticoats round about.
He cut her petticoats up to the knees,
Which made the old woman to shiver and freeze.

When this little woman first did wake,
She began to shiver, and she began to shake;
She began to wonder, and she began to cry—
"Lawkamercyme, this is none of I!"

"But if it be I, as I do hope it be,
I've got a little dog at home, and he'll know me;
If it be I, he'll wag his little tail,
And if it be not I, he'll loudly bark and wail."

Home went the little woman, all in the dark,
Up got the little dog, and he began to bark;
He began to bark, so she began to cry,
"Oh! deary, deary me, this is none of I!"

("Lawkamercyme" 539–40)

The old woman, on the way to market to sell her wares, falls asleep on
the side of the road. As she sleeps, a peddler comes along and violates her
by cutting off the garment that covers, and thus stands for, an identity
that, as the woman's reaction to the violation suggests, had not been a
subject of reflection until that moment. The woman's "shiver[ing] and
freez[ing]" is clearly emotional as well as physical; the trauma is profound enough to set her wondering whether she is she and whether if
one being can take something away from her, another can restore it. She
seems to hope that what she sees, however unfamiliar, is, indeed, "she,"
and sets off for home, where she trusts that her "little dog" will recognize what she, herself, cannot. When the woman arrives home "all in the
dark," her dog barks at her, confirming her suspicion that she is not she.

Yet, we might ask, is the old woman asking the right questions? What
is "none of I"? The grammatical incongruity with which she articulates
her dilemma suggests a conceptual one. "This is none of I" is grammati-
cally incorrect, although the existential stakes in asking the question are
clear. But doesn't language perhaps protect us from asking too much of
prepositional situations by enforcing the use, after a preposition, of the
objective pronoun? Although the spectacle of herself that she confronts
upon awakening might indeed be "none of I" (her presence to herself
as subject, or what William James would call "substantial identity"),
it is not necessarily "none of me" (her presence to herself as mediated
through her presence to others, or "functional identity"). In other words,
what the woman confronts upon awakening needs to be seen as a product of her actions in time (falling asleep on the way to market) as well as
of the agency of another person (the "pedlar"). Might, then, the change
be in the length of her petticoats, rather than in her "self"? Might it not
be better for the woman not to "worry about identity," to get herself to
the market and sell her eggs before she goes home and subjects herself to
the test of the dog? Moreover, can the old woman expect that an identity that seems to require immediacy ("I am I") be restored by the dog's

(or anyone's) agency? And, finally, might she be wrong about the dog's wagging its tail if she is she and barking if she is not? Might the dog be repeating her own bafflement, her shock of "recognition and nonrecognition," in seeing the clearly familiar in an unfamiliar guise? Might she be underestimating her dog's subtlety or misinterpreting his barking?[12]

The kind of thinking about the self that depends upon recognition by another can culminate in the desperate situation in which the old woman in "Lawkamercyme" finds herself. Like the old woman, Stein has suffered an alteration in her relation to herself in the process of taking her wares to market. Although Stein, unlike the old woman, has indeed been successful in marketing her wares and has only been violated to the extent that literary reception is necessarily a violation of the author's relation to her own work, she is no longer the same "she." Success forces her to regard her writing as mediated through the instance of its reception: "You are you because your little dog knows you, but when your public knows you and does not want to pay for you and when your public knows you and does want to pay for you, you are not the same you" (EA 46).

In *Everybody's Autobiography*, Stein represents herself as realizing that, in order to write again, she must reestablish the old relation with herself. And since it is her "outside" circumstances, rather than anything intrinsically "inside" herself that has changed (i.e., not her writing, but its reception), she can rectify her relation with herself only by changing her attitude toward her audience, her relation to the "outside."[13] Both in *Everybody's Autobiography* and in *The Geographical History of America*, the other text Stein wrote upon her return from America, she effects the transformation of self-positioning vis-à-vis her audience by exploring the capacities of the "little dog." Always juxtaposing her original statement, "I am I because my little dog knows me," with a revised representation of the dog, Stein gradually liberates her self-determination from the instance of the dog's recognition. Thus, in *The Geographical History of America* Stein writes:

Chorus: I am I because my little dog knows me.
Chorus: That does not prove anything about you it only proves something about the dog. (103)

And "I am I because my little dog knows me, even if the little dog is a big one, and yet the little dog knowing me does not really make me be

I no not really because after all being I I am I has really nothing to do with the little dog knowing me, he is my audience, but an audience never does prove to you that you are you" (104–5). Unlike the old woman in "Lawkamercyme," who remains trapped within the crisis of identity she has constructed for herself by depending upon her "little dog" for recognition and affirmation, Stein comes to recognize the identity, the independence, and perversity, of the dog:

> The question of identity has nothing to do with the human mind it has something although really nothing altogether to do with human nature. Any dog has identity.
>
> The old woman said I am I because my little dog knows me, but the dog knew that he was he because he knew that he was he as well as knowing that he knew she.
>
> Dogs like knowing what they know even when they make believe that they do not not that they do not like it but that they do not know. (134)

Like "Lawkamercyme" and unlike so much of Stein's other work, *Everybody's Autobiography* tells a story, one that might be regarded as a working-through of the double-bind with which "Lawkamercyme" ends. The narrative of *Everybody's Autobiography* demonstrates how Stein arrived at the intellectual/philosophical position she assumes in *The Geographical History*. *The Geographical History of America* works through many of the same issues as does *Everybody's Autobiography*, but it does so aphoristically and philosophically. The plot of *Everybody's Autobiography*—the chapter titles outline this plot: "What Happened after The Autobiography of Alice B. Toklas," "What Was the Effect on Me of the Autobiography," "Preparations for Going to America," "America," and "Back Again"—allows Stein to chronicle her recognition of the character of America and Americans in order to show how her crisis of audience and identity is resolved through her recognition of what an (American) audience is. If "Lawkamercyme" culminates with the old woman's self-denial in response to her dog's barking, *Everybody's Autobiography* ends with a declaration of independence from the instance of the dog's recognition, the realization that "perhaps I am not I even if my little dog knows me but anyway I like what I have and now it is today" (*EA* 328). In the discussion that follows I want to discuss how it is that through repatriation—the encounter and identification with America and Americans—Stein constructs a knowledge of "strangers" and "herself" that enables her to resume her writing career in France.

III

Everything changes I had never had any life with dogs and now I
had more life with dogs than with any one. . . . And then he said
what would I want if I went over. Well I said of course Miss Toklas
would have to go over and the two dogs. Oh he said.

— Everybody's Autobiography

Stein called America "the country that made me what I am" but claimed to need distance from it in order to "make anything inside [herself] that is entirely out of what is in [her]." Given the role America played in Stein's mythology of creation, a return to America in order to rectify the relation between inside and outside, between her writing self and her audience, seems a particularly—and promisingly—perverse strategy. The third chapter of *Everybody's Autobiography*, "Preparations for Going to America," registers the fits of resistance and rituals of justification punctuating Stein's ruminations about returning to the United States: "All that time America was coming nearer. Not that it had ever really been far away but it was certainly just now coming nearer that is to say it was getting more actual as a place where we might be. . . . As I say I am a person of no initiative, I usually stay where I am. . . . So it used to be Paris and Spain and then it was Paris and Bilignin and what was I to do in America when I got there. After all I am American all right. Being there does not make me more there" (114–15). But perhaps—and this had long been Stein's contention—*not* being there does indeed make her more there; Stein's hesitation might thus be bound up with an anxiety that the confrontation with America would indeed challenge the personal mythology that locates America wherever Gertrude Stein happens to be. What, indeed, is Stein to do if the "inside" is suddenly not only "outside" but everywhere? How should this self-proclaimed (and, in her French context, unchallenged) "representative" American represent America in America and to Americans? What, furthermore, is Stein to do with the stimuli—intellectual, emotional, social—that have no place in her mythology, either because they don't fit or because of the thirty-year hiatus since her last contact with the country? And finally, how will this writer police the boundary between inside and outside against the flood of personal memory, kept at bay during her expatriation through physical distance and art?

In the course of her "Preparations for Going to America," Stein performs the textual tasks that will make it possible for her to confront her native land with equanimity. By "writing about" the questions of "identity and memory and eternity" (*EA* 119) that most "worry her" before she records making the decision to visit America, she puts them behind her, as it were, in advance.[14] She placates the ghosts of her American past by rehearsing the story of her family: "We had a mother and a father and I tell all about that in The Making of Americans which is a history of our family, but I can tell it all again, why not if it is interesting" (139). Thus, instead of presenting the prospect of repatriation in terms of memory and nostalgia, Stein can now project America as a sort of new frontier where the promise of celebrity in its American form supersedes the crisis precipitated by the publication of *The Autobiography of Alice B. Toklas*:

> People always had been nice to me because I am pleasing but this was going to be a different thing. We were on the Champlain and we were coming.
>
> I used to say that was long ago in between I never had thought of going, I used to say that I would not go to America until I was a real lion a real celebrity at that time of course I did not really think I was going to be one. But now we were coming and I was going to be one. (*EA* 173)

Moreover, by calling attention to the contemporary moment and place of writing (France in 1937)—using it as the reference point in relation to which all the meditations and anecdotes acquire currency—she enforces the impression that she has not only survived repatriation but, more generally, has wrested control of the place the past is to occupy in the (continuous) present of her writing.

Stein attempts to put the issue of identity to rest by squaring her notion of genius—and of herself as a genius—with the demands of repatriation.[15] As I have argued, for Stein, the problem with "identity" is that it involves a recognition by the subject of the recognition of it by something external to it. Because this recognition involves indirection, it is by definition a distortion. If "human mind" is always changing within itself, then memory (the recognition by the subject of something that has become external to it through the agency of time rather than space), too, represents a serious distortion. Genius, in Stein's formulation, involves mind's ability not to be distracted, lured into indirection by anything external to it: "And so I do know what a genius is, a genius is some one who does not have to remember the two hundred years that everybody else has to remember" (*EA* 125). The much-maligned American talent for ignoring the past is, according to this logic, a particularly American disposition for genius: if "genius . . . is the existing without any internal recognition of time" (251), then "a genius has to be made in a country which is forming itself to be what it is but is not yet that is what it is is not yet common property" (94). Such a country does not have the vantage point of group memory ("common property") whence identity can be pondered. The inside/outside paradigm that first structured Stein's access to creativity and then stymied it is disenabled; to write America is to record it, rather than to reflect on it: "Now I am writing about what is which is being existing" (258).

In *The Making of Americans*, Stein explains how America's hostility to "singularity that is neither crazy, sporty, faddish, or a fashion, or low class with distinction" causes "queer people" to "fly to the kindly comfort of an older world accustomed to take all manner of strange forms into its bosom" (21). In the course of living in this "older world," however, exchanging the position of involuntary outsider (exile at home) for that of voluntary outsider (expatriate), Stein comes to identify her "queerness" with her genius as well as with being American. The flux and historical callowness of America may not be congenial to "singularity," but "singularity" is congenital to America. In *Everybody's Autobiography*, Stein claims that while genius needs the binary structuring of inside/outside to recognize itself, it can realize itself only through the sublation of these categories (much as, in *The Making of Americans*, "singularity" recognizes itself against the backdrop of "conventional respectability" even if it needs "others who can know it, time and a certainty of place and means" in order to realize itself). In America, the problems of "identity" that ensued from the publication of *The Autobiography* are less resolved than suspended, since, as an "American genius" in America, Stein can present herself as tautological and, in a sense that she will have to define, representative rather than conflicted and aberrant.

In a move that is particularly "queer" in Stein's sense of the term as well as in its current designation of the cultural field generated by non-normative sexualities, Stein "prepares" to rectify the relation between inside and outside by sublating it, by rendering inoperative the distinction that structures the relation.[16] Whereas the American living among French people profits from the oppositions upon which the French have structured their society for themselves and lives unbothered since "their life belongs to them so your life can belong to you," the American in America is, like every other American, "singular," and is most supremely so when she is *not* left alone: "I used to say that I would not go to America until I was a real lion a real celebrity at that time of course I did not really think I was going to be one. . . . In America everybody is but some are more than others. I was more than others" (*EA* 173). Although it is important to recall that Stein can make the narrative of her "singularity" into *Everybody's Autobiography* only once she has returned to France, having revamped and reassumed the inside/outside binary that America suspends for her, I wish now to examine the fruits and real hazards of this suspension.

IV

Dogs have not changed they have been dogs for a long time but
now they never howl or bark at the moon because no matter how
small any village or how far away they have electric light to light it
and if they do not then automobiles pass and make more light than
any moon and the dogs see it so often they know light when they
see it and so now they never see the moon.
                              —*Everybody's Autobiography*

American society as Stein presents it in *Everybody's Autobiography* looks like a realization of the continuous present that is the hallmark of her aesthetic program. Because America lacks—and resists—those "European" demarcations of class, place, and historical determination that would make it accessible to traditional modes of representation and because Stein wants to reinforce the impression that she is writing *Every-body's Autobiography* in her "home town," Paris, she finds it useful to compare America to French society in order to highlight what she terms the former's "lack of connection." In French society, manners enforce distinctions that make existence seem organized—or rather, that make people live as though their existence were organized: "The French they are not foolish, they know that as there are occupations and habits and character and intelligence and personality and force and dullness that all that always does make a class, anything you do every day makes a class that will stay, and so they admit the class as a class but that has nothing to do with the being as a being. . . . Every class has its charm and that can do no harm as long as every class has its charm, and anybody is occupied with their own being" (*EA* 172–73). America, on the other hand, offers no perceptible principle of social organization, no relief from the recognition that "since the earth is all covered over with every one there is really no relation between any one" (102). If there is no "connection between any one and anyone," there is also no "daily life" in the traditional, European sense of the phrase. "Daily life," conceived along "European" lines, derives from historical process that makes it seem motivated and meaningful. For instance, Stein relates the anecdote of her servant, Hélène's, astonishment that Stein would inquire into her husband's voting behavior: "Is it a secret I said, no she said no it is not a secret but one does not tell it" (105). People do things because people have always done things that way, and even if we no longer know precisely why this is so, we assume that there is a historically determined reason that is encoded in particular behavior. Such manners are a form of cultural memory, a code that, however arbitrary, implies a narrative of the meaningfulness of the gestures that organize daily life.

In Stein's paean to American "wooden houses" and shutterless windows, she makes it clear what in her native land replaces the forms of closure and concealment that govern European quotidian culture. The flat, painted surfaces of wooden houses ("there are so many of them an endless number of them and endless varieties in them" [*EA* 188]) and the "windows in a building" that "are the most interesting thing in America" testify to a culture displaying endless variation without difference. As "interesting" as these surfaces may be, they are—unlike European surfaces—entirely and pragmatically, but not at all naively, innocent:

Less and less there are curtains and shutters on the windows bye and bye there are not shutters and no curtains at all and that worried me and I asked everybody about that. But the reason is easy enough. Everybody in America is nice and everybody is honest except those who want to break in. If they want to break in shutters will not stop them so why have them and other people looking in, well as *everybody is a public something and anybody can know anything about any one and can know any one then why shut the shutters and the curtains and keep any one from seeing, they all know what they are going to see so why look.* I gradually began to realize all this. (188–89, emphasis added)

Flat surfaces "take" paint; unshuttered windows provide uncomplicated access that shutters would simply complicate. The crystalline logic of American publicity includes the privacy for which Europeans need to create systems and structures: "It is what in America is very different, each one has something and well taken care of or neglect helps them, helps them to be themselves each one of them" (188). The American aesthetic coincides with its ethics.

Although America has no "daily life," it would thus be wrong to conclude that America does not have its codes. Whereas the coding of European society is essentially metaphoric, based on the ability of appearances to negotiate the realities they both mask and express, American coding is metonymic. Stein's description of the American latitude that so frustrated Henry James in his search for "manners" ("thin and clear and colorless, what would it ever say 'no' to?" [AS 54]) reads like an articulation of her aesthetic principles: "I always explained everything in America by this thing, *the lack of passion that they call repression* and gangsters, and savagery, and *everybody being nice, and everybody not thinking because they had to drink and keep moving,* in Europe when they drink they sit still but not in America no not in America *and that is because there is no sky, there is no lid on top of them and so they move around or stand still and do not say anything*" (EA 209, emphasis added). Stein's conclusion that "that makes that American language that says everything in two words and mostly in words of one syllable" explains her own response to almost everything in America, a phrase that punctuates the American section of *Everybody's Autobiography* like a leitmotif: "we liked it."

"We liked it" resembles the noncommittal but unshakable American friendliness ("everybody being nice") so irritating—because unreadable—to Europeans. It is tempting to imitate the response of so many Europeans confronted with American "niceness" and read the phrase as an insipid response to insipid stimuli, and certainly in some cases such a reading is valid. But I think more is going on behind, as it were, this leitmotif. "We liked it," or its less-common variant, "I liked it," affords Stein the opportunity of marking the presence of a response without committing herself to its contents. The formula enables Stein to maintain a representational and self-representational discourse that negotiates her reactions to America with that "lack of passion they call repression."

Stein would, of course, be the first to object to the applicability here of the surface/depth model that governs the dynamics of "repression"; one cannot, however, do justice to the work of *Everybody's Autobiography* and what it tells us of the experiences of ex- and repatriation without accounting for what this "lack of passion" is, if it is, indeed, not "repression." If "they" call it repression, what name does Stein give to that American "lack of passion" that I have tentatively called "indifference"? In "What Is English Literature," Stein writes of "the disembodied way of disconnecting something from anything and anything from something" that she terms "the American one." She continues, "Some say that it is repression but no it is not repression it is a lack of connection, of there being no connection with living and daily living because there is none, that makes American writing what it always has been and what it will continue to become" ("English Literature" 57). By discovering within America and within herself that democratic indifference, that "lack of passion they call repression," Stein delivers a key to both the poetics and the psychology of her encounter with America. In her use of the "continuous present," Stein brings present, past, and future into a textual surface that yokes them together without violating their lack of connection. *Everybody's Autobiography* is thus supremely American in the sense that it reproduces the experience of "seeing by looking" that Stein describes as the goal of American cultural production: "In America they want to make everything something anybody can see by looking. That is very interesting, that is the reason there are no fences in between no walls to hide anything no curtains to cover anything and the cinema that can make anything be anything anybody can see by looking" (*EA* 202).

Yet if this text exploits and projects the American innocence that Stein has read in the country's unshuttered windows, it does not do so naively. Stein's reference to the cinema makes it clear that "making everything something anybody can see by looking" is a calculated and technically sophisticated undertaking, albeit one whose methods and goals might be so antithetical to European notions of art and manners as to remain invisible to Europeans or those infatuated with the canons of European aesthetics and ethics. But the spectacle that reads as American innocence is as deliberate and sophisticated a cultural production as is Stein's rendition of the confrontation between the "lack of connection" with her native country that has made it possible for her to write quintessentially American literature and the "lack of connection" that she takes to be the quintessence of America.

V

Of course you remember something, two little terriers . . . began
fighting . . . and the two of them a wire-haired and a black Scottie
both females they should not but they do were holding each other
in a terrifying embrace. . . . I remembered in the books you pour
water on them so I called for cold water in a basin and poured it on
them and it separated them. The white one was terribly bitten.
                                        — *Everybody's Autobiography*

What happens when two little dogs recognize each other? Throughout the sections of *Everybody's Autobiography* dedicated to preparing to visit America, Stein's meditations about identity addressed the question of "am I I because my little dog knows me." This form of "worrying about identity," of projecting the instance of recognition as markedly Other and the process of recognition as falsification, is generally absent from the sections of the book dealing with the visit to America itself perhaps because, as I have just suggested, in America, Stein sees herself as one of "everybody"—in kind if not in degree. In place of her broodings about audience and identity, Stein chronicles a casual, untroubled, superficial interaction with everyone and whomever:

> Everybody speaking to you everybody knowing you, everybody in a hotel or restaurant noticing you everybody asking you to write your name for them . . . the people were American people but that was not such a difficult thing.
>
> I have always been accustomed to talking to anybody and to have anybody talk to you, it always happened in America when I was there and before I came over here and it has always happened over here and then went on over there, more of them of course but once you admit adding what is the difference to your feeling. None. (*EA* 184)

Yet a democratic dynamics of recognition, where the Other is the Same, where the outside (the landscape) mirrors the inside, has perils of its own, and there are two conspicuous moments in the record of Stein's repatriation where her equanimity falters, where her mastery of the terrain gives way to a vexed and adamant refusal to recognize it. Both of these moments occur when she is confronted not with individuals but with scenes of her earlier life, first in Cambridge and then, most pronouncedly, in Oakland.

Stein presents her return to Cambridge as a parenthesis in her account of a sojourn in New York:

> We went to Cambridge overnight and I spoke in Radcliffe and at the Signet Club at Harvard. It was funny about Cambridge it was the one place where there was nothing that I recognized nothing. Considering that I had spent four years there it was sufficiently astonishing that nothing was there that I remembered nothing at all. New York Washington East Oakland Baltimore San Francisco were just about as they were they were changed of course but I could find my way there anywhere but Cambridge not at all. I did not go back again perhaps I might have begun again but that day *Cambridge was so different that it was as if I had never been there there was nothing there that had any relation to any place that had been there. I lost Cambridge then and there. That is funny.* (*EA* 192, emphasis added)

Here, Stein makes Cambridge vanish into thin air, closes the parenthesis, and terms the experience "funny." If, however, we recall that for Stein, the truly important things are the ones it is difficult to remember (she writes of American wooden houses, "It is hard to remember them because they are so interesting" [188]), we are justified in wondering whether "funny" might be masking a more complex reaction. And when she experiences a comparable—although far more shattering—loss of orientation in East Oakland, where she, according to all accounts except perhaps her own, spent the most difficult years of her youth and adolescence, the complexity of her response engages directly the terms in which she has presented both her preparations for and accommodations to America.

Driving north from Los Angeles toward the San Francisco Bay Area, "our California the California we had come from" (*EA* 292), Stein and Toklas stop in Yosemite Park to see "the big trees": "The thing that was most exciting about them was that they had no roots did anybody want anything to be more interesting than that that the oldest and the solidest and the biggest tree that could be grown had no foundation, there it was sitting and the wind did not blow it over it sat so well. It was very exciting. Very beautiful and very exciting" (295). The redwoods that Stein, with flamboyant poetic license, thoroughly fabulously records as having no roots impress and reassure because of the paradox she has invented of their rootlessness, on the one hand, and their endurance, solidity, and bulk, on the other.[17] Like the American who is most American when she is not planted in her home soil, these fantastic trees gain in strength in proportion to their lack of foundation (we recall the distinction she drew in "An American in France" between the country "where I made what I made" and that which "made me"). When Stein confronts her own "roots," the landscape of "the California [she] had come from," she is inexplicably troubled; her own endurance, solidity, and bulk seem as nothing against the world around her:

> Then we left for San Francisco and Oakland there I was to be
> where I had come from, we went over the green rounded hills
> which are brown in summer with a very occasional live oak tree
> and otherwise empty and a fence that does not separate them but
> goes where the hill has come to come down . . . and they made me

feel funny, yes they were like that that is what they were and they did trouble me they made me very uncomfortable I do not know why but they did, it all made me uncomfortable it just did.

Then slowly we came into San Francisco it was frightening quite frightening driving there . . . Alice Toklas found it natural but for me it was a trouble yes it was, it did make me feel uncomfortable. (297)

Whence all this vulnerability, all this discomfort, this sudden fear of her favorite pastime, driving? Confronted with a place that threatens to make autobiographical claims upon her, Stein loses the equanimity of affect and tone with which she has hitherto presented her adventure of repatriation in *Everybody's Autobiography*. Here, suddenly, personal, "singular" claims cannot be generalized or made a matter of degree ("I was more than others" [*EA* 173]) rather than of kind. Without the distinctions of class, occupation, and métier, with "shutters [that] are open or none of them and no walls around gardens or anything" (218), the "singular" individual is unprotected in her unmediated encounter with memo*ries* that exceed and resist the regulatory agency of memory. If in Cambridge she willfully repressed the map of the city ("I lost Cambridge then and there"), here she looks at the map and balks at navigating the terrain.

Stein's first reaction to Oakland takes her response to Cambridge one step further. If she could "lose Cambridge," she needs to deny Oakland: "What was the use of my having come from Oakland it was not natural to have come from there yes write about it if I like or anything if I like but not there, *there is no there there*" (*EA* 298, emphasis added). But effacing Oakland neither works nor does it perform the work Stein needs to do. It seems as though she needs the affect of the encounter with her childhood home:

And I asked to go with a reluctant feeling to see the Swett School where I went to school and Thirteenth Avenue and Twenty-fifth Street where we lived which I described in The Making of Americans. Ah Thirteenth Avenue was the same it was shabby and overgrown the houses were certainly some of them those that had been and there were not bigger buildings and they were neglected and, lots of grass and bushes growing yes it might have been the

Thirteenth Avenue when I had been. Not of course the house, the house the big house and the big garden and the eucalyptus trees and the rose hedge naturally were not any longer existing, what was the use, if I had been I then my little dog would know me but if I had not been I then that place would not be the place that I could see, I did not like the feeling, who has to be themselves inside them, not anyone and what is the use of having been if you are to be going on being and if not why is it different and if it is different why not. I did not like anything that was happening. (300)

Throughout Stein's meditations, the test of identity has been her "little dog's" recognition of her. In this passage, the test of positive recognition by an Other does not begin to tell her what she has to know; only a negative logic in which she herself is the agency of recognition can situate her vis-à-vis the spectacle of her roots: "If I had not been I then that place would not be the place that I could see." Her ability to see "this place" that has "made her what she [is]" tells her she is she. Because she cannot help but see what she does not want to see—and cannot help but experience the unpleasant feelings the encounter generates—she must be who she is. This dynamics of perception is the logical consequence of her pursuit of and identification with America. She is the representative American because she can see America in the—very uncomfortable— terms of perception it dictates, terms that make her see herself in a manner that makes her very uncomfortable. When two little dogs recognize each other, they get into a fight. One of them gets badly hurt.

VI

I am I not any longer when I see.
This sentence is at the bottom of all creative activity.
It is just the exact opposite of I am I because my little dog knows me.
                    —"HENRY JAMES," IN *Four in America*

Stein risks rendering the reencounter with Oakland because it is the site where Gertrude Stein's autobiography can become *Everybody's Autobiography*, where Gertrude Stein can become the representative American.

The shattering experience in which she confirms both her "singularity" and her Americanness through her thoroughly dysphoric recognition of the landscape of her past frees her from the traditional logic of *nostos*, in which the homecomer's "identity" is confirmed by the recognition of others, rather than by her recognition of them. Stein's experience of Oakland and her curiously negative self-affirmation are based not on what she sees, but on what she doesn't see but remembers ("the house . . . and the big garden . . . were no longer existing") and whose absence she brings into the continuous present ("were no longer existing") of her text. Unlike the romantic exile, whose relation to home is determined by nostalgia and whose return can only deflate the edifice on which he has constructed his poetic persona, Stein recognizes that to be American means that one has no claim to—but also no power to deny—the roots that would make homecoming either an affirmation of self or the predictable moment of consoling disillusion in the romantic plot. Homecoming can only affirm—redundantly, tautologically—the same lack of connection that has been her aesthetic doctrine all along. "The lack of passion they call repression" is nothing but lack of connection. To call a lack of passion "repression" presupposes an Old World scheme of inside/outside, surface/depth that has no relevance in a country that has "no lid" on it. Without closure there can be no economy of affect: "There is no sky, there is air and that makes religion, and wandering and architecture" (*EA* 208). Americans, Stein points out, are anxious; her most American moments, then, occur when, confronted with a site of memory, she recognizes herself through her anxious apprehension of "the country that made me what I am."

It is sorely tempting to psychoanalyze this dynamic, but Stein withholds the material we would need to do so.[18] In its place, I think we can, however, attempt a "queer" reading, in which Stein suggests that in a society in which inside/outside distinctions are inoperative, everybody is, by definition "out." She is representative not because she is like everyone else, but because, like everyone else, she is different. Like Stein, who has left America in order most forcefully to render the American "inside" herself, America, in its quest for self-recognition, has recourse to mythologies and ideologies (religion and architecture and wandering) that propose to express but also to limit, navigate, map, and render habitable its boundlessness. It is, she suggests, these technologies of self-limitation that make those Americans "who never anyway can understand why such ways and not the others are so dear to us" and that have sent those "queer people" into traditional, romantic exile ("we fly to the kindly comforts of an older world accustomed to take all manner of strange forms into its bosom"). But by staking her claim to America, on the one hand, and foregrounding the purely pragmatic function of expatriation for writing, on the other hand, Stein unwrites the narrative of romantic exile she sketched in *The Making of Americans*. Her text of repatriation, *Everybody's Autobiography*, makes the claim and demonstrates that it is precisely the queer autobiography (the "simple narrative of what is happening not as if it had happened not as if it is happening but as if it is existing simply that thing" [*EA* 312]) that tells the story of the "singular," "disconnected" American who is "everybody":

> Then [in *The Making of Americans*] I was wanting to write a
> history of every individual person who ever is or was or shall be
> living and I was convinced it could be done as I still am but now
> individual anything as related to every other individual is to me no
> longer interesting. At that time I did not realize that the earth is
> completely covered over with every one. In a way it was not then
> because every one was in a group and a group was separated from
> every other one, and so the character of every one was interesting
> because they were in relation but now since the earth is all covered
> over with every one there is really no relation between any one
> and so if this Everybody's Autobiography is to be the Autobiogra-
> phy of every one it is not to be of any connection between any one
> and any one because now there is none. (102)

But this is not the entire story. In the process of denying Oakland, Stein wrote, "yes *write about it if I like* or anything if I like *but not there*, there is no there there" (*EA* 298, emphasis added). Although the confrontation with Oakland does in fact do much of the work of forging the self-identification as the representative queer American, Stein makes it very clear that Oakland is not a place where she can write about Oakland. The "there" that is not "there" is the place where she can write. Throughout *Everybody's Autobiography*, Stein calls the reader's attention to the fact that she is writing the book in France and that the "present" of her "continuous present" is that of her "daily life" in France.

However indispensable Stein's return to her "country," she needed to return to her "home town," Paris, to communicate what she had discovered about the lack of differentiation that is, paradoxically, both America's difference and the sophistication that characterizes America's innocence. And whatever rootless experience of her roots led to the self-denial qua self-affirmation in Oakland, it is the denial of the need for such experiences that Stein will choose to canonize:

> I think I must have had a feeling that [I had lost my roots] or I
> should not have come back. . . . I went to California. I saw it and
> felt it and it had a tenderness and a horror too. Roots are so small
> and dry when you have them and they are exposed to you. You
> have seen them on a plant and sometimes they seem to deny the
> plant if it is vigorous. . . . Well, we're not like that if you think
> about it, we take our roots with us. I always knew that a little and
> now I know it wholly. I know it because you can go back to where
> they are and they can be less real to you than they were three
> thousand, six thousand miles away. Don't worry about your roots.
> . . . The essential thing is to have the feeling that they exist, that
> they are somewhere. They will take care of themselves, and they
> will take care of you, too, though you may never know how it has
> happened. To think of going back for them is to confess that the
> plant is dying. (Cited in Brinnen 329)

For Stein, being in France stands for and enables the continued denial of the need for a direct confrontation with the American world that made her what she is. Indeed, we could go so far as to regard the "mak[ing] of what [she] made" as the continuous(ly present) performance of this denial. Yet the passage above—Stein at her most Jamesian—is briefly nostalgic in its suggestion that she "must have had a feeling" that she had lost her roots. The success of *The Autobiography of Alice B. Toklas*—its launching of Gertrude Stein into the public domain—so disturbed the homeostasis of "inside" and "outside" that the "plant" seems to have feared it was "dying." Having proved, through the narrative rendition of her temporary repatriation, the unfoundedness of this fear ("we take our roots with us. I always knew that a little and now I know it wholly"), she can continue to cultivate her roots at a safe distance from their native soil. It is significant, then, that Stein's most confident assertions of her dual citizenship date from the period immediately following her return to France.

But it is not the question of her national identity that occupies Stein in *Everybody's Autobiography* but that of identity *tout court* and especially the relation of identity to writing. Here, she begs the question of national identity by demonstrating that "American identity" is an oxymoron; the question of identity, as she defines it, is begged by the conditions of existence in America—especially if one doesn't have to live there. By characterizing American indifference as everybody's difference, Stein is able to reinstate herself as the quintessential American writer; the challenge from the "outside" that precipitated her crisis of identity is resolved in the process of conceiving of America as a mirror of Gertrude Stein and vice versa. Confronted with "what made [her] what she [is]," Stein risks that "making the distant approach nearer" that she calls "adventure," which, she insists, "those that create things do not need." But this adventure needs to be put behind her, embalmed, as it were, in the obsolete shape of nineteenth-century narrative so that Stein can proceed with the invention of the twentieth century.

What else does Stein put behind her when she leaves America? It strikes me as not accidental that Stein's account of leaving America is truncated; after her account of the confrontation with Oakland, she seems anxious to get the trip over with and to tackle the business of being "back again" in France. Yet in these scant four pages, Stein records the achievement that actually crowns her sojourn in the United States and that seems to rectify permanently the disequilibrium between inside and outside that motivated her journey in the first place: she finds a library for her works ("And now a young fellow from Berkeley . . . writes to me and tells me he has collected everything that has been printed that I have written and he will give it to the University" [*EA* 302]) and exacts a promise from Bennett Cerf: "Whatever you decide each year you want printed you tell me and I will publish that thing, just like that I said, just like that, he said, you do the deciding" (304). Although she makes it clear that Robert Haas's proposal to begin a Gertrude Stein collection at Berkeley reaches her after her return to France ("And now a young fellow . . . writes to me"), Stein mentions it in the course of her account of her visit to Berkeley. She exploits the associational logic that links Berkeley to Oakland and her visit to Oakland with the letter from Berkeley that would situate a Gertrude Stein archive in her native land, so that the "there" that is not "there" in Oakland promises to take up residence just across the Bay. The trauma of Oakland thus initiates, through a narrative sleight of hand, what we might call a project of canonization. This project of canonization—the transition from ephemeral media "lion" ("It always did bother me that the American public were more interested in me than in my work" [51]) to literary institution—begins in America. "Gertrude Stein" is no longer simply a spectacle of flashing in lights on Times Square,[19] but the name of a permanent (published, collected) American body of work. We might go so far as to say that Stein's oeuvre supplants her roots.

Once Stein has associated her native land with her literary immortality, there is no reason to be there any more. And of course, the conceit on which *Everybody's Autobiography* is based is that she is not "there," any more, but rather, "here," in France. Having done the work of poetically transforming the "outside" of America into a simulacrum of her "inside," Stein can take it all back with her to France ("we take our roots with us") and undertake the project of systematizing the relation between inside and outside, of identity and nationality, that occupies her throughout the second half of the 1930s. The writer who has remade herself as an American is always already "back home" in France, that place of writing that she has restored to herself and without whose romance the account of this restoration would not exist.

Postscript

BREATHES there the man with soul so dead,
Who never to himself hath said,
"This is my own, my native land!"
Whose heart hath ne'er within him burn'd
As home his footsteps he hath turn'd
From wandering on a foreign strand?
If such there breathe, go, mark him well;
For him no Minstrel raptures swell;
High though his titles, proud his name,
Boundless his wealth as wish can claim;
Despite those titles, power, and pelf,
The wretch, concentred all in self,
Living, shall forfeit fair renown,
And, doubly dying, shall go down
To the vile dust from whence he sprung,
Unwept, unhonour'd, and unsung.

SIR WALTER SCOTT'S "INNOMINATUS" represents repatriation as the supreme test of an individual's moral fettle. The person who returns to his native land and fails to evince a convincing frisson of pride and identification is represented as a monster of selfishness who has sacrificed his roots for "titles, power, and pelf." The man whose vanity is unmoved by the passions set into motion by repatriation has doomed himself to an obscurity so profound that it can achieve representation only through the invocation of what he has forfeited; his image must be retrieved from the oblivion of a double death—physical death and oblivion—in order that he be presented as a negative exemplum: "If such there breathe, go, mark him well;/For him no Minstrel raptures swell."

The vehemence of Scott's condemnation of the person whom Henry James might have called the "unrepentant absentee" may be taken as an index of the ambivalences mobilized by repatriation as well as of the stakes for the writer who defies "double death" by chronicling the experience of return. If, as James Baldwin claimed, living in Europe sets "what it means to be an American" in broad relief, return challenges these constructions. The positive sense of national identity of the American in Paris is determined by his or her difference from the surrounding culture: "The French, they surround you with a civilised atmosphere and they leave you inside of you completely to yourself" (*Paris, France* 57). The freedom that Gertrude Stein attributed to the tact of the French is, to a large extent, the *Narrenfreiheit* that all foreigners enjoy when the culture in which they live exempts them from the kinds of claims it makes on its citizens. At the moment of return, these claims reassert themselves with a twofold vengeance: not only are the returnees confronted with the particular demands of and responsibilities toward their native country, but they must become reacquainted with the burden of being subject to such demands at all. If, in Paris, Baldwin found himself to "be as American as any Texas GI" because "divorced from their origins . . . white Americans . . . were no more at home in Europe than I was," the return to America enmeshes him in the spoken and "unspoken. . . assumptions on the part of the people" that legislate for whom America is rightly "home" ("Discovery" 172, 175).

For Baldwin, the day when the American discovers that "it would be simpler—and corny as the words may sound, more honorable—to *go* to Little Rock than sit in Europe on an American passport, trying to explain it" is "a personal day, a terrible day, the day to which his entire sojourn has been tending" ("Discovery" 174–75). On this day, the American discovers that "the responsibility for his development [is] where it always was: in his own hands" (175). In the texts I have discussed in this study, the process of telling the story of repatriation—of "writing back"—represents the taking into the writer's "own hands" of this responsibility. In each of these texts, the writer needs to justify expatriation and claim its yield in the face of a return that, in its most extreme form, calls into question the necessity and validity of this experience. The feeling of never having been away cohabits with an equally compelling feeling of acute strangeness; the "uncanniness" that Priscilla Wald associates with narratives of national identity haunts the "shocks of recognition and nonrecognition" that attend repatriation. Wald writes: "Freud's *uncanny* recognition . . . turns on the discovery that the unfamiliar is really familiar (the stranger as self) but also that the familiar is unfamiliar (the self as stranger). [He] locates uncanniness . . . in the experiences of an altered self that calls the fundamental assumptions of what the self is and whence it derives into question. Ultimately . . . the uncanny sends us home to the discovery that 'home' is not what or where we think it is and that we, by extension, are not who or what we think we are" (7).

For James, Stearns, Cowley, and Stein, the process of writing about repatriation represents a negotiation with the uncanny yield of return. "Writing back" both confirms the self's disjunctive relation with home and deploys this disjunction in a reassertion of an identity that, in each case, makes claims to be a national identity. James's text of return renews and ratifies his thirty-seven-year-old avatar's recognition of the "burden" of the American writer, who must "deal with Europe" even in his dealings with America (*Complete Notebooks* 214). Stearns represents his ability to return from abjection and find a measure of renewed success in America as proof positive of the vision of America implicit in his earlier critique. The collective biography that Cowley projects in *Exile's Return* represents his blueprint for the "intellectual odyssey" of the American man of letters; the struggle to plant the seeds of high culture in native earth that occupies the Lost Generation upon its return from Europe both enforces the differences between the intellectual caste and mainstream America and confers upon it the legitimacy to speak in the name of American culture. Stein's brilliant and brazen equation of her and America's continuous present reinstates the expatriate as the quintessential American and the expatriate writer as the spokesperson for America. In the process of generating these claims, however, each writer takes stock of the incommensurabilities that must be both acknowledged and negotiated in the process of "writing back." In each text, the reencounter—or deliberate failure to reencounter—the place where each writer stakes his or her "roots" is notably and strategically troubled: the New York and Boston of James's childhood are in the process of disappearing; Stearns can never get himself to return to Boston and telephones his dying mother as he watches the boat to Boston cruise up the East River; Cowley's "urn of native soil" only belatedly returns to its source in the graveyard invocation of his mother's memory; when Stein returns to Cambridge she cannot recognize it, and upon reencountering her childhood home in Oakland she remarks famously, "there is no there there" (*EA* 298).

We can only speculate about the individual psychology behind these elisions and evasions of sites of childhood and youth—or indeed, whether these elisions and evasions correspond at all to the psychological state of the writer. Their textual function, to which we do have access, seems fairly clear: with the obscuring or erasure of such sites, the writer is making space for a new beginning in the terms established not by the old landmarks left behind upon expatriation but by the new persona of the repatriated writer. This process is, of course, not without its pathos; the text of return always leaves space for a nostalgia that, because it controls the image of the lost past, can be put in service of the new beginning constituted by the text.

Crucial to the texts of return that I have discussed here is the radical dissociation between continents experienced in the years prior to transatlantic air travel. The expatriate of the 1920s and 1930s knew that return was a cumbersome affair: Harold Stearns's allusion to his contemporaries' casual mobility notwithstanding, transatlantic travel required more planning and was more expensive, in terms of both time and money, than it is today. Expatriation was hence a more absolute matter; sojourns abroad tended to be unbroken and longer; return was correspondingly more ceremonious, its impressions more likely to register the passage of years than of days, weeks, or months. This spatial and temporal dissociation fostered both the imperative to make sense of return and the prospect of the new beginning that these texts enact. Technological progress—air travel, widespread telephonic communication, television, and, most recently, the Internet—make it not only possible but necessary that more recent generations of expatriates remain in much closer contact and even dialogue with home than did the writers whose texts I have examined here. James Baldwin considered himself a commuter rather than an expatriate; certainly his ability to engage the country toward which he was so ambivalent depended on his distance from it, but the authority of his engagement required his regular presence.

The narrative of return implicates the personal in the national narrative—and vice versa—at the same time as it demonstrates their incommensurability. Baldwin wrote that "the time has come . . . for us to examine ourselves, but we can do this only if we are willing to free ourselves of the myth of America and try to find out what is really happening there" ("Discovery" 175). This appeal echoes—of course, with a difference—Henry James's observation during an 1872 sojourn in Italy that "it's the same world there after all and Italy isn't the absolute any more than Massachusetts. It's a complex fate, being an American, and one of the responsibilities it entails is fighting against a superstitious valuation of Europe" (*Letters* 1: 274). The process of "writing back" requires a double emancipation—from the myths of America and from those of Europe. The American who knows both cultures from the outside but finds him- or herself back inside American culture and subject again to its myths has the difficult but crucial task that Baldwin outlines when he writes, "In this endeavor to wed the vision of the Old World with that of the New, it is the writer, not the statesman, who is our strongest arm" ("Discovery" 176).

NOTES

Introduction

1. For Stein, James's oeuvre stands for the difference between English and American literature: "Henry James just went on doing what American literature had always done, the form was always the form of the contemporary English one, but the disembodied way of disconnecting something from anything and anything from something was the American one. The way it had of often all never having any daily living was an American one" ("English Literature" 57).

The dynamics of Stein's identification with James and the relation of this identification to Stein's aesthetics are clearest in the portrait "Henry James" in "Four Portraits": "A narrative of Henry James told by one who listened to some one else telling about some one entirely different from Henry James. . . . She was entirely a different kind of human being from Henry James . . . and did lead an entirely different kind of life. She lived alone and in the country and so did Henry James. She was heavy set and seductive and so was Henry James. She was slow in movement and light in speech and could change her speech without changing her words so that at one time her speech was delicate and witty and at another time slow and troubling and so was that of Henry James. She was not at all at all at all resembling to Henry James and never knew him and never heard of him and was of another nationality and lived in another country. . . . This one the one telling the story had always admired Henry James" (326–27).

See also Charles Caramello's discussion of James and Stein in *Henry James, Gertrude Stein, and the Biographical Act*.

2. See ch. 1, nn. 4 and 5.

3. The phrase "collective autobiography" is John Hazlett's. See *My Generation* 3 and passim.

4. My readings of *The American Scene* and *Everybody's Autobiography* focus entirely on the textual evidence in James's and Stein's writings and letters. In the chapters on Cowley and Stearns, I might seem to succumb to the temptation to indulge in literary gossip about the 1920s. Although this gossip is helpful in establishing the context in which the two men lived and wrote, it is nowhere invoked as evidence in my arguments.

5. Caren Kaplan's *Questions of Travel* is a powerful critical summary of recent discourse about national identity, travel, tourism, and exile, and has been very helpful in delineating the scope of this project. See also Anderson, Bammer, Bartkowski,

Baudrillard, Bhabha, Braidotti, Chambers, Clifford, MacCannell, Pratt, Tabori, and Van Den Abbeele.

6. There is an extensive literature on repatriation, almost all of which is historical, political, or sociological in nature, concerned with the return home of refugee populations. Although the psychology of repatriation that such studies discover bears considerable similarity to the structures of ambivalence that characterize the texts I examine here, any comparison between the conditions determining both "exile" and "return" in historical situations of displacement such as those of *Gastarbeiter* and victims of political persecution and natural disaster and the self-willed emigration of middle-class intellectuals and writers verges on the obscene. The essays in Hirsch and Miller explore precisely the "complex interaction between the affects of belonging and the politics of entitlement in a diasporic world, rethinking and retheorizing beyond the boundaries of either field, the complex interactions between loss and reclamation, mourning and repair, departure and return" (5).

7. See Perl. Studies such as Perl's remain touchingly innocent of the political implications of equating expatriation and exile, failing even to pay adequate attention to the ways in which the texts on which they base their paradigms acknowledge the difference between the two.

8. Shari Benstock's *Women of the Left Bank* is the classic account of the culture of American expatriate women during the period chronicled by Cowley. For an account of a woman journalist's expatriate life in London and a return to America that occasions what she calls a "remaking," see Banks.

9. Cowley understood more than he let on. His poem "Harold Stearns" ("Three Americans in Paris" 351) correctly marks the dissociation between the cultural critic who is said to have initiated the intellectual migration to Paris in the 1920s and Stearns's expatriate persona, and even intimates a connection between Stearns's relation to women and the enigma he represents:

> Amidst the racket, Harold Stearns is quiet. He
> In fact is strangely quiet for this Latin,
> Ebullient city, where such piety
> Is rarer than in puritan Manhattan;
> And rather would he brave the fires of Hades
> Than meet the glances of the Paris ladies.
> And does he then, remembering his article,
> Expound to us Three Roads Proposed to Freedom!
> And does he paint the town? No, not a particle;
> His eyes are innocent as those of Edom.
> Less bad than bashful, less in joy than fear,
> He hides his glances in a glass of beer.

10. Of course, when Malcolm Cowley published *Exile's Return* in 1934, he considered himself a Marxist, and his insistence on the representative, transpersonal narrative is in keeping with the political convictions he had embraced. It is necessary

to note, however, that the 1951 reissue of *Exile's Return* retains the notion of social determination even as it repudiates the Marxism of the first edition.

11. Strictly speaking, *The Odyssey* is only about exile in a limited sense. Odysseus's departure for Troy was reluctant but voluntary; as soon, however, as he is detained against his will by Circe and then Calypso, he can be said to be in exile.

12. In a far lighter vein, Bill Bryson evokes the temporal dissociations involved in returning to America after a long absence: "Coming back to your native land after an absence of many years is a surprisingly unsettling business, a little like waking from a long coma. Time, you discover, has wrought changes that leave you feeling mildly foolish and out of touch. You proffer hopelessly inadequate sums when making small purchases. You puzzle over ATM machines and automated gas pumps and pay phones, and are astonished to discover, by means of a stern grip on your elbow, that gas station maps are no longer free" (2).

13. Chambers writes that "to travel implies movement between fixed positions, a site of departure, a point of arrival, the knowledge of an itinerary. It also intimates an eventual return, a potential homecoming." He equates homecoming with "completing the story, domesticating the detour" (5). To extend this formulation to expatriation involves emphasizing less the movement of travel than the voluntary nature of the displacement and the option of returning home.

14. In an essay entitled "The Role of Separation in Understanding Home," the geographer James L. Kelly concludes from his readings of the works of American expatriate writers of the 1920s that "people living away from home do not acquire new information about the home place, but they are able to obtain new insights into the realities of home because they are free of the constraints of home, have fewer local responsibilities, can distinguish the significant features from the insignificant ones and can look at responsibilities with more maturity and objectivity" (63). It is interesting that he doesn't question how these "insights into the realities of home" affect the writer—and his or her works—when he or she returns.

15. General studies of expatriation in United States cultural history include Rahv; Susman; Ernest Earnest, *Expatriates and Patriots: American Artists, Scholars, and Writers in Europe* (Durham, NC: Duke UP, 1968); John Bainbridge, *Another Way of Living: A Gallery of Americans Who Choose to Live in Europe* (New York: Holt, Rinehart & Winston, 1968); Herbert R. Lottman, *The Left Bank: Writers, Artists, and Politics from the Popular Front to the Cold War* (Chicago: U of Chicago P, 1981); Michel Fabre, *La Rive noire: De Harlem à la Seine* (Paris: Lieu commun, 1985); Humphrey Carpenter, *Geniuses Together: American Writers in the 1920s* (Boston: Houghton Mifflin, 1987); Christopher Sawyer-Lauçanno, *The Continual Pilgrimage: American Writers in Paris, 1944–1960* (New York: Grove Press, 1992); Benstock; Kennedy; Stovall; and Pizer.

The seemingly endless list of personal memoirs of expatriate writers includes Banks; Paul Bowles, *Without Stopping: An Autobiography* (New York: Ecco Press, 1972); Hemingway, *A Movable Feast*; Chester Himes, *The Quality of Hurt: The Early Years; The Autobiography of Chester Himes*, vol. 1 (New York: Thunder's Mouth

Press, 1972) and *My Life of Absurdity: The Later Years; The Autobiography of Chester Himes*, vol. 2 (New York: Thunder's Mouth Press, 1976); McAlmon and Boyle; Gertrude Stein, *The Autobiography of Alice B. Toklas*; Dos Passos; Shirer; and Josephson, *Life among the Surrealists.*

16. In *Exile's Return*, Cowley cites this exchange to illustrate the new perspective that their European sojourn has afforded his "exiles," albeit with some embroidery (Burke's letter becomes "an article in *Vanity Fair*"), emendations (the allusion to Harold Stearns is nastier, as are his characterizations of London, Berlin, and Paris), and concessions to taste ("cunt-lapping" becomes "degenerate"). See 118–19.

17. Robert Edwards cites classical sources in which exile from home is equated with alienation from the self. Invoking Ovid's description of Alcmeon as "*exsul mentis domusque*" ("an exile from mind and home"), Edwards concludes that "the eidetic structure of exile is an uprooting from native soil and translation from the center to the periphery, from organized space invested with meaning to a boundary where the conditions of experience are problematic. . . . The fact of exile tests notions of self and social order, and as it does so each of the terms transforms" (16–17).

18. See, for instance, the epigraph from Melville that Matthew Josephson chose for *Portrait of the Artist as American*: "I feel I am an exile here" (n.p.).

19. This flight from America has an economic dimension as well (see Banks): in the nineteenth and early twentieth centuries, writers, artists, and intellectuals moved to Europe because they could live more cheaply there; in what is only an apparent reversal of this paradigm, many of today's expatriates are ambitious employees of international corporations for whom several stints abroad are prerequisite for eventual advancement at home.

20. This latter figure might be more accurately described as a *nomad*. The plea for the intellectual nomad has been made most recently, with reference to Nietzsche and Deleuze, by Rosi Braidotti. She distinguishes the nomad from both the migrant and the exile: "The nomad does not stand for homelessness, or compulsive displacement; it is rather a figuration for the kind of subject who has relinquished all idea, desire, or nostalgia for fixity" (22).

21. See Ian Buruma's review of Said's autobiographical memoir, *Out of Place: A Memoir*: "The hero emerging from his memoir is not the Palestinian activist so much as the alienated intellectual. The modern image of the heroic intellectual is that of a marginal figure, the lonely champion of the truth, the deconstructionist of official 'narratives,' the 'exile.' One finishes his book with the strong impression that Said presses the suffering of the Palestinian people into the service of his own credentials as an intellectual hero" (10).

22. Of course, the figure of the artist as exile pervades the literature of modernism. Andrew Gurr writes, "the normal role for the modern writer is to be an exile. He is a lone traveler in the countries of the mind. . . . The intellectual is committed either physically or spiritually to a homeless existence" (14). Typically, Gurr fails to sustain the distinctions he occasionally draws between "physical" and "spiritual" exile, and hence elides the difference between a self-exile chosen as "the prerequisite for freedom

in . . . art" and true exile, in which "freedom in art" can at best be a compensation for real homelessness.

23. This list reads like the cast of characters of Freud's "Familienroman des Neu-rotikers" or Malcolm Cowley's *Exile's Return*. The native country, like the "real" parents of the "Familienroman," must be abandoned because it does not live up to the grand ambitions and projections of the dissatisfied individual. On the other side of the boundary that the individual imposes between him- or herself and "home," however, the music of home, the native language, becomes a kind of fetish on which the "exile" bestows all the love that has been withdrawn from its "proper" object.

24. Even a writer such as Van Wyck Brooks, who believed that American artists should stay home and forge a native culture, had a fundamentally pessimistic view of the options historically open to the American writer: He saw the American artist as torn between the "ordeal" of staying in America and sacrificing one's art to the con-ventions of a Puritan society and the "pilgrimage" of the expatriate, through which one lost touch with one's cultural specificity.

The first chapter of Susman ("Pilgrimage to Paris") is a fine summary of the deter-minants of expatriation in American intellectual history. Susman stresses two different, although related, phenomena: first, the intellectual alienation that oppressed American intellectuals and artists in the increasingly mercantile post–Civil War period and that caused many to want to escape America, and second, the attraction of Europe to those, like James and Stein, whose upbringings had been cosmopolitan or to those, like Stearns and Cowley, whose educations had put them in touch with the European cul-tural past. For these writers, the "pilgrimage" to Europe represented a return, either real or imaginary, to the sources of their cultural legacy.

25. Nostalgia plays an important role in Cowley's narrative, but it is a nostalgia for an idealized, lost rural home and not for the America he left or to which he returns.

Chapter One. Framing the Un-Scene / Writing the Wrongs

1. James's expatriation is, of course, a critical touchstone as well: In his study of James's life and work, Van Wyck Brooks regarded James's childhood European travel and his adult expatriation as determining his character and hence both the strengths and, more often, the weaknesses of his fiction: "He was more passive than his brother; he could not so easily react; he received impressions and he retained them. Europe was a paradise. America was a wilderness—it signified nothing but calamity, destruction, oblivion. . . . The life and writings of Henry James were to manifest the effects of all these early—shall we call them—illusions? They grew, they flourished. . . . He accepted these idols of the provincial cave that had been bred so naturally by the character, the circumstances, the solicitude of his father, by the situation of his family, and all the influences of his childhood contributed to foster them" (19).

In addition to the almost ritual invocation of James's life in discussions of the "in-ternational theme" in his work, expatriation is also a touchstone for current reevalua-tions of the relations between James's art and his politics. In an idiosyncratic argument that, as he himself almost admits, works less well for James than for Henry Adams,

Ezra Pound, or T. S. Eliot, Alex Zwerdling sees the turn back toward the "older [European] legacy" as "interrupt[ing] and complicat[ing] the standard teleological account of America's gradual cultural emancipation." Zwerdling attributes their expatriation to a "changing of the guard, as the patricians of the eastern seaboard were supplanted both by the plutocrats newly in control and by the swelling waves of immigrants" that challenged their sense of privilege and offended their sense of what art and culture should be (x–xi).

2. This drama of nostalgia takes concrete form in James's response to the disappearance, in the course of his Boston sojourn, of his childhood home in Ashburton Place. During his first visit, he revels in the persistence, despite so much "raw clearance" in the name of "improvement," of the "pair of ancient houses I was in quest of." Upon returning a month later, "(a justly-rebuked mistake) to see if another whiff of the fragrance were not to be caught, I found but a gaping void, the brutal effacement, at a stroke, of every related object, of the whole precious past. Both the houses had been leveled and the space to the corner cleared. . . . It was as if the bottom had fallen out of one's own biography, and one plunged backward into space without meeting anything. That, however, seemed to give me . . . the whole figure of my connection with everything about. . . . Thus it was the sense of the rupture, more than of anything else, that I was . . . to carry with me" (AS 228–30).

3. In the famous journal entry of 29 March 1905, in which James meditates on his strategies for representing his Cambridge sojourn, he is particularly careful to distinguish between the personal and the professional, between the memories his return to Cambridge revives and the representational "economy" of his travel narrative. He writes: "Oh, the division [into sections devoted to different regions] is good, I see—the 'three' will do beautifully and so for winding up the little *New England*, will Cambridge and its accessories. I feel as if I could *spread* on C., and that is my danger, as it's my danger everywhere. For *my* poor little personal C. of the far-off unspeakable past years, hangs there behind, like a pale pathetic ghost, hangs there behind, fixing me with tender, pleading eyes, eyes of such exquisite pathetic appeal and holding up the silver mirror, just faintly dim, that is like a sphere peopled with the old ghosts." In the journal entry, James succumbs to the appeal of these ghosts, enters the looking glass, and pursues exquisite and far-ranging memories that take him back to considering the sources of his "own vision-haunted migration": "Oh, strange little intensities of history, of ineffaceability; oh, delicate little odd links in *the long chain, kept unbroken for the fingers of one's tenderest touch!* Sanctities, pieties, treasure, abysses!"

As if in reaction against the "unbroken" chain of personal memory, James recoils and remembers the demands of his art: "But these are wanton lapses and impossible excursions; *irrelevant strayings of the pen, in defiance of every economy. My subject awaits me, all too charged and too bristling with the most artful economy possible*" (*Complete Notebooks* 238–39, emphasis added).

4. For a comprehensive critical overview of reviews of The American Scene and scholarship until 1977, see Hewitt. After a lull in the 1980s, discussion of The American Scene picked up considerably in the 1990s. The 1995 publication of an issue of

the *Henry James Review* dedicated to *The American Scene* documents the renewed interest in James's reencounter with America. See n. 5, below.

5. The renaissance of interest in *The American Scene* since the 1990s has centered on reappraisals of the politics and issues of national identity represented and negotiated by the text. See especially studies by Buelens (*Henry James and the "Aliens"*), Blair (*Henry James and the Writing of Race and Nation*), Graham, Freedman ("Henry James and the Discourses of Antisemitism"), Haviland (*Henry James's Last Romance*), McCall, Posnock (*Trial of Curiosity*), Schoenbach, Seltzer, Warren, Washington, Wilson, and Zwerdling, as well as the forum on *The American Scene* in the *Henry James Review* Fall 1995.

6. See Mae Henderson's "Introduction" to *Borders, Boundaries, and Frames* for a general discussion of "framing" in cultural studies. She writes that "the term 'frame' itself refers both to the edges that contain each image and to the internal image contained by the outer borders. Thus the frame generates meaning through its internal arrangement of space as well as through its definition of the boundary between images" (21). See also Derrida and Caws.

7. James writes, "Crowned not only with no history, but with no credible possibility of time for history, and consecrated by no uses save the commercial at any cost, they [the buildings that constitute the New York skyline] are simply the most piercing notes in that concert of the expensively provisional into which your supreme sense of New York resolves itself. They never begin to speak to you, in the manner of the builded majesties of the world as we have heretofore known such . . . with the authority of things of permanence or even of things of long duration. One story is good only till another is told, and sky-scrapers are the last word of economic ingenuity only till another word be written" (*AS* 77).

8. Posnock writes, "For an alien to be at home is as oxymoronic as calling oneself . . . a 'restored absentee.' . . . 'Being at home' for James . . . is not to rest in the stable continuity of tradition but to embrace a 'strange' contradiction—that being at home and being an alien are identical" (278).

James's encounter, in the New Hampshire hills, with a foreign-looking young man whose failure to respond to James's appeal for directions first in English, then in French and Italian, is generally read as a dramatic document of James's dismay at the infiltration of foreigners even in areas where one would least expect them (see, e.g., Zwerdling 198). A closer reading of the passage suggests a more subtle response on James's part. The passage continues, "'What are you then?' I wonderingly asked—*on which my accent loosened in him the faculty of speech*. 'I'm an Armenian,' he replied" (*AS* 119, emphasis added). By the time James returned to America, his accent, while perhaps not entirely English, was also no longer entirely American. In James's rendering of this situation, it is his (foreign) accent—a sign that identifies him with the "alien"—that establishes the connection with the young Armenian, who, quite obviously, understands and speaks enough American to bring the encounter to a satisfying conclusion.

9. Ross Posnock's brilliant reading of *The American Scene* (see esp. chs. 3 and 8)

constantly dovetails with my own, although Posnock sees James's uncertainties about the direction that American democracy is taking as far more positively productive than I see them.

10. See Winnett, Intro. and ch. 3, and Bentley, esp. ch. 3.

11. See Roland Barthes, "La Bruyère," in *Essais Critiques* 22, for a discussion of the "inland" and "outland" of *mondanité* that has significantly influenced my understanding of the function of manners in literary discourse.

12. See chapter 2, 121–24, for a discussion of James's reflections on masculinity, femininity, and gender relations in the United States.

13. Martha Banta concludes that "Philadelphia's Society [in contrast to New York's]—blank, bland, static, forever indifferently dancing apart from its own terrible City—is already dead" ("Strange Deserts" 8). Given her generally thematic focus, this conclusion is certainly justifiable; given Philadelphia's importance in James's scheme of representation, however, its status is more complex. See also Gooder, esp. 23–29, and Otter, ch. 3.

14. For discussions of romance in relation to *The American Scene*, see Beverley Haviland's extended argument in *Henry James's Last Romance* and Ross Posnock's comments throughout *The Trial of Curiosity* about James's ability to suspend "his will to originate, to order and master, preferring from the start to let impressions fall into 'the train of associations. . . . The mimetic has begun to act itself out in the style and conduct of James's sentences" (165). Without wanting to diminish the power and seductiveness of Posnock's argument, I think it is necessary to acknowledge the very powerful—and, to my mind, decisive—contrary movement in James back toward frames, limits, and control, toward an ethos of representation that Posnock would have him superceding. The fundamental difference in our readings becomes clearest in our interpretations of the word *margin*, which Posnock sees as a "zone of uncertainty . . . a veritable quicksand engulfing all pretensions to mastery, control, and stable identity" (88), whereas I regard James's margin as the locus whence he attempts to recover "mastery, control, and stable identity."

15. The debate around James's attitude toward Jews has intensified in the past decades, with most commentators, myself included, trying to find a framework in which the most egregious of his utterances both make some kind of tolerable sense in the immediate context and correspond to his stated political and social positions. Even Alex Zwerdling, the thesis of whose study centers on the "Improvised Europeans'" retreat from what they perceived as their cultural displacement in the United States, is incapable of calling James an anti-Semite. See Buelens, Blair, Justin D. Edwards, Freedman ("Henry James and the Discourses of Antisemitism"), Haviland ("The Return of the Alien"), and Posnock ("Affirming the Alien"; *Trial of Curiosity*).

16. Balzac's France, James wrote, was "a subject vast and comprehensive enough, yet with definite edges and corners . . . both inspiring enough for an immense prose epic and reducible enough for a report or a chart" ("Honoré de Balzac, 1902" 92–93).

17. See *Le Père Goriot*, where Balzac has Eugène de Rastignac recognize the sordid realities of Parisian life: "Il vit le monde comme il est: les lois et la morale impuissantes

chez les riches, et vit dans la fortune *l'ultima ratio mundi*. 'Vautrin a raison, la fortune est la vertu!' se dit-il" [He saw the world as it is: that law and morals are without power among the rich, and wealth is the *ultima ratio mundi*. "Vautrin is right, success is virtue," he told himself (89)].

18. At various points in his life, James advised other people to focus their attention on America. He wrote, for instance, to Edith Wharton that she should "profit, be warned, by my awful example of exile and ignorance. You will say that *j'en parle à mon aise*—but I shall have paid for my ease, and I don't want you to pay (as much) for yours. . . . *Do New York!*" (*Letters* 4: 236), and he urged William James to arrange for his children to know their native country: "What I most of all feel, and in the light of it conjure you to keep doing for them, is their being *à même* to contract local saturations and attachments in respect to their *own* great and glorious country, to learn, and strike roots into, its infinite beauty, as I suppose, and variety" (100).

These utterances are often taken as James's statement of regret about his own choices, as is the confession reported by Hamlin Garland in *Roadside Meetings*: "If I were to live my life over again . . . I would be an American. I would steep myself in America, I would know no other land. I would study its beautiful side" (461).

James's advice to others is rarely self-serving, and what he advises others to do may be a product of his experience, without necessarily casting the necessity of his experience into question. The confession that Garland attributes to James is not confirmed and was, in any case, made before—and not, as Zwerdling mistakenly reports—after James's 1904 trip to America (204).

19. James remembers "William's inspired transcript, on the exquisite little Florentine urn of Alice's ashes, William's divine gift to us, and to *her,* of the Dantean lines—*Dopo lungo exilio e martiro / Viene a questa pace*—". *Paradiso* 10, 128–89, correctly reads: "ed essa da martiro e da essilio venne a questa pace" (*Complete Notebooks* 240).

20. Compare: "and out of Erebus they came, / flocking toward me now, the ghosts of the dead and gone . . . / . . . But I . . . sat down on alert there and never let the ghosts / of the shambling, shiftless dead come near that blood / till I had questioned Tiresias myself" (Homer 250–51).

21. In a 1874 letter to Grace Norton from Florence, James wrote, "The great fact for us all there [in America] is that, relish Europe as we may, we belong much more to that than to this and stand in a much less factitious and artificial relation to it. I feel forever how Europe keeps holding one at arm's length, and condemning one to a meagre scraping of the surface" (*Letters* 1: 428).

22. See Kenneth W. Warren's reading of "The Jolly Corner," which also sees Brydon falling back into the ethos and the aesthetic of a bygone era (126–30).

23. The passage continues: "It is an extraordinary world, an altogether huge 'proposition,' as they say there, giving one, I think, an immense impression of material and political power; but almost cruelly charmless, in effect, and calculated to make one crouch, ever afterwards, as cravenly as possible, at Lamb House Rye—if one happens to have a poor little L.H.,R., to crouch in" (*Letters* 4: 397).

24. In *Henry James and the Writing of Race and Nation*, Sara Blair claims that what she terms James's "documentary" project "is in dialogue and contest with the framing power of visual, or 'phantasmagoric,' technologies to document race and thus to manage the range of bourgeois America's ongoing responses to the question of how national culture and citizens are made" (162). While I see James as engaging an American raw material that demands representational strategies other than his own, I do not see him actually acknowledging those technologies. On the contrary, I see *The American Scene* as characterized by the willful self-limitation to the literary.

Chapter Two. An Intellectual Is Being Beaten

1. Stearns did, of course, notice the badge, and Cowley must have known it; the memoir to which he alludes in the footnote cited above records the scene in detail: "At six o'clock the next evening I arrived at the Pennsylvania Station where Malcolm Cowley—and this certainly would not happen today—greeted me with a typical booster's 'Welcome To Our City' banner. He invited me to his apartment, where Peggy, his wife, and he and myself had a dinner, washed down with a bit of the synthetic gin of the era. Anyway it was jolly" (*Street* 250).

2. Stearns's own description of his writing assignments, "anything I could pick up" (*Street* 128), unfairly minimizes the respect he and his work enjoyed at the time. William Shirer, for instance, describes Stearns as "one of my heroes, one of the brightest of all the young intellectuals who in Greenwich Village were stirring up the country, shaming it for its lack of culture and taste and goading it to take notice of the new young writers and the new young literature. . . . He had become a leading contributor to the newly founded *New Republic* and later the youthful editor of *The Dial*, and in 1921, when he was thirty, he had sent to the publishers a book he had conceived and edited, *Civilization in the United States*, which had burst upon the country and shaken it up—and shaken me up—when it came out a year later. I had got the news of it in the college library one day. Thumbing through *The Nation* I had come across the book section, then edited by Carl Van Doren, which was devoted in its entirety to six reviews of the book. . . . It and a book of his own essays . . . *America and the Young Intellectual*, aroused me from my provincial slumbers" (219).

3. See also Ford 134–35.

4. It is interesting to note that in Stearns's controversial volume, *Civilization in the United States*, so often regarded as the manifesto of the kind of expatriates for whom Cowley, for one, had such contempt, the author of the chapter "Sex," Elsie Clews Parsons, writes: "The American case of sex . . . may be said to present symptoms of arrested development. Together with the non-realism of childish or senile formula, there is here the kind of emotionalism which checks emotional vitality and which is fed upon the sense of crisis. . . . The emotions of crisis are statutory, pre-determined, conventionalized; neither for oneself nor for others do they make any demands upon imagination, or insight, or spiritual concern" (315).

5. Stearns says much the same of "Hem" in *The Street I Know*. Describing the period when his fortunes were at their nadir, he writes: "He[mingway] did what he

could—that is, he got my typewriter out of pawn, gave me some cash, paid for my hotel, and tried to suggest one or two possible markets for some articles. But by this time he was definitely out of the newspaper game—I think he was glad of it, too—and he had no leads to give me looking towards a regular newspaper job in Paris. He probably didn't realize the difficulties I was up against anyway in getting a job in Paris on a newspaper—how, by this time, the myth had grown that I could always make money 'on my own' at the track and that I didn't need a job anyway, not to mention the fact, of course, that the whispering campaign about my health stood me in no good purpose either. However, this much I can say for Hemingway—and I am glad to say, too: He always has acted the way you would expect a friend to act in all the years I have known him; he has never 'let me down;' and, what I think I like best of all, he has always been honest with me. As probably he would write it, he has never kidded me" (367–68).

Ford cites a letter from Hemingway to Fitzgerald that reveals Hemingway's impatience with Stearns: "Hemingway wrote to Fitzgerald that it was useless to try to reform a has-been who had done nothing for almost two years. Any softness toward the down-and-out Stearns was misplaced, Hemingway advised. Except for giving Stearns money . . . and being nice to him, there was nothing anyone could do. The 'poor bastard lives altogether in his imagination,' Hemingway explained. 'I always get awfully sorry for people and especially for liars, drunks, homely whores, etc. . . . After all, panhandling is no damned fun. A gent who's drinking himself to death ought not to be constantly having to raise the funds to do it with. I do think Harold had a pretty damned good head. Also think he destroyed it or completely coated it with fuzz by drinking.'

"Having given Fitzgerald the lowdown on Stearns, Hemingway asked him to keep it confidential. It would only make life tougher if Harold were to think Hemingway did not believe in him. Watching the man decline was 'pretty sad,' but nothing could be done about it" (111).

6. This nickname reflects both Stearns's passion for horse racing and his "long silences and paradoxical dignity" (Sarason and Strickland 359).

7. Jolas's remark is recorded in Sarason and Strickland 360. The phrase "a reformed character" is Cowley's (*Exile's Return* [1951] 285).

8. William Shirer's version of Stearns's departure follows similar lines: "Having sent his two books to the printer, Harold Stearns had taken his own advice and . . . boarded ship for Europe. A dozen reporters had come to the gangplank in New York to chronicle the departure of the young literary lion and to note his last words. 'How long are you going to stay away?' one asked. 'Perhaps forever,' Stearns said" (219). In his introduction to *Confessions of a Harvard Man*, the 1984 reissue of *The Street I Know*, Hugh Ford embroiders on a version of the story that, as he acknowledges, he owes to Cowley. After a paraphrase of Cowley's description, he adds, "He was going to Europe, he announced, because there people knew how to live" (*Confessions of a Harvard Man* xv).

I have been unable to find the slightest mention of this event in the New York newspapers of the time. Although the sailing of the *Berengaria* and the names of some of the passengers aboard are mentioned in both the *New York Times* and the *New York World* of 5 July 1921, Stearns's name appears nowhere.

Cowley's representation of Stearns's departure retains a hold over representations of it and of its importance for the early 1920s. Most recently, Michael North writes: "Perhaps the most celebrated such departure [of a generation that fled from America to France in order to rediscover art] at the time was Harold Stearns' in 1921. In his preface to *Civilization in the United States* . . . Stearns complained that 'the most moving and pathetic fact in the social life of America to-day is emotional and aesthetic starvation. . . . Stearns loudly departed the United States for France, where he was to end his aesthetic starvation as a racetrack columnist" (181). As so often happens, North launches a critique of Stearns while ultimately subscribing to Stearns's critique of America or at least affirming that this critique was shared by most of Stearns's contemporaries.

9. Warren Susman, too, in "Pilgrimage to Paris," sees Stearns as representing a generation older and more ensconced in the institutions of American culture than Cowley and the "young intellectuals" whose cause he is espousing: "He is, in part, cut off from the special currents of the new expatriation because he did not serve in the war, because he had a considerable career in America before he came to France . . . because he was not directly associated with any of the little magazines or special intellectual or artistic groups of Americans in Paris, and because there is little evidence that he felt the particular impact of current French intellectual and artistic currents. . . . Even as a critic of American life Stearns was somehow outside the newer expatriate tradition. It is too often maintained that *Civilization in the United States*, for example, because it was published the same day Stearns dramatically withdrew from the country, represented the kind of criticisms that led to expatriation. Yet of the 'Thirty Americans' who contributed to that symposium only Stearns and Conrad Aiken could be considered expatriates . . . and only Stearns sought France as the center of his life in exile. The contributors were too well established and secure in positions within the American scene. Further, many of the more significant younger expatriates, many of the expatriate magazines—while still critical of the United States—specifically attacked the famous symposium. It was the work, after all, of individuals who had played a role in the pre-war attempt to achieve the fulfillment of the American promise, written from their own special viewpoint, their own sense of American failure. The younger expatriates had had no such experience in American life; their criticisms were often differently directed. Often the authors of the symposium were as much under attack by the younger expatriates as was a critic like Stuart Sherman, so much the earlier enemy of Harold Stearns" (268–69).

10. Hugh Ford sees Alice MacDougal's death as the "main, if not the sole reason that Harold Stearns left the United States" (93). Susman, who is ultimately not sympathetic to Stearns, distinguishes between the cultural drama of Stearns's departure from America and its personal motivations, although he makes Stearns himself responsible for the drama: "Harold Stearns, with his dramatic withdrawal from the United States after concluding his inquiry into *Civilization in the United States*, his earlier defiant

'what can a young man do?—get out!' attempted to leave little doubt that his reasons for expatriation were cultural, that his expatriation was a strategy for dealing with intolerable situations in the United States and a means of indicating his criticism of life for the intellectual in the United States. Yet a reading of his autobiography—written three years after his return it is true—suggests that there were clearly personal psychological motives in his case; he had been tragically upset by the death of his wife in childbirth, he had lost any sense of assurance in himself, and he had encountered other personal difficulties in his sex life which reinforced the feeling Blackmur described: 'he couldn't stand himself in America'" (210).

I have searched in vain for any indication in *The Street I Know* of "other personal difficulties in his sex life." Stearns does allude to a "happy household" he shared with a former girlfriend who lived in the same house as he and who did what she could to comfort Stearns after Alice's death. This woman, Felicia, had many lovers but "'would not permit anybody to live with her.' . . . There was not then, there never was later . . . any question of Felicia and myself 'living together.' But we both understood each other and could get along and manage things better than most such strange ménage à deux combinations. And it was a happy household, for we both had many friends in common" (191). As I hope to demonstrate, the sexual politics of Cowley's generation and the critics who base their understandings of Stearns on Cowley's rendition of him make it impossible to imagine that Stearns seems actually to have liked women and chosen their company.

11. Mark Orwoll's biography of Stearns, "Gathering Legends: Harold Stearns and the Lost Generation," has not been published, and Orwoll has denied me access to the manuscript. In the three-page précis of the biography that he sent to publishers and that he also made available to me, Orwoll claims that Stearns was "born a bastard."

12. "I am developing into a disagreeable prig and a good deal of a snob," Cowley wrote in a letter to Kenneth Burke (cited in Bak 49). In another letter, he elaborates, "Harvard has made me healthy. It has made me respect myself, and at the same time made me snobbish. It has ruined me as an author, and made me a much better citizen. It has taught me to kiss girls without blushing. The old views are dropping off one by one" (Jay 25).

Hans Bak does not defend Cowley's snobbishness, but explains it as follows: "Prerequisites for success in the Harvard club system were rigid and complicated. Cowley, doubtless aware of the hopelessness of his case, might claim that the club system was beyond his ambition, yet he could not refrain from toying with the possibility, and had secret hopes of making at least the Dickey. Rubbing elbows with the social elite on the Gold Coast, Cowley could not help feeling uneasy about his own social status. Knowing himself barred from eligibility to any of the Harvard clubs—he made neither the Institute nor the Dickey—Cowley, as if in compensation, was tempted to adopt the manners and modes of those inside the club system. Since he was neither an 'in' nor a complete outsider, his social position at Harvard remained uncertain and amphibious" (59–60).

13. Christine Stansell writes, "Art . . . was deemed to be a peculiarly feminine

interest at the end of the [nineteenth] century and artists as a group were considered vaguely compromised men. Insipid female taste supposedly dominated American culture, and in this mental frame, male artists ran the risk of emasculation, prevented by sentimental women from creating the virile work demanded by the times. In truth, there was little substance to the charge, but the 'feminization of American culture,' an idea born of reactions against the small gains New Women did make in public life, was a truism by the end of the century and nagged at the self-assurance of men who made art" (*American Moderns* 32). See also Ellison (603, nn. 12 and 13), Lears, Kimmel, Bederman, and Persons.

14. Is it worth noting here that this second move in Stearns's argument, the association of practical thought with women and abstract thought with men, has a "European" genealogy. Rousseau, for instance, writes, "The quest for abstract and speculative truths, principles, and axioms in the sciences, for everything that tends to generalize ideas, is not within the competence of women. All their studies ought to be related to practice. It is for them to apply the principles man has found, and to make the observations which lead man to the establishment of principles" (*Emile* 386).

15. Stansell's omission of any reference to Stearns is the most recent and surprising instance of this phenomenon. It is equally interesting to note that accounts of his tenure with the *Dial* are taken almost exclusively from his own account of it in *The Street I Know*; even there, his contribution seems to have left no mark or at least to have resisted assimilation into any grand narrative of the *Dial*'s designs. See Joost.

16. "He was a very attractive man, women did indeed flock to him, but he didn't have a strong interest in romantic relationships" (Mark Orwoll, pers. comm., 28 April 2000).

17. Stearns's second wife's fortune contributed significantly to the comfort of his "later" years (Ford 134). My limited access to biographical material makes it impossible to confirm his financial arrangements in the late 1930s and early 1940s.

18. Stearns's paean to his deceased friend Walter Franzen picks up on this incompatibility of "real intellectual work" and the market: "If one wanted an indictment of modern education and modern civilization, I still believe that the fact that Walter Franzen was permitted to wander round New York, without finding any outlet for his great talents, would furnish a better indictment than all the Socialist orators have ever been able to draw up since before Debs. Sometimes, when discouraged at the difficulties always faced in this country by anybody trying to do honest and unbiased intellectual work, I think of Walter—and, if perhaps not all the bitterness, the discouragement goes. At least, I have been permitted to survive, though, perhaps, that is because I have not quite the same kind of courage he had. Or better luck" (*Street* 131).

19. Traditional psychoanalytic discussions of masochism see it as "a sublimated expression of desire for the father." Carol Siegel sketches Gilles Deleuze's description of its dynamics: "Masochism is a (male) strategy for receiving sexual pleasure without experiencing the castration anxiety that results from identification and rivalry with the father. The masochist gives up paternal/phallic power by contract to a woman who then acts as his agent to punish him *as* a representative or impersonator of the father.'"

She then cites Deleuze: "'What is beaten, humiliated, and ridiculed in him is the image and the likeness of the father'" (198). Given Stearns's fatherlessness, we would have to propose the following variation on this pathology: Stearns's masochism enables him to produce the (missing) father and simultaneously enter into oedipal struggle with him while both "pay[ing] tribute to [his mother's] indomitable spirit" (*Street* 13) and recognizing that the "indomitable" mother has been the bearer of the phallus all along. As should become clear, however, a reading of Stearns's masochism as the appropriate response to a cultural situation of a subject with his personal history is far more productive in this context.

20. Note, in this context, George Santayana's comments on Stearns's "Preface" to *Civilization in the United States*. In response to the passage in which Stearns bemoans the "sharp dichotomy between preaching and practice; we let our right hand know what our left hand doeth. . . . The moral code resolves itself into . . . the fear of what people will say," Santayana writes: "I see the fact which Mr. Stearns points to here, but not as he sees it. The American conscience is not insincere; it is only belated, inapplicable. The sanctities are traditional; sentiment preserves and requires the habits and language of an elder age; it has all the sincerity of instinct. But it does not exactly fit the exigencies of public life, which has been transformed and accelerated in a way which conscience can't keep up with, yet is dazzled by and has not the heart to condemn; for it has to keep house, as it were, with an obstreperous younger brother, the conscience of emancipated human nature, with its new set of illusions and its pride in its thundering, pushing life. The American intellect is shy and feminine; it paints nature in watercolours; whereas the sharp masculine eye sees the world as a moving-picture—rapid, vulgar, to be glanced at and used merely as a sign of what is going to happen next. Mere man in America hardly has an articulate logic in which to express his practical convictions, and I doubt if even this book will supply the want. I won't say that it is itself genteel; that would enrage its revolutionary authors too much; they may have forgotten that Emerson and Thoreau and Brook Farm were revolutionary. But if not genteel and not specifically American, the spirit of these critics is one of offended sensibility. Things shock them; and their compensatory ideals and plans of reform are fetched from abstract reflection or irrelevant enthusiasms. They are far from expressing the manly heart of America, emancipated from the genteel tradition. They seem to be morally underfed, and they are disaffected" (161–62).

Santayana's need to sharpen, as it were, precisely the point that Stearns is making, and will make in precisely Santayana's terms later in the volume, reinforces my sense that American male intellectuals were so oppressed by the imputed gender of their enterprise that they could not even recognize a discourse that articulated their own agenda.

21. See Benjamin, Bersani, Burgett, Savran, Stewart, and Silverman.

22. Ford writes, "The bonding elements in their marriage were Alice's devotion to Harold and Harold's humility toward his wife" (91).

23. Stearns's understanding of how the war challenged and even warped contemporary constructions of masculinity is eloquently demonstrated in his explanation

qua defense of Ernest Hemingway's machismo: "A good deal of the false and over-emphasized masculinity in the writing of a man like Hemingway—who after all was a young man then and *was* fighting himself—is in reality due to the feeling of disgust with this safe-at-home, civilian virtue-standards blindness of those who could still talk about correct and moral acts at the very moment the vilest and most immoral acts—the slaughter of the world's youth in a senseless war—were not merely being condoned but applauded. There is much more—and much subtler, because not quite fully conscious—criticism of war-mindedness in Hemingway's specious (yet seductive) enthusiasm for gore than a romantic critic might surmise" (*Street* 164).

24. Alice seems to have echoed many of Stearns's idiosyncrasies: she postponed informing her parents of the marriage because "her mother was ill in California . . . and she didn't want any news to upset her"; on the evening of their wedding, she attended a business dinner and he kept a poker date; they continued to keep separate apartments after their marriage: "until both of us were more definite in our plans of future work, we should not attempt to live together" (*Street* 177–78).

25. Recall the "Preface" to *The Ambassadors*, in which James writes of "the dreadful little old tradition, one of the platitudes of the human comedy, that people's moral scheme *does* break down in Paris; that nothing is more frequently observed; that hundreds of thousands of more or less hypocritical or more or less cynical persons annually visit the place for the sake of the probable catastrophe" (*Art of the Novel* 316).

26. Note Stearns's description of Joan, a "divorcee considerably older than myself, but attractive, intelligent, witty, and a good sport, if the world ever produced one" with whom he kept company in 1924, prior to his short trip back to America. "Joan," Stearns continues, "was—and, indeed, still is—my ideal of what a woman companion can be, but only so infrequently is. . . . Joan was a sure exit from the psychopathic ward. A woman who had two grown-up daughters and a grown-up son naturally understood the *essential childishness of most men* and might not even be abashed at the particularly absurd form it took with me" (*Street* 222–23, emphasis added).

27. It would be misleading to suggest that Stearns's life in Paris was a life without women; without the friendship and generosity of women, it is likely that he would not have survived. Early in his sojourn, his always meager journalist's income was supplemented by the contributions of a series of female companions; in fact, it was "Joan" who was perspicacious enough to recognize Stearns's need to see his young son and entirely planned and financed his trip to America in 1924. But Stearns's mission in Paris was not to live a good or wholesome or even happy life; his mission was abjection, and given the conscientiousness with which he pursued it, it is a miracle that he survived as long as he did.

28. Stearns did, it was true, move from the *Chicago Tribune* to the *British Daily Mail*; it is significant that the onset of his truly desperate times coincides with this move away from the American microcosm of the *Tribune*. Stearns reflects, "most of us, whether we know it or not, are homesick for our own kind at least now and then, and if your own kind is slightly mad, that makes no difference either. It is all in the accent, the point of view, the curious assumptions that, naturally, we take for granted—until,

of course, we go with an alien crowd and find that we cannot take their assumptions for granted, that in cold fact we often do not even know what those assumptions are. Most American expatriates in Paris, for instance, would not stay there ten weeks—unless there were other American expatriates with whom they could talk things over" (*Street* 338).

29. This need for what I here call a "superstructure of compulsion" is a leitmotif in Stearns's life, one that he recognized precociously, even if he was unable to redress it. In one of his earliest articles, "The Confessions of a Harvard Man," Stearns takes Harvard to task for not having better enforced the symbolic order that it represents: "It fails to stimulate the majority of its students to take advantage of this rich opportunity. It furnishes a totally inadequate intellectual discipline. And instead of teaching a man good habits of work and steady concentration, it encourages lazy and vicious habits" (819).

30. We find, in *The Street I Know*, vestiges of a relation to his mother that could, indeed, support a psychoanalytical reading of Stearns as "abject": "The abjection of self would be the culminating form of that experience of the subject to which it is revealed that all its objects are based merely on the inaugural *loss* that laid the foundations of its own being. . . . Even before things for him *are*—hence before they are signifiable—he drives them out . . . and constitutes his own territory, edged by the abject. . . . What he has swallowed up instead of maternal love is an emptiness, or rather, a maternal hatred without a word for the words of the father; that is what he tries to cleanse himself of, tirelessly" (Kristeva 5–6).

What remains is to reconcile Stearns's American masochistic pathology and its European abjection: as long as Stearns regarded himself as inscribed within the problematic space he called "Civilization in America," he was also subject to its constitutive institutions and hierarchies. His subject-formation clearly depended upon a relation to these instances that both clung desperately to them and challenged their authenticity; hence the masochism he suggests in his "sensual" life and its extension into his relation to the social and cultural institutions of America. Having set himself loose from this highly ambivalent determining matrix, Stearns entered what Kristeva calls the "abject," that relation of self-loathing without context, "that disturbs identity, system, order. What does not respect borders, positions, rules" (Kristeva 4). His return to America would thus be a reinscription of himself within the constitutive institutions whose internalizations abjection expels.

31. "A Prodigal American Returns" was published in *Scribner's Magazine* 94 (May 1932): 293–95. It was reprinted as the first chapter of *Rediscovering America*, from which I cite here. It is interesting to note that he sees "the new [Soviet] Russian attitude toward women" as having "at least on the surface . . . so much in common with our own" (23).

Chapter Three. Wo Mama war, soll Dada werden

1. Lewis P. Simpson describes this aspect of Cowley's work most eloquently: "We see running through the whole range of his work as a twentieth-century poet, critic,

and literary and cultural historian a basic motive of alienation. As both a creator and an interpreter of the literature of the lost generation, Cowley is a contributor to one of its leading aspects: a myth or a legend of creativity which is definable as a poetics of exile" ("Malcolm Cowley" 225). Writing about *Exile's Return* in particular, Simpson continues, "The most dramatic evidence of this condition he finds in the exile of this generation of writers from the fundamental aspect of reality in America, childhood. It was not a normal separation of childhood from adulthood. The country of childhood cast them out, though surviving in their minds as their 'most essential baggage.' . . . The deracination of the lost generation was inherent in the condition of American life" (228).

2. Unless otherwise specified, citations are taken from the 1934 edition of *Exile's Return*.

3. To his credit, Cowley's rejection of the oedipal diagnosis seems not merely defensive, but true to the facts as he presents them. He continues, "They [the symptoms of the Oedipus complex] would be hard to find. I never quarreled with Popsie, never felt him to be a rival, and always respected him for holding fast to his beliefs, including those I rejected. Instead of rebelling against him, I nodded my head and silently disregarded his advice. . . . Usually he let me have my way, as he also let Mother have hers" ("Mother and Son" 32–33).

4. This ambivalence is far more artistically productive—although certainly more personally crippling—than the more unilaterally "destructive" emotions that Douglas describes.

5. Homecoming and return—indeed, like the particular Odyssean allusion—proved to be particularly productive topoi with which to evaluate the relation between the self-willed "new" and the ambivalent past that lent both meaning and urgency to the project of modernism. James Joyce's *Ulysses* and Ezra Pound's *Cantos* explicitly exploit the structural and cultural resonances of the classical topos for their fictions. See Perl, esp. Prologue and ch. 8. Cowley, on the other hand, deploys the topos in service of autobiographical narrative.

6. When Cowley published *A Second Flowering: Works and Days of the Lost Generation* in 1973, he designated "Fitzgerald, Hemingway, Dos Passos, Cummings, Wilder, Faulkner, Wolfe, and Hart Crane, all born between 1894 and 1900" as "representative" of an "age group" that had "more experiences in common and was more conscious of possessing shared purposes than the groups that preceded or followed it" (vii). Although the generation Cowley invokes in *Exile's Return* is slightly more comprehensive—including Cowley himself as a major player, as well as the friends, like Kenneth Burke, Matthew Josephson, and S. Foster Damon, with whom he played—he takes pride in allowing the "great" names to stand for the enduring achievement of the generation as a whole. See also n. 8.

7. In a 1922 letter to John Brooks Wheelwright, Cowley is explicit about the size of this group: "I think we are all fools if we don't work and if we don't work together. The requisite for an intelligent literature (as distinguished from an emotional literature) is an intelligent society, and an intelligent society may consist of only half a dozen

people. It would be a mistake to found a school; that would mean that these half dozen men had only one idea. Many ideas can be born and be polished by rubbing against each other" (cited in Kempf 76).

8. When Cowley reexamined this period in *A Second Flowering* (1972), he half-addressed the white, male bias of his generation-making. Attributing the scope of his canonization to his desire "to present the [lost] generation in terms of eight representative figures . . . born in the years from 1894 . . . to 1900," he assesses the consequences of this decision: "That choice of years has reasons behind it and explains the absence of other representative figures, for instance, Katherine Anne Porter, Elizabeth Madox Roberts, Henry Miller, Djuna Barnes, Archibald MacLeish, and Edna St. Vincent Millay, all a little older, and Steinbeck, Cozzens, and Nathaniel West, among others a little younger. There are no women among the eight, a fact being that the admired writers of the generation were men in the great majority. The time of famous women storytellers and poets was, in this country, either a little earlier or twenty years later. I feel a lasting gratitude [!] for the work of Caroline Gordon, Louise Bogan, Dawn Powell, and one or two other women of the generation, but they have been less widely read than male contemporaries of no greater talent.

"The famous Jewish novelists of later years were little boys or babies in the 1920s. So were the famous Black writers except Richard Wright, who was in his teens, and there are no representatives here of ethnic groups" (240).

Cowley walks a tightrope here: his desire to present himself as a contemporary of the great and famous writers of his time is stronger than his zeal, often expressed, to be the discoverer or champion of less-well-known and deserving authors. That "the men of the Lost Generation were white, middle-class, mostly Protestant by upbringing" seems less to disturb than to reassure him, and Cowley saves his true regret "for not having devoted" more attention to members of his cohort such as Edmund Wilson, Allen Tate, and Kenneth Burke. As in *Exile's Return*, Cowley's tactic is to dismiss with faint praise or actively ignore those figures who don't anchor him in the midst of the literary life of his time.

9. Cowley alludes to the French notion "to be very busy *à l'américaine*" (ER 162).

10. There is considerable evidence that the Dada that Cowley and his friends regarded themselves as introducing to New York was already well established there—primarily but not only in the visual arts—when they returned from their "exile." Naumann documents both the origins of New York Dada and its interactions with European Dada in the years between 1915 and 1922.

11. The general issue of the gender of modernity has been addressed most pertinently by Huyssen and Felski. North and Stansell (*American Moderns*) are most helpful in mapping the contours of this issue in American culture.

12. Matthew Josephson recalls the Cowley household in precisely such terms: "On occasion, I would come in to see Malcolm in the evening and find his home in complete disarray, a noisy game of cards in progress, and soiled dishes, empty wine bottles, and also flowers everywhere about. But in a corner of the kitchen, Malcolm had set up a small table with a portable typewriter and his papers and books. Here everything

was beautifully neat and clean, so that his little writing corner was in marked contrast with the rest of the place. At times, he would go into his corner and set to work doggedly—for he had great resolution—while the poker game raged around him all night." For the record, Josephson continues, "In the end, however, literature prevailed over poker and wine; he and Peggy were divorced, and he married a younger woman who, besides having other virtues, kept his household in beautiful order" (*Life among the Surrealists* 49–50).

13. In fact, at least as Cowley related it to Hans Bak, his marriage did "cause" severe illness. While Cowley was finishing his degree at Harvard, Peggy had been unfaithful and contracted syphilis. Bak reports: "A source of shame and humiliation, [what Cowley called "the most sinister of diseases"] was associated with images of leprosy and mutilation, of madness, the possibility of a slow, disgraceful death. For half a year Cowley and Peggy subjected themselves to courses of medical treatment at free clinics in Manhattan and became intimately familiar with conventional remedies of the time. . . . For the duration of the treatment they were locked to each other, much like 'prisoners in the same cell.' After six months they were pronounced cured and discharged, but the emotional and psychological wounds were slow to heal. More than fifty years later Cowley still recalled the intense feelings of estrangement brought on by the disease, as if through the experience he had been given a 'passport into the underworld' " (158).

14. It is interesting to note that while Cowley was writing to John Brooks Wheelwright about the need for "an intelligent society" of "half a dozen men" (see n. 4), Peggy Baird Cowley was writing to the same correspondent that a "woman in these days can't afford to be feminine unless some nice kind of man has an income of ten thousand to spend on her" and a "good majority of the present day women have got to be ready to face any emergency and to stand on their own feet at any moment" (Bak 126).

15. For detailed accounts of Cowley's productivity and the ideas that occupied him prior to 1921, see Bak and Kempf. Cowley's letters to Kenneth Burke (Jay) document his struggles as a poet and as an aspiring intellectual.

16. See Felski, Huyssen, Siegel, and Stewart for discussions of the crisis of gender in European modernism.

17. Cowley remains contemptuously innocent of the discourses suggesting affinities between the avant-garde and the feminine. For thoroughgoing discussions of this subject see Felski, Friedman, Gilbert and Gubar, Huyssen, Jardine, and North.

18. In *Die realen Frauen der Surrealisten*, Unda Hörner presents an intellectual biography of Simone Breton, Gala Élouard, and Elsa Triolet and details the conflicts between their substantial cultural and artistic interests and the demands of the men whose "wives and mistresses" they were.

19. Stearns's account of this episode could not have pleased Cowley. He refers to it in the course of his excursus on American men in Paris, presenting it as a prime example of "the arrogance of being an American": "The sad truth is that these great literary discoverers of new forms were only Americans after all[,] that is to say, bel-

ligerent when crossed. . . . When Cowley, then Macalmon [*sic*], then others got into violent fisticuff encounters, or became screaming and loud, or, when ignored, even insulting to the French 'bourgeois' who did not even know who they were or what they stood for, let alone had done them any harm—when all this happened, they were not fighting the great literary battle they imagined. They were trying, in a war-weary and cynical Paris, which already had had some experience with the run-of-the-mill kind of American soldier during the war, to impress on a people, who didn't even care if it was true, that Americans were as up-to-date in literary fashions and absurdities as were the French themselves. . . . In the old days, our youngsters used to come to Paris looking for culture; I suppose it was a mark of something or other in intellectual progress that at that time they came over looking for trouble. It was a strange form of New Nationalism, which I deliberately put in capitals just to annoy them—for afterwards, when they got home, they couldn't get on the Russian bandwagon fast enough. Impolite and aggressive Americans abroad, they became European and Russian yearners when they got back home—I wondered then, if there was not a certain connection between these two phenomena; if, in fact, they were not really two aspects of the same thing" (*Street* 298–99).

20. Although Caren Kaplan's discussion of *Exile's Return* has a very different emphasis, her conclusion is similar to my own. She writes, "The displacements of 'exile' have brought the modernists of Cowley's group not to a fuller understanding of the histories and particularities of the places they have traveled through but to a will to power that consolidates nationalist identities and confirms a repressive hierarchy of values. In this narrative of modernity, the 'international aesthetic' is no match for the 'business picture' and its allied nationalist agendas" (49).

21. Adam Gussow argues that Cowley's career was "a persistent attempt to reroot his life and his language in his native earth, to rewrite the fable of his tribe's deracination" (6 and passim).

22. Such speculation is supported by Cowley's later admission that he did not really consider Crosby's story as significant as *Exile's Return* suggests and that he "had failed to show its connection with the rest of the narrative." In the "Prologue" to the 1951 revised edition of *Exile's Return*, he confesses, "I had written at length about the life of Harry Crosby, whom I scarcely knew, in order to avoid discussing the more recent death of Hart Crane, whom I knew so well that I still couldn't bear to write about him" (11).

Crosby's biographer, Geoffrey Wolff, particularly resists Cowley's claim that Crosby "died in those endless moments [in Verdun] when he was waiting for the road to be cleared. In his heart he felt that he belonged with his good friends Aaron Davis Weld and Oliver Ames Jr., both killed in action. Bodily he survived . . . but only to find that something was dead inside him—his boyhood" (*ER* 246). He writes, "In Cowley's thesis, much depends on one's willingness to assume that there is such an odd creature as a literary generation. . . . . More important, it also depends on an attractive and far-fetched assumption about Harry's suicide: that it was a second rather than first death. . . . What had in fact died . . . was Harry's innocence. . . . [Harry's] story is remarkable not for its illustration of general principles or its symbolic burden, but for its isolation, its lonely singularity" (*Black Sun* 307–8).

23. Stearns concludes his contribution to *America Now*, the essay "The Intellectual Life, " which was designed to echo and revise the essay on the same subject that he wrote for *Civilization in the United States*, with a recognition of the "willingness on the part of most Americans to undertake the great adventure of intellectual co-operation": "Every reader of this book will think of different exemplifications of this desire of ours to learn more and to think a bit straighter: How many more examples there are than one can recall offhand, like the New School for Social Research; the Town Hall; the radio programs devoted to science; adult education, as it is called; unions organizing workers' classes; civic centers and the like; vocational training camps; university 'extension' classes; even correspondence schools" (381–82). See Huyssen for a discussion of modernism's association of mass culture with the feminine.

24. In *White Logic*, his study of alcoholism in American modernist fiction, John W. Crowley claims that "the chief modernist vice was habitual drunkenness." He cites Robin Roon's discovery of "a clear association of problematic drunkenness not only with American writers, but with a particular generational cohort that came of age in 1909–1921." His list of "significant American writers, born before 1921, who were known for habitual drunkenness" includes not only such legendary alcoholics as O'Neill, Crane, Fitzgerald, Hemingway, and Stearns but also Cowley himself and most of the members of his inner circle (35, 39).

25. For a discussion of the psychosocial dynamics of men's groups and organizations in American cultural history, see Nelson.

Chapter Four. Everybody's Autobiography

1. Most notable in this regard is Shirley C. Neuman's brilliant study, *Gertrude Stein: Autobiography and the Problem of Narration*, which, in its exposition of Stein's autobiographical strategies in the text, never once mentions what *Everybody's Autobiography* is "about." See also Gallow.

In "The Re-Vision of America," Alfred Hornung discusses *Everybody's Autobiography* and *The American Scene* in terms of their representation of repatriation. M. Lynn Weiss's *Gertrude Stein and Richard Wright* is the first full-length study I have found that takes the thematics of repatriation into account in its discussion of *Everybody's Autobiography*. Charles Caramello's essay "Coming Across America" sketches a project quite similar to my own, but in the four pages devoted to the subject, can only suggest what the dynamics of Stein's confrontation with America might be.

Priscilla Wald's chapter on *The Making of Americans* in *Constituting Americans* discusses Stein's (self)-production of a writerly national identity in a way that prepares for this discussion of her return to America.

2. See, for instance, Elizabeth Sprigge's biography of Stein. The chapter entitled "Lectures in America," which chronicles Stein's trip, "is based on the description of the American visit in *Everybody's Autobiography*" (184).

3. In *Imagining Paris*, J. Gerald Kennedy summarizes Stein's motivations for leaving the United States as follows: "partly to rejoin Leo . . . and partly to escape the chagrin of an abandoned medical career at Johns Hopkins and an awkward romance with a young woman named May Bookstaver. Headstrong and unconventional, Stein moved to France to refashion her life and to free herself from prudish attitudes about the role and behavior of young women" (40). Sarah Jackson Meroni concurs, while accepting even less of Stein's personal myth-making: "Contrary to some popular myths (many of them promulgated by Stein herself), the actual reasons for Gertrude Stein's expatriation appear to have been rather banal. Professionally, Stein was adrift. Medicine had lost its appeal for her and, as she failed and refused to repeat a required course at Johns Hopkins, her medical career came to an end. Personally, Stein had been involved in a love affair with a woman in New York that had unfortunately reached an unpleasant and disappointing impasse. By going to Paris, Stein was hoping to give herself some direction. . . . In this sense Stein's move eastward across the Atlantic is an echo of the American move westward across the plains" (26–27).

4. In a particularly intelligent discussion of the "relations of lesbian and nationalism [via] the question of lesbianism and representation," Julie Abraham suggests a way to reconcile the artistic and sexual motivations for Stein's expatriation: "Stein established both her interest in America and her lesbianism as the source of her expatriation in the opening of *The Making of Americans*. . . . Stein split her nation and habitation to claim both nationality and personal freedom" (511).

5. See, for instance, *Paris, France* 5.

6. Corinne E. Blackmer notes, "Through a supreme act of ventriloquism of Toklas's distinctive voice, Stein authorizes her claims of centrality within the narrative of modernism . . . and thus achieves literary and public recognition. Stein, through Alice's voice, can proclaim her own genius; more important, however, she can seize control of the processes of her own reputation making and impel critics to confront her on her own territory, from the standpoint of her own artistic assumptions and narrative of self-creation. Alice becomes a link between the domestic and public realms, an authorizing presence who permits Stein to state her claims for public recognition and refute the arguments of her detractors" (245).

7. "In later years perhaps it had to do with the Autobiography and how it affected me but anyway there has been a tendency to go out more and see different kinds of people. In the older days mostly they came to see me but then we began to go out to see them. . . . And now after the Autobiography and Bernard Fay had translated it and they all had read it we began to naturally be going out more to meet French literary people" (*EA* 33–34).

8. I emphasize the issue of the chronology of *Everybody's Autobiography*, since it seems to differ somewhat from that which we can glean from Stein's biography. The heightened attention to identity that she represents in *Everybody's Autobiography* as a result of the success of *The Autobiography of Alice B. Toklas* seems actually to have been a result of the trip to America and return to France. Yet it seems crucial to a

reading of *Everybody's Autobiography* that we accede to the chronology she presents in the text, since in her representation of her sojourn in America, this reconfrontation with her native land enables her to work through the issue of identity.

9. See Stein, "What Are Master-pieces" 151. William Gass's articulation of the distinction between "human nature" and "human mind" is particularly clear and bears citation: "Human nature is incapable of objectivity. It is viciously anthropocentric, whereas the human mind leaves all personal interest behind. It sees things as entities, not identities. It is concerned, in the Kantian sense, with things-in-themselves. The human mind knows that men must die that others may live; one epoch go that another may take its place; that ideas, fashions, feelings, pass. The human mind neither forgets nor remembers; it neither sorrows nor longs; it never experiences fear or disappointment. In the table headed Human Nature there is, therefore, time and memory, with all their beginnings, their middles, and their ends; there is habit and identity, storms and hilly country, acting, audience, speaking and adventure, dogs and other animals, politics, propaganda, war, place, practice and its guiding truths, its directing sciences, while in the table of the Human Mind there's contact rather than connection, plains, space, landscape, math and money, not nervousness but excitement, not saying but showing, romance rather than mystery, masterpieces moreover, and above all, Being" (William Gass, "Introduction," Stein, *Geographical History of America* 39).

10. See Neuman: "'I am I because my little dog knows me' is not 'representative' of thought or even a metaphor for it, since representation demands that the two things, thought and its formalization, share an essential identity. Rather it is a recreation in the present of the act of meditating on identity. The meditation is realized, not represented, in the use of the nursery rhyme. The rhyme is similarly recreated" (39).

11. Neuman, who resolutely refuses to discuss *Everybody's Autobiography* in terms of its obvious subject matter—Stein's trip to America—does, however, remark that "*Everybody's Autobiography* bears insistent testimony to the fact that the success of *The Autobiography of Alice B. Toklas* coupled with this discernible and appreciative audience [during the American tour] evoked a rather idiosyncratic identity crisis in Stein" (59). While I agree that the success of the *Autobiography* sparked the crisis, I consider the American trip to have been part of the cure.

I am grateful to Herwig Friedl for his provocative insistence on the anti- and non-narrative emphasis in Stein's writing. See his "Lively Sense."

12. Stein's preoccupation with "the little dog" and its capacity for recognition pervades her writings in the mid- and late thirties. Its presence as a leitmotif in this text of homecoming necessarily invokes that homecoming narrative par excellence, *The Odyssey*. The passage from *The Odyssey* in which Odysseus's dog, Argos, recognizes his long-lost master serves as a foil both to "Lawkamercyme" and to Stein's use of the "little dog" motif in *Everybody's Autobiography*; see epigraph to section II. Alone among the inhabitants of Ithaca, the old dog recognizes the disguised Odysseus; he wags his tail, and, his longings realized, dies. The traditional reading of the passage sees the loyal and incorruptible dog as affirming the identity that Odysseus will need his wiles and wits to prove to the human inhabitants of the polis. Argos's recognition

of his master proves something about the dog, much as the self-restraint that forces Odysseus not to acknowledge his recognition of the dog proves something about Odysseus. Odysseus's survival depends upon his ability to distinguish between the dog's recognition and the exigencies of his situation, which forbid him to reciprocate the dog's response.

13. This statement would seem to be challenged by Stein's assertion that "everything that summer was in confusion just as it is this summer, only then the confusion was inside me and not outside me and now it is outside me and not inside me" (*EA* 132). But the confusion inside her must be seen as being caused not by a "confusion . . . outside" but by a very clear and unconfused set of new circumstances with which Stein has not yet come to terms.

14. Stein's formula for passing over old acquaintances in order to make way for new ones suggests a strategy for dealing with anticipated problems as well: "Having written all about them they ceased to exist. That is very funny if you write all about any one they do not exist any more, for you" (123).

15. See Will's chapter on *EA*, "From Genius to Celebrity," and Leick.

16. See Eve Kosofsky Sedgwick's consideration of the semantic field occupied by the word *queer*: "The open mesh of possibilities, gaps, overlaps, dissonances and resonances, lapses and excesses of meaning when the constituent elements of one's gender, of anyone's sexuality, aren't made (or can't be made) to signify monolithically. . . . A word so fraught as 'queer' is . . . never can only denote; nor can it only connote; a part of its experimental force as a speech act is the way in which it dramatizes locutionary position itself. . . . 'Queer' seems to hinge . . . on a person's undertaking particular, performative acts of experimental self-perception and filiation" (*Tendencies* 8–9).

17. Although redwoods do indeed have roots, and hence a foundation, their root systems are peculiar, and it is perhaps this peculiarity to which Stein refers. Instead of having a single taproot, redwoods "form a shallow network of relatively small roots that extend radially, up to a hundred feet from the base. The ends of the roots are fibrous, allowing them maximum surface area to obtain moisture and nutrients. If a flood buries the roots too deeply in silt, they have the ability to grow and explore their way toward more oxygenated soil" (Humboldt Redwoods State Park, http://humboldtreds.org\info.htmp). Perhaps Stein was attracted to the notion of roots that were broadly ranging rather than deep, multiple rather than singular, and capable of escaping the perils of depth through lateral movement.

It is interesting to note the similarity between this image and Deleuze's figuration of the rhizome, described by Braidotti as "a root that grows underground, sideways; Deleuze plays it against the linear roots of trees. By extension, it is 'as if' the rhizomatic mode expressed a nonphallogocentric way of thinking: secret, lateral, spreading" (23).

18. One notable exception that suggests the direction such an analysis might take is a passage concerning Stein's much maligned sister, Bertha: "One thing I can always remember going back again to East Oakland is wearing gloves and books. Bertha was being put at another school and I went with her and while they were talking to her I was left in the superintendent's room and there was a bookcase there. I was wearing

gloves I was just beginning to wear them and I saw a book and I began reading, it was Jane Eyre and I had not read it and I held it tightly and I read it and then suddenly I saw that my thumb had made a black mark on the page I was holding.

"I can never touch a book with a glove on and I get very troubled when any one touches a book and they have a glove on. Dirty hands do not dirty a book as much as a glove can" (*EA* 155).

In this condensation of *Jane Eyre*, where Bertha is the girl going to school, is Gertrude then the madwoman in the attic? If there were more such passages in the text, one could, perhaps, undertake a reading where Stein's "lack of passion" could, perhaps, be read as repression. In such a reading, books and writing would, of course, play a central role.

19. ". . . and then we saw an electric sign moving around a building and it said Gertrude Stein has come and that was upsetting. Anybody saying how do you do to you and knowing your name may be upsetting but on the while it is natural enough but to suddenly see your name is always upsetting. Of course it has happened to me pretty often and I like it to happen just as often but always it does give me a little shock of recognition and nonrecognition. It is one of the things most worrying in the subject of identity" (*EA* 180).

Aaron, Daniel. *Writers on the Left: Episodes in American Literary Communism*. New York: Harcourt, Brace & World, 1961.

Abrahams, Julie. "'We Are Americans': Gertrude, *Brewsie and Willie*." *Modern Fiction Studies* 42.3 (1996): 508–28.

Anderson, Benedict. *Imagined Communities: Reflections on the Origin and Spread of Nationalism*. London: Verso, 1983.

Bak, Hans. *Malcolm Cowley: The Formative Years*. Athens: U of Georgia P, 1993.

Baldwin, James. "The Discovery of What It Means to Be an American." 1959. *The Price of the Ticket: Collected Nonfiction, 1948–1985*. New York: St. Martin's/Marek, 1985. 171–76.

———. "Alas, Poor Richard." 1961. *The Price of the Ticket: Collected Nonfiction, 1948–1985*. New York: St. Martin's/Marek, 1985. 269–87.

———. "No Name in the Street." 1972. *The Price of the Ticket: Collected Nonfiction, 1948–1985*. New York: St. Martin's/Marek, 1985. 449–552.

Balzac, Honoré de. *Le Père Goriot*. 1835. Paris: Garnier-Flammarion, 1966.

———. "Avant-propos." 1842. *La Comédie humaine*, vol. 1, *Etudes de moeurs: Scènes de la vie privée*. Paris: Bibliothèque de la Pléiade/Gallimard, 1976. 7–20.

Bammer, Angelika, ed. *Displacements: Cultural Identities in Question*. Bloomington: Indiana UP, 1994.

Banks, Elizabeth. *The Remaking of an American*. 1928. Intro. Jane S. Gabin. Gainsville: UP of Florida, 2000.

Banta, Martha. "'Strange Deserts': Hotels, Hospitals, Country Clubs, Prisons, and the City of Brotherly Love." *Henry James Review* 17.1 (1996): 1–10.

———. "Men, Women, and the American Way." *Cambridge Companion to Henry James*. Ed. Jonathan Freedman. Cambridge: Cambridge UP, 1998. 21–38.

Barthes, Roland. "La Bruyère." *Essais critiques*. Paris: Seuil, 1964. 221–37.

Bartkowski, Fran. *Travelers, Immigrants, Inmates: Essays in Estrangement*. Minneapolis: U of Minnesota P, 1995.

Baudrillard, Jean. *Amérique*. Paris: Grasset, 1986.

Bederman, Gail. *Manliness and Civilization: A Cultural History of Gender and Race in the United States, 1880–1917*. Chicago: U of Chicago P, 1998.

Benjamin, Jessica. *The Bonds of Love: Psychoanalysis, Feminism, and the Problem of Domination*. New York: Pantheon, 1988.

Benstock, Shari. *Women of the Left Bank, 1900–1940*. Austin: U of Texas P, 1987.

Bentley, Nancy. *The Ethnography of Manners: Hawthorne, James, Wharton*. Cambridge Studies in American Literature and Culture. Cambridge: Cambridge UP, 1995.

Berman, Jessica. "Feminizing the Nation: Woman as Cultural Icon in Late James." *Henry James Review* 17.1 (1996): 58–76.

Bersani, Leo. *The Freudian Body: Psychoanalysis and Art*. New York: Columbia UP, 1986.

Bhabha, Homi. *Nation and Narration*. London: Routledge, 1990.

Blackmer, Corinne E. "Selling Taboo Subjects: The Literary Commerce of Gertrude Stein and Carl Van Vechten." *Marketing Modernisms: Self-Promotion, Canonization, Rereading*. Ed. Kevin J. H. Dettmar and Stephen Watt. Ann Arbor: U of Michigan P, 1996. 221–52.

Blair, Sara. "Documenting America: Racial Theater in *The American Scene*." *Henry James Review* 16.3 (1995): 264–72.

———. *Henry James and the Writing of Race and Nation*. Cambridge: Cambridge UP, 1996.

Boym, Svetlana. *The Future of Nostalgia*. New York: Basic Books, 2001.

Braidotti, Rosi. *Nomadic Subjects: Embodiment and Sexual Difference in Contemporary Feminist Theory*. New York: Columbia UP, 1994.

Brinnin, John Malcolm. *The Third Rose: Gertrude Stein and Her World*. Gloucester, MA: P. Smith, 1968.

Brooks, Van Wyck. *The Pilgrimage of Henry James*. London: Jonathan Cape, 1928.

Bryson, Bill. *I'm a Stranger Here Myself*. New York: Broadway Books, 1999.

Buelens, Gert. "James's 'Aliens': Consuming, Performing and Judging the American scene." *Modern Philology* 96.3 (1999): 347–63.

———. *Henry James and the "Aliens" in Possession of the American Scene*. Amsterdam: Rodopi, 2002.

Burgett, Bruce. "Masochism and Male Sentimentalism: Charles Brockden Brown's *Clara Howard*." *Sentimental Men: Masculinity and the Politics of Affect in American Culture*. Ed. Mary Chapman and Glenn Hendler, Berkeley: U of California P, 1999. 205–25.

Buruma, Ian. "Misplaced Person." *New York Times Book Review* 3 Oct. 1999: 10.

Butler, Judith. *Bodies That Matter*. New York: Routledge, 1993.

Caramello, Charles. "Coming Across America: Stein and Federman." *Near Encounters: Festschrift for Richard Martin*. Ed. Hanjo Besserem and Bernd Herzogenrath. Frankfurt am Main: Peter Lang, 1995. 47–56.

———. *Henry James, Gertrude Stein, and the Biographical Act*. Chapel Hill: U of North Carolina P, 1996.

Caws, Mary Ann. *Reading Frames in Modern Fiction*. Princeton, NJ: Princeton UP, 1985.

Chamberlain, Mary. *Narratives of Exile and Return*. Warwick U Caribbean Series. London: Macmillan, 1997.

Chambers, Iain. *Migrancy, Culture, Identity*. London: Routledge, 1994.

Cixous, Hélène. *The Exile of James Joyce*. Trans. Sally A. J. Powell. New York: David Lewis, 1972.

Clifford, James. *The Predicament of Culture: Twentieth-Century Ethnography, Literature, and Art*. Cambridge, MA: Harvard UP, 1988.

———. "Notes on Theory and Travel." *Inscriptions* 5 (1989): 177–88.

Cowley, Malcolm. "This Youngest Generation." *Literary Review of the New York Evening Post* 15 Oct. 1921: 81–82.

———. "Three Americans in Paris." *Literary Review of the New York Evening Post* 14 Jan. 1922: 351.

———. "Young Mr. Elkins." *Broom* Dec. 1922: 52–56.

———. *Exile's Return: A Narrative of Ideas*. New York: W. W. Norton, 1934.

———. *Exile's Return: A Literary Odyssey of the 1920s*. New York: Viking Press, 1951.

———. "The Two Henry Jameses." *A Many-Windowed House: Collected Essays on American Writers and American Writing*. Ed. Henry Dan Piper. Carbondale: Southern Illinois UP, 1970. 89–99.

———. *A Second Flowering: Works and Days of the Lost Generation*. New York: Viking, 1973.

———. *And I Worked at the Writer's Trade: Chapters of Literary History, 1918–1978*. New York: Viking, 1978.

———. *The Dream of the Golden Mountains: Remembering the 1930s*. Harmondsworth, UK: Penguin, 1981.

———. "Mother and Son." *American Heritage* 34.2 (1983): 28–35.

———. "The Urn." *A Life. Blue Juniata*. New York: Penguin, 1985. 151–53.

———. "John Cheever: The Novelist's Life as a Drama." *Faulkner* 402–16.

———. "Looking for the Essential Me." *Faulkner* 579–84.

Crowley, John W. *The White Logic: Alcoholism and Gender in American Modernist Fiction*. Amherst: U of Massachusetts P, 1994.

DeKoven, Marianne. *Rich and Strange: Gender, History, Modernism*. Princeton, NJ: Princeton UP, 1991.

Denning, Michael. *The Cultural Front: The Laboring of American Culture in the Twentieth Century*. London: Verso, 1998.

Derrida, Jacques. *La Verité en peinture*. Paris: Flammarion, 1978.

Dolan, Marc. *Modern Lives: A Cultural Re-reading of "The Lost Generation."* West Lafayette, IN: Purdue UP, 1996.

Dos Passos, John. *The Best Times: An Informal Memoir*. New York: New American Library, 1966.

Douglas, Ann. *The Feminization of American Culture*. New York: Avon, 1978.

———. *Terrible Honesty: Mongrel Manhattan in the 1920s*. New York: Farrar, Straus & Giroux, 1995.

Edwards, Justin D. "Henry James's 'Alien' New York: Gender and Race in *The American Scene*." *American Studies International* 6.1 (1998): 66–80.

Edwards, Robert. "Exile, Self, and Society." *Exile in Literature.* Ed. María-Inés Lagos-Pope. London: Associated University Presses, 1988. 15–31.

Ellison, Julie. "The Gender of Transparency: Masculinity and the Conduct of Life." *American Literary History* 4.4 (1992): 584–606.

Emerson, Ralph Waldo. "The American Scholar." 1837. *Essays and Lectures.* Ed. Joel Porte. New York: Library of America, 1983.

Faulkner, Donald W., ed. *The Portable Malcolm Cowley.* New York: Viking, 1990.

Felski, Rita. *The Gender of Modernity.* Cambridge, MA: Harvard UP, 1995.

Fogel, Daniel Mark, ed. *A Companion to Henry James Studies.* Westport, CT: Greenwood Press, 1993.

Ford, Hugh. *Four Lives in Paris.* San Francisco: North Point Press, 1987.

Freedman, Jonathan. "Henry James and the Discourses of Antisemitism." *Between Race and Culture.* Ed. Brian Cheyette. Stanford, CA: Stanford UP, 1996. 62–83.

———, ed. *The Cambridge Companion to Henry James.* Cambridge: Cambridge UP, 1998.

Freud, Sigmund. *Drei Abhandlungen zur Sexualtheorie.* 1905. Frankfurt am Main: S. Fischer, 1982. Vol. 5 of *Studienausgabe.* 39–145.

Friedl, Herwig. "'A Lively Sense of Being Part of Being': Ontological Universalism in Gertrude Stein's *The Making of Americans.*" *The American Dream: Festschrift for Peter Freese on the Occasion of His Sixtieth Birthday.* Ed. Carin Freywald and Michael Porsche. Essen: Die Blaue Eule, 1999. 213–34.

Friedman, Susan Stanford. *Penelope's Web: Gender, Modernity, H.D.'s Fiction.* Cambridge: Cambridge UP, 1990.

Galow, Timothy W. "Gertrude Stein's *Everybody's Autobiography* and the Art of Contradictions." *Journal of Modern Literature* 32.1 (2008): 111–28.

Garland, Hamlin. *Roadside Meetings.* New York: Macmillan, 1930.

Germain, Edward, ed. *Shadows of the Sun: The Diaries of Harry Crosby.* Santa Barbara, CA: Black Sparrow Press, 1977.

Gide, André. *Le Retour de l'enfant prodigue.* Paris: Gallimard, 1948.

Gilbert, Sandra M., and Susan Gubar. *The War of the Words.* New Haven, CT: Yale UP, 1988. Vol. 1 of *No Man's Land: The Place of the Woman Writer in the Twentieth Century.*

Gooder, R. F. "The American Scene, or Paradise Lost." *Cambridge Quarterly* 37.1 (2008): 16–29.

Graham, Wendy. "Notes on a Native Son: Henry James's New York." *American Literary History* 21.2 (2009): 239–267.

Gurr, Andrew. *Writers in Exile: The Identity of Home in Modern Literature.* Brighton, UK: Harvester Press, 1981.

Gussow, Adam. "'Whatever Roots We Had in the Soil': Malcolm Cowley and the American Scholar." *Horns of Plenty: Malcolm Cowley and His Generation* 1.1 (1988): 5–15, 19–24.

Gygax, Franziska. *Gender and Genre in Gertrude Stein.* Contributions in Women's Studies. Westport, CT: Greenwood Press, 1998.

Harrison, Gilbert A., ed. *Gertrude Stein's America*. New York: Liveright, 1974.

Haviland, Beverly. "The Return of the Alien: Henry James in New York, 1904." *Henry James Review* 16.3 (1995): 257–63.

———. *Henry James's Last Romance: Making Sense of the Past and of the American Scene*. Cambridge: Cambridge UP, 1997.

Hazlett, John D. "Conversion, Revisionism, and Revision in Malcolm Cowley's *Exile's Return*." *South Atlantic Quarterly* 82.2 (1983): 179–88.

———. *My Generation: Collective Autobiography and Identity Politics*. Madison: U of Wisconsin P, 1998.

Hemingway, Ernest. *Fiesta: The Sun Also Rises*. 1926. London: Arrow, 1994.

———. *A Movable Feast*. London: Jonathan Cape, 1964.

Henderson, Mae, ed. *Borders, Boundaries, and Frames: Essays in Cultural Criticism and Cultural Studies*. New York: Routledge, 1995.

Hewitt, Rosalie. "Henry James's *The American Scene*: Its Genesis and Its Reception, 1905–1977." *Henry James Review* 1.2 (1980): 179–96.

Hirsch, Marianne, and Nancy K. Miller, eds. *Rites of Return: Diaspora Poetics and the Politics of Memory*. New York: Columbia UP, 2011.

Hobhouse, Janet. *Everybody Who Was Anybody: A Biography of Gertrude Stein*. London: Weidenfeld & Nicolson, 1975.

Hoffmann, Monika. *Gertrude Steins Autobiographien*: The Autobiography of Alice B. Toklas *und* Everybody's Autobiography. Mainzer Studien zur Amerikanistik. Frankfurt am Main: P. Lang, 1992.

Hofmannsthal, Hugo von. "Französische Redensarten." 1897. *Gesammelte Werke*, vol. 3. Berlin: S. Fischer, 1924. 135–41.

———. "Die Briefe des Zurückgekehrten." 1907. *Gesammelte Werke in Einzelausgaben, Prosa*, vol. 2. Frankfurt am Main: S. Fischer, 1959. 279–310.

Holland, Laurence Bedwell. *The Expense of Vision: Essays on the Craft of Henry James*. Princeton, NJ: Princeton UP, 1964.

Hollier, Denis. "Letter from Paris (Foreign Mail)." Suleiman, 89–108.

Homer. *The Odyssey*. Trans. Robert Fagles. New York: Viking Penguin, 1996.

Hornung, Alfred. "The Re-vision of America: European Experiences and American Autobiography." *Visions of America since 1492*. Ed. Deborah Madsen. London: Leicester UP, 1994. 94–110.

Hörner, Unda. *Die realen Frauen der Surrealisten*. Frankfurt am Main: Suhrkamp, 1998.

Huyssen, Andreas. *After the Great Divide: Modernism, Mass Culture, Postmodernism*. Bloomington: Indiana UP, 1986.

James, Henry. "Review of Hippolyte Taine's 'Italy: Rome and Naples.'" 1868. *Literary Criticism: French Writers* 826–31.

———. "Review of Hippolyte Taine's *History of English Literature*." 1872. *Literary Criticism: French Writers* 841–48.

———. "Review of Hippolyte Taine's *Notes on Paris*." 1875. *Literary Criticism: French Writers* 848–51.

———. *Hawthorne.* 1879. *Literary Criticism: Essays on Literature* 315–457.

———. "The Art of Fiction." 1884. *The Future of the Novel.* Ed. Leon Edel. New York: Vintage, 1956. 3–27.

———. "Honoré de Balzac, 1902." 1902. *Literary Criticism: French Writers* 90–115.

———. *The Ambassadors.* 1903. Harmondsworth, UK: Penguin, 1986.

———. *William Wetmore Story and His Friends.* 2 vols. Edinburgh: William Blackwood & Sons, 1903.

———. *The Golden Bowl.* 1904. Harmondsworth, UK: Penguin, 1987.

———. "The Lesson of Balzac." 1905. *Literary Criticism: French Writers* 115–39.

———. "The Speech of American Women, Part One." *Harper's Bazaar* Nov. 1906: 979–82.

———. "The Speech of American Women, Part Two." *Harper's Bazaar* Dec. 1906: 1103–6.

———. *The American Scene.* 1907. Bloomington: Indiana UP, 1968.

———. "The Manners of American Women, Part Four." *Harper's Bazaar* July 1907: 646–51.

———. "The Jolly Corner." 1908. *Complete Stories, 1898–1910.* New York: Library of America, 1996.

———. *The Art of the Novel: Critical Prefaces.* Ed. R. P. Blackmur. New York: Scribner's, 1934.

———. *Letters,* Vol. 1, *1843–1875.* Ed. Leon Edel. Cambridge, MA: Harvard UP, 1974.

———. *Letters,* Vol. 4, *1895–1916.* Ed. Leon Edel. Cambridge, MA: Harvard UP, 1984.

———. *Literary Criticism: Essays on Literature, American Writers, English Writers.* New York: Library of America, 1984.

———. *Literary Criticism: French Writers, Other European Writers, the Prefaces to the New York Edition.* New York: Library of America, 1984.

———. *The Complete Notebooks of Henry James.* Ed. Leon Edel and Lyall H. Powers. New York: Oxford UP, 1987.

———. *Collected Travel Writings: Great Britain and America.* New York: Library of America, 1993.

Jankélévitch, Vladimir. *L'Irréversible et la nostalgie.* Paris: Flammarion, 1974.

Jardine, Alice. *Gynesis: Configurations of Woman and Modernity.* Ithaca, NY: Cornell UP, 1985.

Jay, Paul, ed. *The Selected Correspondence of Kenneth Burke and Malcolm Cowley, 1915–1981.* New York: Viking, 1988.

Jewell, Phebe Beth. "The Foreign Mirror: Exile, Identity, and the Creative Process in Stendhal, Gertrude Stein, and Samuel Beckett." Diss. U of Washington, 1994.

Jolas, Eugene, and Elliot Paul. "A Review." *American Expatriate Writers: Paris in the Twenties.* Ed. Matthew Bruccoli and Robert W. Trogdon. Vol. 15 of *Dictionary of Literary Biography: Documentary Series.* Detroit: Gale Research, 1997. 247–51.

Joost, Nicholas. *Scofield Thayer and* The Dial. Carbondale: Southern Illinois UP, 1964.

———. *Years of Transition: The Dial, 1912–1920*. Barre, MA: Barre Publishers, 1967.

Josephson, Matthew. *Portrait of the Artist as American*. New York: Harcourt, Brace, 1930.

———. *Life among the Surrealists: A Memoir*. New York: Holt, 1962.

———. *Infidel in the Temple: A Memoir of the Nineteen-Thirties*. New York: Knopf, 1967.

Joyce, James. *Portrait of the Artist as a Young Man*. 1916. New York: Viking, 1969.

Kaplan, Caren. *Questions of Travel: Postmodern Discourses of Displacement*. Durham, NC: Duke UP, 1998.

Kazin, Alfred. *Starting Out in the Thirties*. Boston: Little, Brown, 1962.

Kelly, James L. "The Role of Separation in Understanding Home." *Journal of Geography* Mar.–Apr. 1985: 61–63.

Kempf, James Michael. *The Early Career of Malcolm Cowley: A Humanist among the Moderns*. Baton Rouge: Louisiana State UP, 1985.

Kennedy, J. Gerald. *Imagining Paris: Exile, Writing, and American Identity*. New Haven, CT: Yale UP, 1993.

Kimmel, Michael. *Manhood in America: A Cultural History*. New York: Free Press, 1996.

Kristeva, Julia. *Powers of Horror: An Essay on Abjection*. Trans. Leon S. Roudiez. New York: Columbia UP, 1982.

Kronenberger, Louis. "Return from Venusberg." *New Republic* 22 Jan. 1936: 318–19.

Kundera, Milan. *Ignorance*. Trans. Linda Asher. New York: HarperCollins, 2000.

Lagos-Pope, Mariá-Inés. *Exile in Literature*. Lewisburg, PA: Bucknell UP, 1988.

Lane, James W. "Pleasantly Disconcerting." *Commonweal* 25 May 1934: 110.

Lauter, Paul. "Race and Gender in the Shaping of the American Literary Canon: A Case Study from the Twenties." *Feminist Studies* 9.3 (1983): 435–63.

"Lawkamercyme." *A Dictionary of British Folk-Tales in the English Language Incorporating the F. J. Norton Collection, Part A: Folk Narratives*. Ed. Katharine M. Briggs. Vol. 2. Bloomington: Indiana UP, 1970. 539–40.

Lears, T. J. Jackson. *No Place of Grace: Antimodernism and the Transformation of American Culture, 1880–1920*. Chicago: U of Chicago P, 1994.

Leed, Eric J. *No Man's Land: Combat and Identity in World War I*. New York: Cambridge UP, 1979.

Leick, Karen. *Gertrude Stein and the Making of an American Celebrity*. New York: Routledge, 2009.

Leverenz, David. *Manhood and the American Renaissance*. Ithaca, NY: Cornell UP, 1989.

MacCannell, Dean. *The Tourist: A New Theory of the Leisure Class*. New York: Schocken, 1976.

MacLeish, Archibald. "American Letter." 1930. *New and Collected Poems, 1917–1976*. Boston: Houghton Mifflin, 1976. 62–65.

———. "America Was Promises." 1939. *New and Collected Poems, 1917–1976*. Boston: Houghton Mifflin, 1976. 323–31.

Martin, Biddy, and Chandra Talpade Mohanty. "Feminist Politics: What's Home Got to Do with It?" *Feminist Studies/Critical Studies*. Ed. Teresa de Lauretis. Bloomington: Indiana UP, 1986. 191–212.

McAlmon, Robert, and Kay Boyle. *Being Geniuses Together, 1920–1930*. Garden City, NY: Doubleday, 1968.

McCall, Dan. *Citizens of Somewhere Else: Nathaniel Hawthorne and Henry James*. Ithaca, NY: Cornell UP, 1999.

McCarthy, Mary. "A Guide to Exiles, Expatriates, and Internal Emigrés." Robinson 49–58.

McWhirter, David Bruce, ed. *Henry James's New York Edition: The Construction of Authorship*. Stanford, CA: Stanford UP, 1995.

Mellow, James R. *Charmed Circle: Gertrude Stein and Company*. New York: Praeger, 1974.

Meroni, Sarah Jeanne Jackson. "Gertrude Stein and Expatriation." *Prospero* 1 (1994): 25–34.

Miller, Henry. *Aller Retour New York*. 1935. New York: New Directions, 1991.

Monk, Craig. *Writing the Lost Generation: Expatriate Autobiography and American Modernism*. Iowa City: U of Iowa P, 2008.

Naumann, Francis M. *New York Dada: 1915–23*. New York: Harry N. Abrams, 1994.

Nelson, Dana D. *National Manhood: Capitalist Citizenship and the Imagined Fraternity of White Men*. Durham, NC: Duke UP, 1998.

Neuman, Shirley C. *Gertrude Stein: Autobiography and the Problem of Narration*. ELS Monograph Series. Victoria, BC: English Literary Studies, Dept. of English, U of Victoria, 1979.

The New English Bible with the Apocrypha. New York: Oxford UP, 1971.

North, Michael. *Reading 1922: A Return to the Scene of the Modern*. New York: Oxford UP, 1999.

Novick, Sheldon M. *Henry James: The Young Master*. New York: Random House, 1996.

Offutt, Chris. *No Heroes: A Memoir of Coming Home*. New York: Simon & Schuster, 2002.

Otter, Samuel. *Philadelphia Stories: America's Literature of Race and Freedom*. New York: Oxford UP, 2010.

Orwoll, Mark P. Summary of "Gathering Legends: Harold Stearns and the Lost Generation," 1999.

Perl, Jeffrey M. *The Tradition of Return: The Implicit History of Modern Literature*. Princeton, NJ: Princeton UP, 1984.

Persons, Stow. *The Decline of American Gentility*. New York: Columbia UP, 1973.

Pizer, Donald. *American Expatriate Writing and the Paris Moment: Modernism and Place*. Baton Rouge: Louisiana State UP, 1997.

Posnock, Ross. *The Trial of Curiosity: Henry James, William James, and the Challenge of Modernity*. New York: Oxford UP, 1991.

———. "Henry James and the Limits of Historicism." *Henry James Review* 16.3 (1995): 273–77.

————. "Affirming the Alien: The Pragmatist Pluralism of *The American Scene*." Freedman 224–24.

Pratt, Mary Louise. *Imperial Eyes: Travel Writing and Transculturation*. London: Routledge, 1992.

Przybylowicz, Donna. *Desire and Repression: The Dialectic of Self and Other in the Late Works of Henry James*. Tuscaloosa: U of Alabama P, 1986.

Rahv, Philip. *The Discovery of Europe: The Story of American Experience in the Old World*. Boston: Houghton Mifflin, 1947.

Reising, Russell J. "Figuring Himself Out: Spencer Brydon, 'The Jolly Corner,' and Cultural Change." *Journal of Narrative Technique* 19 (Winter 1989): 116–29.

————. *Loose Ends: Closure and Crisis in the American Social Text*. New Americanists. Durham, NC: Duke UP, 1996.

Robinson, Marc, ed. *Altogether Elsewhere: Writers on Exile*. San Diego: Harcourt, Brace, 1994.

Rotundo, E. Anthony. *American Manhood: Transformations in Masculinity from the Revolution to the Modern Era*. New York: Basic Books, 1993.

Rousseau, Jean-Jacques. *Emile: or, On Education*. 1762. Trans. Allan Bloom. New York: Basic Books, 1979.

————. *The Confessions*. 1782. Trans. J. M. Cohen. Harmondsworth, UK: Penguin, 1954.

Ruddick, Lisa Cole. *Reading Gertrude Stein: Body, Text, Gnosis*. Ithaca, NY: Cornell UP, 1990.

Rutherford, Jonathan. *Men's Silences: Predicaments in Masculinity*. London: Routledge, 1992.

Said, Edward. "Reflections on Exile." Robinson 137–49.

————. *Representations of the Intellectual*. New York: Vintage, 1994.

Santayana, George. "Marginal Notes on *Civilization in the United States*." *George Santayana's America*. Comp. and ed. James Ballowe. Urbana: U of Illinois P, 1967. 160–76.

Sarason, Kerin R., and Ruth L. Strickland. "Harold Stearns." *American Writers in Paris: 1920–1939*. Ed. Karen Lane Rood. Vol. 4 of *Dictionary of American Biography*. Detroit: Gale Research, 1980. 358–60.

Savran, David. *Taking It Like a Man: White Masculinity, Masochism, and Contemporary American Culture*. Princeton, NJ: Princeton UP, 1998.

Schoenbach, Lisi. "A Jamesian State: *The American Scene* and the 'Working of Democratic Institutions.'" *Henry James Review* 30.2 (2009): 162–179.

Schriber, Mary Suzanne. *Writing Home: American Women Abroad, 1830–1920*. Charlottesville: UP of Virginia, 1997.

Sedgwick, Eve Kosofsky. *Epistemology of the Closet*. Berkeley: U of California P, 1990.

————. *Tendencies*. Durham, NC: Duke UP, 1993.

Seidel, Michael. *Exile and the Narrative Imagination*. New Haven, CT: Yale UP, 1986.

Seltzer, Mark. *Henry James and the Art of Power*. Ithaca, NY: Cornell UP, 1984.

Shirer, William L. *Twentieth-Century Journey: A Memoir of a Life and the Times.* Boston: Little, Brown, 1984.

Shklar, Judith N. "Obligation, Loyalty, Exile." *Political Theory* 21.2 (1993): 181–98.

Siegel, Carol. *Male Masochism: Modern Revisions of the Story of Love.* Bloomington: Indiana UP, 1995.

Silverman, Kaja. *Male Subjectivity at the Margins.* New York: Routledge, 1992.

Simpson, Lewis P. "Malcolm Cowley and the American Writer." *Sewanee Review* 84 (1976): 221–47.

———. "Cowley's Odyssey: Literature and Faith in the Thirties." *Sewanee Review* 89 (1981): 520–39.

Souhami, Diana. *Gertrude and Alice.* San Francisco: Pandora, 1992.

Spahr, Juliana. *Everybody's Autonomy: Connective Reading and Collective Identity.* Modern and Contemporary Poetics. Tuscaloosa: U of Alabama P, 2001.

Spillers, Hortense J., ed. *Comparative American Identities: Race, Sex, Nationality in the Modern Text.* New York: Routledge, 1991.

Sprigge, Elizabeth. *Gertrude Stein and Her Work.* New York: Harper & Bros., 1957.

Stansell, Christine. "The Strangely Inspired Hermit of Andover." *London Review of Books* June 1997: 29–30.

———. *American Moderns: Bohemian New York and the Creation of a New Century.* New York: Metropolitan Books, 2000.

Stearns, Harold E. "The Confessions of a Harvard Man." *Forum* Dec.–Jan. 1913/1914: 819–26; 69–81.

———. *Liberalism in America: Its Origin, Its Temporary Collapse, Its Future.* New York: Boni & Liveright, 1919.

———. *America and the Young Intellectual.* New York: George H. Doran, 1921.

———, ed. *Civilization in the United States: An Enquiry by Thirty Americans.* London: Jonathan Cape, 1922.

———. "Apologia of an Expatriate." *Scribner's Magazine* Mar. 1929: 338–41.

———. *Rediscovering America.* New York: Liveright, 1934.

———. *The Street I Know.* New York: Lee Furman, 1935.

———. *America: A Re-Appraisal.* New York: Hillman-Curl, 1937.

———, ed. *America Now: An Inquiry into Civilization in the United States by Thirty-Six Americans.* New York: Scribner's, 1938.

———. *Confessions of a Harvard Man: A Journey through Literary Bohemia; Paris and New York in the 20s and 30s.* Rpt. of *The Street I Know.* Ed. Hugh Ford. Sutton West, CA: Paget Press, 1984.

Stein, Gertrude. "Meditations on being about to visit my native land." TS. Gertrude Stein and Alice B. Toklas Papers. Beinecke Rare Book and Manuscript Library, Yale University, 1935.

———. *The Autobiography of Alice B. Toklas.* 1933. Harmondsworth, UK: Penguin, 1966.

———. "Henry James." 1933, published 1947. Meyerowitz 291–330.

———. "What Are Master-pieces and Why Are There So Few of Them?" 1936, published 1940. Meyerowitz 148–56.

———. *Paris, France.* 1940. New York: Liveright, 1970.

———. "What Is English Literature?" 1934, published 1935. Meyerowitz 31–58.

———. *Look at Me Now and Here I Am: Writings and Lectures, 1909–1945.* Ed. Patricia Meyerowitz. Harmondsworth, UK: Penguin, 1967.

———. *Everybody's Autobiography.* 1937. Cambridge, MA: Exact Change, 1993.

———. *The Geographical History of America; or, The Relation of Human Nature to the Human Mind.* 1936. Baltimore: Johns Hopkins UP, 1995.

———. *The Making of Americans.* 1925. Normal, IL: Dalkey Archive Press, 1995.

———. "An American and France." Unpublished manuscript. Gertrude Stein and Alice B. Toklas Papers. Beinecke Rare Book and Manuscript Library, Yale University, [1936].

Stewart, Suzanne. *Sublime Surrender: Male Masochism at the Fin-de-Siècle.* Cornell Studies in the History of Psychiatry. Ithaca, NY: Cornell UP, 1998.

Storti, Craig. *The Art of Coming Home.* Yarmouth, ME: Intercultural Press Nicholas Brealey, 2001.

Stovall, Tyler. *Paris Noir: African Americans in the City of Light.* Boston: Houghton Mifflin, 1996.

Stowe, William W. *Going Abroad: European Travel in Nineteenth-Century American Culture.* Princeton, NJ: Princeton UP, 1994.

Suleiman, Susan Rubin, ed. *Exile and Creativity: Signposts, Travelers, Outsiders, Backward Glances.* Durham, NC: Duke UP, 1998.

Susman, Warren. "Pilgrimage to Paris: The Backgrounds of American Expatriation, 1920–1934." Diss. Madison: U of Wisconsin, 1957.

———. "A Second Country: The Expatriate Image." *Texas Studies in Literature and Language* 3.2 (1961): 171–83.

Sutherland, Donald. *Gertrude Stein: A Biography of Her Work.* Westport, CT: Greenwood Press, 1971.

Tabori, Paul. *The Anatomy of Exile: A Semantic and Historical Study.* London: Harrap, 1972.

Tanner, Tony. *Henry James and the Art of Nonfiction.* Jack N. and Addie D. Averitt Lecture Series. Athens: U of Georgia P, 1995.

Teahan, Sheila. "Engendering Culture in *The American Scene.*" *Henry James Review* 17.1 (1996): 52–57.

Trimberger, Ellen Kay. "Feminism, Men, and Modern Love: Greenwich Village, 1900–1925." *Powers of Desire: The Politics of Sexuality.* Ed. Ann Snitow, Christine Stansell, and Sharon Thompson. New York: New Feminist Library/Monthly Review Press, 1983. 131–52.

Van Den Abbeele, Georges. "Sightseers: The Tourist and Theorist." *Diacritics* 10.4 (1980): 2–14.

Van Doren, Carl. "Life after Legend." *Nation* 13 Nov. 1935: 574.

Wald, Priscilla. *Constituting Americans: Cultural Anxiety and Narrative Form*. Durham, NC: Duke UP, 1995.

Warren, Kenneth W. *Black and White Strangers: Race and American Literary Realism*. Black Literature and Culture. Chicago: U of Chicago P, 1993.

Washington, Bryan R. *The Politics of Exile: Ideology in Henry James, F. Scott Fitzgerald, and James Baldwin*. Boston: Northeastern UP, 1995.

Wasserstrom, William. *The Time of the Dial*. Syracuse, NY: Syracuse UP, 1963.

Weiss, M. Lynn. *Gertrude Stein and Richard Wright: The Poetics and Politics of Modernism*. Jackson: UP of Mississippi, 1998.

Will, Barbara. *Gertrude Stein, Modernism, and the Problem of "Genius."* Edinburgh: Edinburgh UP, 2000.

Wilson, Sarah. *Melting-Pot Modernism*. Ithaca, NY: Cornell UP, 2010.

Winnett, Susan. *Terrible Sociability: The Text of Manners in Laclos, Goethe, and James*. Stanford, CA: Stanford UP, 1993.

Wolff, Geoffrey. *Black Sun: The Brief Transit and Violent Eclipse of Harry Crosby*. London: Hamish Hamilton, 1976.

Young, Thomas Daniel, ed. *Conversations with Malcolm Cowley*. Jackson: UP of Mississippi, 1986.

Ziff, Larzer. *Return Passages: Great American Travel Writing, 1780–1910*. New Haven, CT: Yale UP, 2000.

Zwerdling, Alex. *Improvised Europeans: American Literary Expatriates and the Siege of London*. New York: Basic Books, 1998.

Abraham, Julie, 261n4

alienation: and exile, 7–8, 33, 35, 37–38, 242n17; and expatriation, 41, 243n24

The Ambassadors (James), 1–3, 13, 26–27, 254n25

America: and Americanness, 11, 44, 49, 54, 78, 229; comparisons to Europe, 23–24, 142, 224; Cowley representations of, 96, 184, 191, 200; and expatriation, 22, 24–25, 241–42n15; James's representations of, 48–53, 56–58, 64–82, 87, 88–89, 91; national identity of, 24, 27, 54, 232, 235, 237–38; nostalgia toward, 9, 41, 47; reasons for leaving, 34, 113–14, 206, 242n19, 243n23, 250–51n10, 261nn3–4; significance of, for returnees, 18, 22–30, 42, 145; Stearns critique of, 6–7, 109–12, 114, 124–25, 141–42, 150, 172, 188–89, 198, 250n9, 252n18; Stein representations of, 11–12, 18, 203, 217–24, 236

America and the Young Intellectual (Stearns), 97, 108–9, 140, 141–42, 248n2; "What Can a Young Man Do?," essay in, 111, 112, 114

American Mercury, 184

America Now: An Inquiry into Civilization in the United States (Stearns, ed.), 99, 103, 149–50

The American Scene (James), 18, 43, 44, 53, 81–89, 86; assimilation in, 51, 71, 77–78, 87–88; autobiographical character of, 5, 94, 204; critical overviews of, 244–45nn4–5; framing in, 54, 68, 76, 78; function of money in, 85–86; on gender relations, 121–22; lack of closure in, 63; New York Jewish culture in, 67–68, 75, 76–79; and *The Odyssey,* 90–91, 247n20; Philadelphia representation in, 67–69, 72, 73–75; as precursor text, 4–5; as repatriation narrative, 3, 8, 28, 47, 90, 205; representations of America in, 48–49, 56–57, 64–80, 87; romance in, 70, 246n14; Stearns indebtedness to, 5; Stein autobiography and, 203, 204; title of, 50; writing of, 3

The Art of Coming Home (Storti), 17

The Autobiography of Alice B. Toklas (Stein), 212, 218, 261n6; commercial success of, 11, 203, 208, 209–10, 231, 261n8, 262n11; on France and French, 208

Baird Cowley, Peggy. *See* Cowley, Peggy Baird

Bak, Hans, 181, 251–52nn12–13

Baldwin, James, 26, 34, 235, 237, 238

Balzac, Honoré de, 83–85, 246–47nn16–17

Banta, Martha, 246n13

Being Geniuses Together (McAlmon and Boyle), 103, 105–7

Benstock, Shari, 240n8

Bersani, Leo, 134

The Best Years (Dos Passos), 103

Blackmer, Corinne E., 261n6

Blair, Sara, 248n24

Bourget, Paul, 63, 92

Bourne, Randolph, 124

Boyd, Ernest, 184

Boyle, Kay, 103, 105–7

Boym, Svetlana, 13, 38, 47

Braidotti, Rosi, 242n20

Breton, André, 195

Britten, Clarence, 189

Brooks, Van Wyck, 243n1, 243n24

Broom, 184

Bryson, Bill, 241n12

Burke, Kenneth, 23, 164, 196, 251n12

Buruma, Ian, 242n21

Butler, Judith, 199

Caramello, Charles, 260n1

Cerf, Bennett, 232

Chambers, Iain, 17, 241n13

Chicago Tribune, 97, 102, 254n28

Civilization in the United States
(Stearns, ed.), 108, 146–47, 172,
250n9; Parsons's chapter in, 248n4;
Stearns's essay in, 109–10, 112, 124;
Stearns's preface to, 253n20; and
Stearns's reputation, 97, 101, 130,
248n2

Cixous, Hélène, 38

Clifford, James, 18

Collier's, 101

La Comédie humaine (Balzac), 83–84

Conrad, Joseph, 32

Cowley, Malcolm, 155–202; acrimony
toward Stearns, 9, 99–100, 155, 199,
200, 240n9; ambivalence of, 9, 163,
164, 256n4; on America's cultural
landscape, 170, 189, 198, 259n21;
Aragon influence on, 196; compares

Europe and America, 23–24, 242n16;
and Crosby, 114, 199, 258–59n22;
cultural generalizations of, 9, 100;
and Dada, 193–95, 197, 257n10; as
different from Stearns, 9–10, 98, 100,
107, 172; on exile and expatriation,
41–42, 100, 163, 165, 175; on father,
173; first marriage of, 162, 179–82,
258n13; gender politics of, 101,
165–66, 168, 176–79, 183, 186–88,
257n8; on Greenwich Village, 172,
186–88, 189–90, 201; household
of, 185, 257–58n12; and James, 5;
Kazin portrait of, 200–201; letter to
Burke, 23, 164, 196, 251n12; letter
to Wheelwright, 256–57n7, 258n14;
literary evolution of, 166, 173–74,
177; on Lost Generation, 5, 6, 100,
114, 155, 165–69, 171, 190–92, 202,
236, 256n6; on marriage, 185–86;
and Marxism, 240–41n10; on modernist writers, 193, 256n6; mother of
(Josephine Cowley), 156–59, 161–63,
165, 176, 256n3; mythology of, 171,
173; and *New Republic,* 177–79,
182, 200; on New Woman, 10, 101,
168, 176–79, 186–87, 188–89, 194,
258n17; and nostalgia, 9, 159–60,
164, 172, 173, 176; Paris punching
incident of, 196–97, 258–59n19;
repatriation and return of, 4, 29–30,
155, 197–98, 200, 236–37; representation of Stearns by, 96–97, 98–99,
198, 248n1, 250n8; sentimentalism
of, 101, 159, 255–56n1; snobbishness
of, 117, 251n12; on women, 168,
176–79, 186–87, 188; and World War
I, 155, 169, 187

Cowley, Malcolm, works of: *Blue Juniata,* 156–58, 166, 181, 183, 202;
The Dream of the Golden Mountains,
96–97, 177–81, 183, 185; "Harold

Stearns," 240n9; "Mother and Son," 156, 158, 161, 163, 256n3; "Prayer on All Saints' Day," 156–58, 166, 183, 202; *A Second Flowering: Works and Days of the Lost Generation*, 256n6, 257n8; "This Youngest Generation," 192; "Three Americans in Paris," 200; "The Urn," 160, 166, 202; "Young Mr. Elkins," 200. See also *Exile's Return*

Cowley, Peggy Baird, 162, 179–82, 184, 186, 189, 258nn13–14

Crane, Hart, 9, 114, 179, 180–82, 260n24

Croce, Benedetto, 152

Crosby, Harry, 9, 114, 174, 198, 199, 259–60n22

Crowley, John W., 260n24

Dada, 174–75, 257n10; Cowley and, 193–95, 197

Daily Mail, 102, 254n28

Dante Alighieri, 90, 247n19

Deleuze, Gilles, 252–53n19, 263n17

The Dial, 101, 189, 248n2, 252n15

Dolan, Marc, 171

Dos Passos, John, 103, 106

Douglas, Ann, 118, 164–65, 256n4

Dramatic Mirror, 101

The Dream of the Golden Mountains (Cowley), 96–97, 177–85

Duranty, Walter, 98–99

Edwards, Robert, 242n17

Eliot, T. S., 193

Emerson, Ralph Waldo, 31, 119–20

Europe: American intellectuals and, 23, 31; comparisons to America, 23–24, 142, 224; Cowley and, 23–24, 242n16, 243n24; James and, 43–44, 247n21; Stearns and, 243n24; Stein and, 224

The Europeans, The (James), 43–44

Everybody's Autobiography (Stein), 4, 5, 225–28, 230, 262n12; autobiographical character of, 5–6, 230; on Cambridge, 225–26, 237; chronology of, 212, 261–62n8; "continuous present" in, 206, 218, 220, 223, 229, 230; critical attention to, 10–11, 204–5, 260n1; France function in, 203, 210, 221, 230, 231; as homecoming and repatriation narrative, 14, 203, 205, 213, 223, 230; identity question in, 11–12, 205, 212–13, 220, 232; "inside" and "outside" in, 208, 210, 211, 215; "Lawkamercyme" in, 11, 212–16; "little dog" in, 215–16, 224, 228; plot of, 216; on Oakland, 226–28, 230, 231, 232–33, 237; portrayal of America in, 11–12, 203, 217–19, 220–24; "queerness" in, 6, 205, 220, 229, 230; self-positioning in, 208–9, 215

exile, 7, 33, 35–40, 42; and alienation, 7–8, 33, 35, 37–38, 242n17; artists and, 38, 40, 242–43n22; and expatriation, 34, 35, 38, 240n7; *The Odyssey* and, 13, 241n11; as punishment, 32–33; Said on, 35–38, 242n20

Exile and Creativity (Suleiman), 35

The Exile of James Joyce (Cixous), 38

Exile's Return (Cowley), 4, 112, 163, 183, 202, 259n20; autobiographical character of, 6; Dada in, 192–97; as fairy tale manqué, 172, 174; gender politics of, 8–9, 133, 185–86; Greenwich Village culture in, 172, 186–88, 189–90, 201; Harvard in, 117; as literary odyssey, 171–72, 176, 177, 202, 236, 242n16; as Lost Generation narrative, 100, 133, 155, 165–66, 190–92, 202, 236; as narrative of ideas, 166, 175, 199; nostalgia in, 159–60;

Exile's Return (Cowley) (*cont.*)
  representation of America in, 96, 184,
  191, 200; representation of Stearns in,
  98; representation of women in, 176,
  177, 178, 185; as story of expatriation and return, 107–8, 174
expatriation, 17, 24–25, 35, 237; and
  alienation, 41, 243n24; artistic function of, 206–7; Cowley and, 41–42,
  100, 163, 165; and exile, 34, 35, 38,
  240n7; as hedonistic, 34; and homecoming, 13, 17, 25, 46; James and,
  34, 43, 89, 243–44n1; and language,
  39–40, 243n23; national identity and,
  24, 27, 54, 232, 235; and nostalgia,
  41, 243n25; reasons for, 34, 113–14,
  206, 242n19, 243n23, 250–51n10,
  261nn3–4; Stearns and, 41–42, 100,
  112–14, 141, 249–51nn8–10; Stein
  and, 206–7, 232, 261nn3–4; and
  travel, 31–32; in U.S. cultural history,
  22, 241–42n15; voluntary nature of,
  33–34, 241n13

feminization: of American literary culture, 118–19, 120–21, 251–52n13,
  253n20; Cowley reaction to, 10, 101,
  187, 188–89, 194, 258n17; James on,
  121–24; Lost Generation and, 192;
  Stearns on, 94, 126–27, 135
Fitzgerald, F. Scott, 135–36, 249n5,
  260n24
Ford, Hugh, 249n8, 250n10, 253n22
Four in America (Stein), 212
framing: about, 49, 245n6; James strategies of, 49, 52, 54, 62–63, 76, 82–83,
  92–93, 248n24
France: Balzac's, 83–84, 246–47nn16–
  17; Stearns in, 109, 141–43, 148,
  153, 250n9; Stein on, 203, 221, 230.
  See also Paris
Franzen, Walter, 252n18

Freeman, 101
Freud, Sigmund, 134, 236

Garland, Hamlin, 247n18
Gass, William, 262n9
gender: Cowley reaction to, 101,
  165–66, 168, 176–79, 183, 186–88,
  257n8; and intellectual life, 124, 127,
  135; James on, 121–24; and sex, 126,
  134–35; Stearns on, 10, 125–28, 131,
  135, 152, 252n14. *See also* feminiza-
  tion; masculinity
The Geographical History of America
  (Stein), 212, 215, 216
Gide, André, 21–22
The Golden Bowl (James), 44
Gordimer, Nadine, 3
Gosse, Edmund, 50
Great Depression, 96, 153
Greenwich Village: Cowley and, 172,
  186–88, 189–90, 201; Stearns and,
  129–30, 132
Gurr, Andrew, 242–43n22
Gussow, Adam, 259n21
Guthrie, Ramon, 184

Haas, Robert, 232
Hardy, Thomas, 49
Harper's Weekly, 101
Harvard: Cowley and, 117, 251n12;
  James and, 64–67, 244n3; Stearns
  and, 116–18, 133; Stein and, 225–26,
  237
Harvey, George, 49
Harvey, Paul, 92, 247n23
Hawthorne, Nathaniel, 22, 31, 84
Haywood, Bill, 133–34
Hemingway, Ernest, 260n24; on Stea-
  rns, 97, 103–5, 249n5; Stearns on,
  248–49n5, 253–54n23; works of: *A
  Movable Feast,* 103–4; *The Sun Also
  Rises,* 97, 104–5, 201

Henderson, Mae, 245n6

Hofmannsthal, Hugo von, 40; "Die Briefe des Zurückgekehrten," 15–17, 40–41; "Französische Redensarten," 39–40

Hollier, Denis, 39–40

home and homecoming: expatriates and, 13, 17, 25, 46; *Heimat,* 15–17, 39; and identity crisis, 210–13, 214, 215; James on, 3, 90, 205; "Lawka-mercyme" as narrative of, 213–14; and nostalgic yearning, 33, 47; as notion and trope, 17–18, 256n5; *The Odyssey* and, 13–15; Stearns on, 18, 147–48; Stein on, 14, 46, 145, 203, 205, 213. *See also* repatriation and return

Hörner, Unda, 258n18

Hornung, Alfred, 260n1

Ignorance (Kundera), 20

"Intellectual Exile: Expatriates and Mar-ginals" (Said), 35–36

Irving, Washington, 31

James, Henry, 43–95, 205, 247n18; and "alien," 55, 67, 245n8; on American capitalism and democracy, 58–59, 64, 246n9; and American identity, 30, 49–50, 56, 92–93; on Americans in Europe, 238, 247n21; on America's cultural lacks, 22–23, 56–57, 63; on assimilation, 51, 71, 77–78, 87–88; on Balzac's France, 246n16; on culture, 68, 81; Dante cited by, 90, 247n19; deferral strategy of, 58, 64, 67, 86–87; dissociation notion of, 69; double consciousness of, 41, 46; on English language, 74–75; expatriation of, 34, 43, 89, 243–44n1; framing strategies of, 49, 52, 54, 62–63, 76, 82–83, 92–93, 248n24; on gender

relations, 121–24; on Harvard and Cambridge, 64–67, 244n3; on Haw-thorne, 22, 84; on immigrants, 54, 71, 77–78, 81; and Jews, 48, 67–68, 75–79, 81, 92–93, 246n15; on lan-guage, 74–75; and manners, 59–63, 67, 68, 72, 222; on money in Amer-ica, 55–56, 64, 85–86; on New York, 61–62, 67–68, 71, 75, 76–79, 245n7; and nostalgia, 47, 89–90, 244n2; in Paris, 141, 254n25; on Philadel-phia, 67–69, 72, 73–75; portrayal of America by, 48–53, 57–58, 81–82, 88–89; on repatriation, 27–28, 45–46, 47, 82–83, 89–90, 236; representa-tional strategies of, 70–71, 73; return to America of, 2–3, 4, 44–45, 46–47; self-definition of, 47, 50; on shocks of America, 46, 75–76; on speech of American women, 122; Stearns and, 5, 94–95; Stein and, 5, 239n1; and travel, 45, 52–53, 243n1

James, Henry, letters, 44–47, 48; to Paul Bourget, 63, 92; to Edmund Gosse, 50; to George Harvey, 49; to Paul Harvey, 92, 247n23; to Grace Nor-ton, 247n21; to Edith Wharton, 49

James, Henry, works of: *The Ambassa-dors,* 1–3, 13, 26–27, 254n25; *Com-plete Notebooks,* 34, 41, 44, 45, 90; *The Europeans,* 43–44; *The Golden Bowl,* 44; "The Jolly Corner," 3, 8, 28, 44, 91–92; "The Lesson of Bal-zac," 51; "The Manners of American Women," 122; "The Speech of Ameri-can Women," 122; *William Wetmore Story and his Friends,* 89. See also *The American Scene*

James, William, 214, 247n18; on "hu-man nature," "human mind," and "substantial identity," 212, 262n9

Jankélévitch, Vladimir, 13–14

Jolas, Eugène, 108, 249n7
"The Jolly Corner" (James), 3, 44; as tale of repatriation, 8, 28, 91–92
Josephson, Matthew, 33–34, 184, 242n18; on Cowley, 258–59n12; on Stearns, 103
Joyce, James, 38, 40, 193, 256n5

Kaplan, Caren, 239n5, 259n20
Kazin, Alfred, 200–201
Kelly, James L., 241n14
Kennedy, J. Gerald, 261n3
Kristeva, Julia, 148, 255n30
Kronenberger, Louis, 149
Kundera, Milan, 7–8, 20
Kuttner, Alfred, 113

Lane, James W., 148
language: expatriates and, 39–40, 243n23; James on, 74–75; Stein on, 208, 222–23
Lauter, Paul, 169–70
"Lawkamercyme," 11, 212–16
Liberalism in America (Stearns), 101, 140
Life among the Surrealists (Josephson), 103
Lost Generation: about, 167–69, 256–57n7; *Exile's Return* as narrative of, 100, 133, 155, 165–66, 190–92, 202, 236; gender politics of, 8–9, 168, 169–70, 171, 257n8; as literary generation, 167, 169, 256n6; return from exile of, 166, 167–68; Stearns and, 5, 6, 142–43
Lowell, James Russell, 91

MacDougal, Alice: death of, 102, 113–14, 140, 250n10; Stearns marriage to, 135, 136, 137–40, 253n22, 254n24

manners, 59–63, 67, 68, 72, 222
Martin, Biddy, 17–18
masculinity, 131, 137, 138, 143, 146–47, 253–54n23; and crisis of American male intellectual, 109, 134, 176; "disinterested," 136, 137, 140; perceived threats to, 131, 132, 135
masochism, 134, 252n19; Stearns and, 10, 133, 136, 139, 140, 152, 253n19, 255n30
McAlmon, Robert, 103
McCarthy, Mary, 32–33, 34
Miller, Henry, 18–19, 97
modernism, 130, 171, 261n6; artist-as-exile theme of, 242–43n22
Mohanty, Chanda, 17–18
Monday Night (Boyle), 103, 106
money: Balzac on, 84–85, 246–47n17; James on, 55–56, 64, 85–86; Stein on, 209–11

Neuman, Shirley C., 212, 260n1, 262nn10–11
New Republic: Cowley and, 177–79, 182, 200; Stearns and, 101, 149, 248n2
New York: Cowley on, 29–30, 172, 200; James on, 61–62, 67–68, 71, 75, 76–79, 245n7; Stearns on, 6, 190; Stein on, 30. *See also* Greenwich Village
nomad, 242n20
North, Michael, 250n8
nostalgia, 41, 47, 237, 243n25; Svetlana Boym on, 38–39; Cowley and, 9, 159–60, 164, 172, 173, 176; James and, 47, 89–90, 244n2; Stearns and, 116, 148, 172

The Odyssey, 224, 262–63n12; *American Scene* and, 90–91, 247n20; as narrative of exile and return, 13–15, 20–21, 241n11

Offutt, Chris, 19–20

O'Neill, Eugene, 260n24

Orwoll, Mark, 115, 251n11

Paris: American expatriates and, 235, 255n28; Cowley in, 196–97, 258–59n19; James in, 141, 254n25; Stearns and, 109, 141–43, 148, 153, 250n9, 254n27; Stein and, 210, 231. *See also* France

Paris, France (Stein), 206

Parsons, Elsie Clews, 248n4

Posnock, Ross, 245–46nn8–9, 246n14

Pound, Ezra, 256n5

Prodigal Son, 7, 21–22

Proust, Marcel, 193

queerness, 263n16; Stein and, 6, 205, 220, 229, 230

"Race and Gender in the Shaping of the American Literary Canon" (Lauter), 169–70

Rediscovering America (Stearns), 5, 98, 102, 147–48, 151, 152

"Reflections on Exile" (Said), 37–38

repatriation and return, 12–13, 18–19, 26, 30, 237; ambivalences about, 42, 235; of Cowley, 4, 29–30, 155, 197–98, 200, 236–37; James on, 1–2, 3, 8, 27–28, 45–47, 82–83, 89–92, 205, 236; literature on, 7–8, 240n6; Lost Generation and, 166, 167–68; and national identity, 27, 237–38; *The Odyssey* as narrative of, 14, 20–21; of Stearns, 4, 6, 10, 18, 29, 95, 102, 109, 144–46, 149, 152, 153, 154; Stein on, 14, 28–29, 46, 145, 203, 205, 213, 216–18, 223, 230, 236;

temporal dissociations in, 18, 20, 241nn12–14; for travel writers, 32; as trope, 166, 256n5; "writing back" on, 27–28, 236–38. *See also* home and homecoming

The Return of the Native (Hardy), 49

Return Passages (Ziff), 32

Roosevelt, Franklin D., 96

Rousseau, Jean-Jacques, 132, 252n14

Said, Edward, 33, 35–38

Santayana, George, 124, 253n20

Schriber, Mary Suzanne, 31

Scott, Sir Walter, 234

Scribner's Magazine, 135–36, 146, 154

Second Flowering: Works and Days of the Lost Generation (Cowley), 256n6, 257n8

Sedgwick, Eve Kosofsky, 263n16

Seven Arts, 101

Shipman, Evan, 98

Shirer, William, 103, 106, 145, 249n8

Siegel, Carol, 252–53n19

Simpson, Lewis P., 255–56n1

Stansell, Christine, 130, 176–77, 251–52n13, 252n15

Stearns, Harold E., 96–154; abjection of, 10, 107, 146, 148–49, 153, 199, 202, 255n30; alcoholism of, 199, 260n24; biographical sketch of, 101–3, 248n2; birth of, 115, 251n11; Boyle on, 103, 105–7; character and disposition, 107, 141, 142; Chicago interlude of, 133–34; Cowley acrimony toward, 9, 99–100, 155, 199, 200, 240n9; Cowley compared to, 9–10, 98, 100, 107, 172; Cowley representation of, 96–97, 98–99, 198, 248n1, 250n8; critique of U.S. intellectual life by, 6–7, 109–12, 114, 124–25, 141–42, 150, 172, 188–89, 198,

Stearns, Harold E. (*cont.*)
250n9, 252n18; and *The Dial*, 101,
137, 189, 248n2, 252n15; Dos Passos
on, 103, 106; expatriation of, 41–42,
100, 112–14, 141, 249–51nn8–10;
gender politics of, 10, 125–28, 131,
135, 152, 252n14; and Greenwich
Village, 129–30, 132; and Harvard,
116–18, 133; on Hemingway, 248–
49n5, 253–54n23; Hemingway on,
97, 103–5, 249n5; and horse racing,
105, 106, 143, 249n6; and James,
5, 94–95; literary evolution of, 117,
119, 149; and Lost Generation, 5, 6,
142–43; and Alice MacDougal, 102,
113–14, 135, 136, 137–40, 250n10,
253n22, 254n24; on masculinity, 109,
131, 137, 138, 143, 146–47; and
masochism, 10, 133, 136, 139, 140,
148, 152, 153, 253n19, 255nn29–30;
mother of, 115–16, 129, 146, 152,
255n30; and *New Republic*, 101, 149,
248n2; as newspaper correspondent,
97, 101, 102, 141, 143, 254n28; and
nostalgia, 116, 148, 172; notoriety of,
6, 107, 108; observations on America
by, 125, 146–47, 150–52, 153, 201;
Paris sojourn of, 109, 141–43, 148,
153, 250n9; repatriation and return
of, 4, 6, 10, 29, 95, 98, 109, 144–46,
149, 152, 153, 154, 248n1; reputation of, 6, 100; self-representation
by, 7, 100–101, 146; self-resurrection
of, 9, 199; Shirer on, 103, 106, 145,
249n8; social criticism of, 108–9,
112, 119; support from others to,
131, 252n17; and women, 128–29,
130–32, 135–36, 251n10, 252n16,
254n27; on women and feminization,
125–26, 133, 150–52, 172, 254n26;
and World War I, 136–37, 198; on
younger generation, 111, 113

Stearns, Harold E., works of: *America
and the Young Intellectual*, 97, 108–9,
111, 112, 114, 140–42, 248n2; *America: A Re-appraisal*, 103; *America
Now*, 99, 103, 149–50; "Apologia
of an Expatriate," 135–36; *Civilization in the United States*, 97, 101,
108–10, 112, 124, 130, 146–47, 172,
248n2, 250n9, 253n20; "The Confessions of a Harvard Man," 255n29;
"The Girls," 151; "The Intellectual
Life," 109–10, 112, 124; *Liberalism
in America*, 101, 140; "A Prodigal
American Returns," 150–51, 154,
255n31; *Rediscovering America*, 5,
98, 102, 147–48, 151, 152; "What
Can a Young Man Do?," 111, 112,
140; "Where Are Our Intellectuals?,"
108, 111. See also *The Street I Know*
Stein, Gertrude, 203–33; and Americanness, 228, 229–30, 232, 233; on audience, 209, 212–13, 215–16, 217, 225;
on Cambridge, 225–26, 237; crisis
of identity in, 210–13, 215, 261n7,
262n11, 263n13; double consciousness and citizenship of, 41, 231–32;
definition of "romance" by, 207; expatriation of, 206–7, 232, 261nn3–4;
genius notion of, 218–20; on human
mind and memory, 212, 219; and
identity, 212, 218, 224–25, 228, 229,
232; on James, 5, 239n1; on language,
208, 222–23; "little dog motif" of,
215–16, 224, 228, 262–63n12; on
New York, 30; on Oakland, 226–28,
230, 231, 232–33, 237, 263–64n18;
on Paris and France, 203, 210, 221,
230, 235; and queerness, 6, 205, 220,
229, 230; reasons for leaving U.S.,
206, 261nn3–4; on repatriation and
homecoming, 28–29, 46, 145, 205,
216–18, 236; representation of Amer-

ica by, 11–12, 18, 217–19, 220–24,
236; representation of in America, 4,
205; on roots and rootlessness, 226–
27, 229, 231, 263n17; self-alienation
of, 212; on "shocks of recognition
and nonrecognition," 14, 46, 145,
203; and singularity, 219, 220, 229
Stein, Gertrude, works of: "An American and France," 206–7; The Autobiography of Alice B. Toklas, 11, 203,
208–10, 212, 218, 231, 261nn6–8,
262n11; Four in America, 212; The
Geographical History of America,
212, 215, 216; "Identity a Poem,"
212; "Meditations on being about
to visit my native land," 18, 203–4;
Paris, France, 206; "What Is English
Literature?," 208, 209, 223. See also
Everybody's Autobiography
Sterne, Laurence, 115
Storti, Craig, 17
Story, William Wetmore, 89
Stowe, William W., 31
The Street I Know (Stearns), 4, 109,
115, 128, 153; autobiographical
character of, 94, 102–3; Cowley on
publication of, 99; on French sojourn,
141–44, 153; Alice MacDougal in,
136, 140; representation of America
in, 133, 190, 202; reviews of, 148,
149; and Stearns repatriation, 18,
102, 144–46; World War I representation in, 136–37, 187
Suleiman, Susan Rubin, 35
Susman, Warren, 243n24, 250nn9–10

Taine, Hippolyte, 52–53
Tate, Allen, 169–70
Toklas, Alice B., 4, 261n6

travel: European, 31; and expatriation,
31–32; James and, 45, 52–53, 243n1
Trimberger, Ellen Kay, 130
Tristram Shandy (Sterne), 115
Twentieth-Century Journey (Shirer), 103
Tzara, Tristan, 195

uncanny (Freud), 235–36

Valéry, Paul, 193
van Doren, Carl, 99, 248n2

Wald, Priscilla, 235–36, 260n1
Weiss, M. Lynn, 260n1
Wharton, Edith, 49, 247n18
Wheelwright, John Brooks, 256–57n7,
258n14
William Wetmore Story and His Friends
(James), 89
Wolff, Geoffrey, 259–60n22
women: Cowley portrayal of, 176, 177,
178, 185; Dadaists and, 194–96,
258n18; and emancipation, 186–87;
exclusion from Lost Generation
of, 8–9, 168, 169–70, 171, 257n8;
James's critique of, 122–23; and literary culture, 118–19, 120–21, 126,
251–52n13; and male double standard, 195–96; Stearns on, 125–26,
133, 150–52, 172, 254n26. See also
feminization
writing back: as phrase and act, 27–28;
significance of, 236–38

Ziff, Larzer, 31–32
Zola, Émile, 93
Zwerdling, Alex, 244n1, 246n15,
247n18